PAN-EUROPEAN PERSPECTIVES ON PARTY POLITICS

PAN-EUROPEAN PERSPECTIVES ON PARTY POLITICS

EDITED BY

PAUL LEWIS AND PAUL WEBB

BRILL
LEIDEN   BOSTON
2003

This book is printed on acid-free paper.

Library of Congress Cataloging-in-Publication Data

Pan-European perspectives on party politics / edited by Paul Lewis and Paul Webb.
 p. cm.
 Includes bibliographical references.
 ISBN 90-04-13014-4 (alk. paper)
 1. Political parties Europe. I. Lewis, Paul G., 1945 II. Webb, Paul (Paul D.)

JN50.P36 2003
324.2 094 dc21

2003045165

ISBN 90 04 13014 4

© Copyright 2003 by Koninklijke Brill NV, Leiden, The Netherlands

All rights reserved. No part of this publication may be reproduced, translated, stored in a retrieval system, or transmitted in any form or by any means, electronic, mechanical, photocopying, recording or otherwise, without prior written permission from the publisher.

Authorization to photocopy items for internal or personal use is granted by Brill provided that the appropriate fees are paid directly to The Copyright Clearance Center, 222 Rosewood Drive, Suite 910 Danvers MA 01923, USA.
Fees are subject to change

PRINTED IN THE NETHERLANDS

CONTENTS

Foreword	vii
Introduction: Pan-European Perspectives on Parties and Party Systems	1
Paul Webb	
Electoral Systems and Party Systems in Europe East and West	9
Sarah Birch	
Party Development and the Polish Presidential Election of October 2000	33
Frances Millard	
The Structure and Dynamics of Intra-Party Politics in Europe	55
Françoise Boucek	
On the Predominance of State Money: Reassessing Party Financing in the New Democracies of Southern and Eastern Europe	97
Ingrid van Biezen and Petr Kopecký	
Cartelisation in Post-Communist Politics: State Party Funding in Post-1989 Poland	127
Aleks Szczerbiak	
Are the Exceptions Really the Rule? Questioning the Application of 'Electoral-Professional' Type Models of Party Organisation in East Central Europe	151
Seán Hanley	
Cleavages, Party Strategy and Party System Change in Europe, East and West	179
Nick Sitter	
Europeanisation, Euroscepticism and Party Systems: Party-based Euroscepticism in the Candidate States of Central and Eastern Europe	207
Paul Taggart and Aleks Szczerbiak	
Conclusion: European Parties East and West: Comparative Perspectives	227
Paul G. Lewis	
Notes on Contributors	243

FOREWORD

As editor of the journal Perspectives on European Politics and Society (*PEPS*) I am very pleased to introduce to you this special edited book on political parties. Seven of the ten chapters were first published in a special issue of *PEPS* guest edited by Paul Lewis and Paul Webb (*PEPS*, Vol. 2, No. 3, December 2001). For this revised edition the editors have provided us with a new introduction and conclusion and there are three additional chapters by Paul Taggart and Aleks Szczerbiak (first published in *PEPS*, Vol. 3, No. 1, May 2002) and Françoise Boucek and Nick Sitter (*PEPS* Vol. 3, No. 3, January 2003).

Dr. Cameron Ross (Editor, *PEPS*).

Paul Webb

Introduction: Pan-European Perspectives on Parties and Party Systems

Traditions of party scholarship in Europe

The study of parties and party systems has been a perennial feature of European political science. In this book we seek to draw on this tradition in order to reflect, a dozen or more years after the fall of the Berlin Wall, on the implications of that momentous conjuncture for the study of party politics in Europe. We believe that sufficient time has passed to permit a self-consciously pan-European approach to this subject. In particular, the contributors to the book each address two inter-connected questions:

- To what extent is there evidence of convergence in patterns of party politics across Eastern and Western Europe?
- To what extent has the theory of parties and party systems coped with the emergence of democratic politics in Eastern Europe? Has it proved to be of continuing relevance and utility, or has it been undermined, perhaps to be superseded by quite different models or paradigms?

The latter question derives from the perception of many commentators, succinctly expressed by Stephen Wolinetz, that 'by default and occasionally by design, the comparative party systems literature, like the comparative parties literature . . .

has been largely a Western European literature.'[1] The emergence of this literature was largely a consequence of the democratisation of Western European polities in the late nineteenth and early twentieth centuries. Democratisation, as many have noted, brought with it the advent of the mass party, the chief vehicle by which the newly enfranchised masses were mobilised. The mass party gave expression to new forms of political identity, competition and action for the citizens of Western Europe and spawned a rich and enduring body of theoretical interpretation, the origins of which date back to Max Weber.[2] The most elaborate account of the politics and organisation of the mass party, and its precursors, however, was articulated by Maurice Duverger, whose pioneering study *Political Parties* became a classic which remains a point of almost liturgical reference for today's scholars.[3]

Duverger argued that in the pre-democratic era parties were purely parliamentary alliances of elites who banded together for the purpose of coordinating legislative action; such parties lacked extra-parliamentary national organisations and grass-roots memberships. This elitist organisational ideal-type was referred to by Duverger as the *cadre party*, and its rather restricted form of local organisation as the *caucus*. By contrast, the democratic era saw the invention of the *mass-branch party*, a form of political organisation which depended on large numbers of grass-roots members, and a more centralised national structure. He regarded the mass party as initially a natural form of left-wing political organisation, a 'socialist invention', for two fundamental reasons. First, since political education and integration of the newly enfranchised masses was the primary goal of the left, it was obvious that the mobilisation of as many individual supporters as possible was necessary: 'Without members, the party would be like a teacher without pupils.[4] Second, mass membership had an obvious rationale in terms of resources. Nowhere in Europe could left-wing parties intent on mobilising the working class hope to attract the support of many wealthy backers, but the aggregated subscriptions paid by a mass of ordinary individuals could clearly constitute a significant sum. By contrast, the parties of the right were historically more likely to have their roots in the cadre model, the organisational basis of which was the wealth of parliamentary elites and their sponsors. Nevertheless, Duverger did acknowledge the probability of 'contagion from the left' as cadre parties would seek to extend their appeal by adopting the organisational methods of mass parties. Thus, as the central purpose of parties shifted from coordinated legislative action to the political integration of the masses, the typical organisational structures of political parties changed. By the 1960s, however, West European and American political scientists were pointing to a further evolution in the purpose and style of major parties. Most notably, Otto Kirchheimer argued that such parties were substituting electoral ambition for their role as social integrators. Kirchheimer wrote in the context of the controversial debate about the waning of ideological conflict which engaged social and political theorists during the 1960s. Like a number of other observers, he perceived an attenuation of ideological conflict in western societies. He credited this to the development of more fluid social class situations and the secularisation of societies once firmly influenced by organised religion. His conclusion was that:

> ... the mass integration party, product of an age with harder class lines and more sharply protruding denominational structures, is transforming itself into a catch-all 'people's' party. Abandoning attempts at the intellectual and moral *encadrement* of the masses, it is turning more fully to the electoral scene, trying to exchange effectiveness in depth for a wider audience and more immediate electoral success.[5]

This transformation of West European parties involved not only ideological mutation, but also organisational changes affecting intra-party balances of power between leaders and members, and relations with external non-electoral organisations such as trade unions and churches. This argument was subsequently embellished by Angelo Panebianco, who built directly on Kirchheimer's intellectual foundations in devising his 'electoral-professional' model.[6] For Panebianco, the internal rebalancing of power was vital to the strategic autonomy required by leaders in order to implement their preferred electoral strategies; furthermore, he added significantly to the catch-all model by pointing out that modern electoralist parties also give influential roles to new kinds of 'professional' employee with expertise important to the conduct of election campaigns.

Since Panebianco, other scholars have continued to build upon the intellectual edifice constructed by Duverger and Kirchheimer in order to press the case for new heuristic abstractions such as the 'cartel' or 'business party' models.[7] The first of these has been especially influential in recent years, its unique claim being that many major contemporary Western parties have evolved a new and parasitic relationship with the state. Richard Katz and Peter Mair argue that these parties exploit their access to state resources in order to cement their organisational advantages over others: 'The state ... becomes an institutionalised structure of support, sustaining insiders while excluding outsiders'.[8]

The theoretical significance of the era of democratisation in Western Europe is by no means limited to debates about models of party development. It applies equally to work on party systems. This can be illustrated by reference to two aspects of this literature, the first of which stems from the classic work of S. M. Lipset and Stein Rokkan on cleavage structures and party systems. As is widely known, they emphasised the central importance of two great macro-historical processes rooted far back in Europe's pre-democratic past, each of which generated cleavages of enduring relevance to the democratic era of party politics. The first of these phenomena was that of *national revolution*, which spawned both religious and centre-periphery cleavages, while the second was *industrial revolution*, which generated urban-rural and worker-employer cleavages. The interaction of these macro-historical developments with the initiatives of political 'entrepreneurs' and institutional contexts accounts for the emergence and consolidation of Western European party systems up to the moment of democratisation, at which point patterns of party competition - 'with few but significant exceptions' - became 'frozen'.[9]

The second aspect of the literature on party systems stemming from Western Europe is concerned with the relationship between electoral systems and party systems. Once again, Duverger was the modern instigator of this strand of inquiry, with his famous - though much criticised - 'law' that plurality voting in single member constituencies tends to produce two-party systems.[10] Although subsequent scholarship in this field of inquiry has by no means focussed exclusively on this part of the world, studies of West European cases have remained prominent. It should also be said that these works have carried forward our understanding of the relationship between electoral systems and party systems to a point well beyond that established by Duverger.[11]

While scholars in the US have been quick to note how the theoretical fixation with West European cases helped create a sense of 'American exceptionalism' which was not easily surmounted, the fall of the Soviet Empire in Eastern Europe has created a new set of challenges for party theory. Interestingly, however, notwithstanding the ideological and strategic gulf which separated them until 1989, it is conceivable that the theoretical corpus associated with Western European parties and party systems may yet travel more readily to Eastern Europe than it ever did to the USA. In this issue, we set about investigating this possibility by studying the implications of East European democratisation for comparative theory. To be sure, we cannot pretend to offer definitive answers to the key questions, for these would require a far more comprehensive review of empirical developments than we could possibly manage in the space available. They might also require the passage of a longer period of time than has yet elapsed. Our aim, therefore, is to be selective and illustrative rather than comprehensive, and to take stock of developments to this point in time. This, at least, should be enough to propose some tentative interim conclusions and to supply cues for further research.

The scope of the book

The contributions to this book focus on the three broad themes which I have outlined as being central to traditions of party scholarship in Western Europe. The first theme concerns the interplay of parties and party systems with their institutional contexts. Thus, Sarah Birch provides a succinct but remarkably comprehensive review of the variety of electoral systems which operate across the continent of Europe today, before assessing their impact on party systems. Then Frances Millard uses the case of Poland in order to investigate the capacity of a presidential institutional context to constrain party politics. Francoise Boucek shifts our focus to the internal life of parties by exploring the ways in which different institutions such as electoral systems, procedural legislative devices, and intra-party decisional arrangements can shape intra-party behaviour. Notwithstanding data constraints, she is able to use this analytical framework to assess the implications of institutional contexts in East and Central Europe for intra-party politics.

The second theme is explored in three chapters on party organisational development. In one way or another, each of these chapters tests the utility for Eastern Europe of well established West European models. Thus, while Katz and Mair's cartel party model is the underlying theoretical referent for both the study of party funding supplied by Ingrid van Biezen and Petr Kopecký, and Aleks Szczerbiak's detailed case-study of developments in Poland, Sean Hanley uses the Czech case to explore the limits of Angelo Panebianco's electoral-professional model.

The third theme dealt with in the book is that of party system developments. First, Nick Sitter offers a detailed consideration of the continuing relevance of Lipset and Rokkan's famous 'cleavage model', by applying it to the cases of Hungary, Poland, the Czech Republic and Slovakia. Though there are 'considerable similarities', he points out that the cleavages, relationships between voters and parties, and the very nature of parties, all differ considerably from the early Twentieth Century West European context. Moreover, party strategy emerges as a key variable in explaining patterns of party system stability and change. Finally, Paul Taggart and Aleks Szczerbiak consider the possibility that a post-Rokkan cleavage which has emerged in Western Europe over the past decade might also be impacting on the party systems of Eastern Europe: this is the political fault-line between the supporters and critics of European integration.

Paul Lewis concludes the issue by drawing together the implications of these contributions: his central contention is that the standard West European-inspired models do, on the whole, provide a good fit with the empirical developments in Eastern and Central European party politics since 1989, notwithstanding a 'stubborn residue' of regional and temporal differences. To reiterate, however, we regard this as something in the nature of an academic staging-post, in that it is a suggestive interim conclusion which invites further careful testing and elaboration.

Notes

[1] Stephen B. Wolinetz 'Introduction' in Stephen B. Wolinetz (ed.), *Party Systems* (Aldershot: Ashgate, 1998), p. xii.
[2] Max Weber 'Politics as vocation' in H.H. Gerth and C. Wright Mills (eds.) *From Max Weber: Essays in Sociology* (New York: Oxford University Press, 1972).
[3] Maurice Duverger, *Political Parties: Their Organisation and Activity in the Modern State* (London: Methuen, 1954).
[4] Duverger, *Political Parties*, p. 63.
[5] Otto Kirchheimer, 'The Transformation of West European Party Systems', in Joseph

LaPalombara and Myron Weiner (eds.) *Political Parties and Political Development* (Princeton: Princeton University Press, 1966), p. 185.
6   Angelo Panebianco, *Political Parties: Organisation and Power* (Cambridge: Cambridge University Press, 1988), pp. 262-7.
7   R.S. Katz and Peter Mair, 'Changing Models of Party Organisation and Party Democracy: The Emergence of the Cartel Party', *Party Politics*, 1, 1995, pp. 5-28; J. Hopkin and C. Paolucci, 'The business firm model of party organisation: Cases from Spain and Italy', *European Journal of Political Research*, 35, 1999, pp. 307-39.
8   Katz and Mair, 'Changing models of party organisation', p. 16.
9   S.M. Lipset and S. Rokkan, 'Cleavage Structures, Party Systems, and Voter Alignments: An Introduction', in S.M. Lipset and S. Rokkan (eds.) *Party Systems and Voter Alignments: Cross National Perspectives* (New York: The Free Press, 1967).
10 Duverger, *Political Parties*, p. 217.
11 See also Douglas Rae, *The Political Consequences of Electoral Laws* (New Haven and London: Yale University Press, 1967); and Arend Lijphart *Electoral Systems and Party Systems* (Cambridge: Cambridge University Press, 1994).

Sarah Birch
Electoral Systems and Party Systems in Europe East and West

ABSTRACT

This article assesses the differences in the design of electoral institutions and electoral outcomes in 20 Eastern and 20 Western European democracies. It finds broad similarities between the types of electoral systems that have been adopted in the two parts of the continent. The size and shape of the party systems that have been generated by these systems are also similar overall. Yet statistical analysis demonstrates that the electoral systems of Eastern Europe are doing far more 'work' than their Western counterparts to reduce the size of party systems, and that they are more likely to use exclusionary thresholds to achieve this end than manipulation of constituency size. Possible reasons for these differences are discussed with reference to the factors that impinge on electoral system design.

Introduction

In the summer of 1991 the Soviet Union was in its death throes. A new Union treaty was derailed unconstitutionally by hard-liners, leaving the authoritarian empire naked for all to peer at its most shameful attributes. By this time, all the other states in communist Europe had held competitive multi-party elections, and most of them were well on their way to democracy. The abortive coup in Moscow that August thus represented the end in Europe of a type of system that had come to be known by the somewhat incongruous term of 'really existing communism'. Ten years later, multiparty electoral democracy had been established in all but a handful of the states in the former communist area (exceptions were Belarus, Azerbaijan, and the five ex-Soviet states of Central Asia), leaving 'Europe' radically altered. This chapter will seek to compare and contrast the electoral institutions of post-communist Eastern Europe with those of their Western counterparts and to trace the effects of those institutions on party systems.[1]

The interactions between electoral systems and party systems in established democracies have been carefully studied and well-mapped. But it is worth noting that the majority of such states, are for reasons of historical accident, located in Western Europe. The wave of electoral reform that spread through the continent in the late nineteenth and early twentieth centuries was linked in a number of intricate ways to the subsequent state of development of Western European party systems.[2] The dismantling of communism that occurred in the Eastern portion of the continent in the late 1980s took a rather different course, and it led to the establishment of largely new party systems that reflect the specific features of post-communism.[3] We can thus expect that the development of electoral institutions will have taken different paths, reflecting the different historical trajectories characteristic of the states in the two halves of the continent. We can also anticipate that these differences in institutional design will have had systematic effects on the shape of party systems in East and West.

This article will assess the differences in the design of electoral institutions and electoral outcomes in Eastern and Western European democracies. The first section provides a brief overview of electoral system designs and electoral outcomes in the two parts of the continent, noting both similarities and differences. The second section seeks to account for East-West differences, while the third and final section interprets them. The dataset on which the analysis is based is comprised of electoral legislation and results from the most recent elections (as of 1 July 2001) to the lower or only houses of the national legislatures of 20 emerging Central and East European democracies and 20 established democracies of West Europe.[4] The Central and Eastern European states in question are: Albania, Armenia, Bosnia and Herzegovina, Bulgaria, Croatia, the Czech Republic, Estonia, Georgia, Hungary, Latvia,

Lithuania, Macedonia, Moldova, Poland, Romania, Russia, Slovakia, Slovenia, Ukraine, and FR Yugoslavia. The Western European states are: Austria, Belgium, Cyprus, Denmark, Finland, France, Germany, Greece, Iceland, Ireland, Italy, Luxembourg, Malta, the Netherlands, Norway, Portugal, Spain, Sweden, Switzerland, and the United Kingdom. Turkey was omitted from the analysis due to the fact that it has not been an established democracy for considerably longer than many of the post-communist states, yet at the same time it does not fit easily into the 'Eastern' mould. Belarus and Azerbaijan were also omitted because they cannot be considered to be emerging democracies.

Electoral Institutions in Central and Eastern Europe and Western Europe Compared

During the communist period, elections were conducted throughout communist Europe according to absolute majority systems in single or small multi-member constituencies. In most cases voters had no choice of candidate, and where they could choose the options were individuals with the same political affiliation. Until the late 1980s, there was very little *political* choice in elections held under communism. Since that time virtually all the states of Central Europe and the former Soviet Union have reformed their electoral systems. The only ones not to have done so are Belarus and Turkmenistan - states that are also notable for their failure to democratise.

A cursory overview of electoral systems in Central and Eastern Europe (CEE) ten years after the final collapse of communism indicates a high degree of similarity between electoral processes on the two halves of the continent. The majority of states in the post-communist region have opted for the list proportional model that is the norm in Western Europe (accounting for 14 of 20 cases), rather than for Anglo-American single-member constituency systems. Of the 20 CEE states surveyed here, 12 have adopted list proportional representation and the remaining eight have mixed systems that include a proportional component (see Table 1 below).

As far as electoral institutions are concerned, it is fair to say that many of the differences between East and West are a function of historical point of development. The post-communist states have adopted 'state-of-the-art' electoral regimes complete with all the latest aspects of design innovations current at the end of the twentieth century. The mixed systems adopted by approximately a third of the states in the region are increasingly being favoured the world over by emerging democracies as well as established democracies such as Italy, Germany, New Zealand and Japan.[5] In terms of electoral administrative institutions the CEE states are also generally more advanced than their Western counterparts. Firstly, in keeping with commitments to the OSCE under the 1990 Copenhagen document, they all allow international and domestic observers to be present for the main events of the voting process. Their Western neighbours are also in theory bound by these commitments, yet they often see fit to ignore them. Secondly, the post-communist states have almost all established permanent independent electoral commissions to oversee the electoral process and to ensure that it is not influenced by the interests of current power-holders. Though independent commissions of this type have come to be recognised as 'best practice',[6] the majority of Western European states still allow their elections to be run by a branch of the government - typically the ministry of the interior - which is under political control. Finally, many of the CEE countries have procedures for maintaining the integrity of the electoral process - including arrangements for guaranteeing vote security and accurate tabulation - that are more rigorous than those of Western European states.

Thus, in institutional terms, the post-communist states have taken the Western European model and improved upon it. This has partly been the result of Western assistance programmes that have deemed it necessary to introduce more stringent procedures in the new democracies than they have at home, and partly the consequence of a failure on the part of many Western states to modernise their electoral practices.[7] Though the quality of electoral administration in the newly democratised states is not *in practice* always as high as might be desired, the quality of electoral institution design is in most cases superior to that found in the established democracies. The CEE states will soon undoubtedly be demanding in their negotiations with various supranational European bodies that their Western counterparts come up to the new standards established in the East.

A finding perhaps more interesting from the point of view of political science is that in terms of electoral outcomes the states of Central and Eastern Europe are also approximating the patterns of results we find in Western European elections. Tables 1 and 2 display various measures of the size of

Table 1: Electoral Systems and Electoral Outcomes:
Eastern and Central Europe

Country	Year	Type of Electoral System	Effective Number of Electoral Parties*	Effective Number of Parliamentary Parties*	Seat Share of the Two Largest Parties	Minimum Number Parties to Form a Majority
Albania	1997	Mixed (26% PR, 74% SM)	2.87 (.01)	2.07	81.29%	1
Armenia	1999	Mixed (43% PR, 57% SM)	4.77	3.97	54.96%	2
Bosnia and Herceg.	2000	Regional PR	7.73	7.29	40.48%	3
Bulgaria	2001	Regional PR	3.95	2.92	71.25%	2
Croatia	2000	Regional PR	3.89** (.05)	2.71**	72.55%	2
Czech Republic	1998	Regional PR	4.76	3.70	68.50%	2
Estonia	1999	Regional PR	6.68	5.50	45.54%	3
Georgia	1999	Mixed (64%PR, 36% SM)	3.98** (.01)	2.36**	76.17%	1
Hungary	1998	Mixed (54% PR, 46% SM)	5.04	4.00	63.99%	2
Latvia	1998	Regional PR	6.94	5.49	45.00%	3
Lithuania	2000	Mixed (50% PR, 50% SM)	7.85	6.51	56.74%	2
Macedonia	1998	Mixed (29% PR, 71% SM)	6.55	3.95	64.17%	2
Moldova	2001	PR	3.57	1.85	89.11%	1
Poland	1997	Regional PR	4.55	2.94**	79.34%	2
Romania	2000	Regional PR	5.26	3.57**	72.87%	2
Russia	1999	Mixed (50% PR, 50% SM)	6.34	4.76	41.56%	3
Slovakia	1998	PR	5.26	4.76	56.67%	2
Slovenia	2000	Regional PR	5.14** (.02)	4.55**	53.33%	2
Ukraine	1998	Mixed (50% PR, 50% SM)	9.06***	5.49***	37.11%	4
Yugoslavia	2000	Regional PR	3.19 (.02)	3.12	73.91%	2
Average			5.37	4.08	62.23%	2.15

Notes: Figures in brackets are confidence intervals.
* These measures exclude independent candidates. In mixed systems, the effective number of elective parties is calculated as the weighted average of the effective number of parties in the two votes, except for Armenia and Georgia where list vote percentages only were used, due to lack of adequate single-member vote data.
** These figures exclude ethnic representatives of minority, regional, and overseas groups elected according to different rules and/or through separate processes.
*** Party affiliation is defined here in terms of party membership.
Sources: see Appendix.

Table 2: Electoral Systems and Electoral Outcomes: Western Europe

Country	Year	Type of Electoral System	Effective Number of Electoral Parties*	Effective Number of Parliamentary Parties*	Seat Share of the Two Largest Parties	Minimum Number Parties to Form a Majority
Austria	1999	Regional PR	3.82	3.41	63.93%	2
Belgium	1999	Regional PR	10.32	9.05	30.00%	4
Cyprus	2001	Regional PR	3.77	3.64	69.64%	2
Denmark	1998	Regional PR	4.73	4.72	58.66%	2
Finland	1999	Regional PR	5.90	5.15	49.50%	3
France	1997	SM absolute majority	3.43	2.51	66.72%	2
Germany	1998	Mixed (50% PR, 50% SM)[9]	3.29	2.91	81.17%	2
Greece	2000	Regional PR	2.64	2.21	94.33%	1
Iceland	1999	Regional PR	3.55	3.45	68.25%	2
Ireland	1997	Single-Transferable Vote	4.03	3.00	78.92%	2
Italy	2001	Mixed (25% PR, 75% SM)	2.55**	2.04**	96.82%	1
Luxemb.	1999	Regional PR	4.62	4.34	56.67%	2
Malta	1998	Single Transferable Vote	2.04	1.99	100.00%	1
Netherlands	1998	PR	5.14	4.82	55.33%	2
Norway	1997	Regional PR	5.07	4.36	54.55%	2
Portugal	1999	Regional PR	3.06	2.61	85.22%	2
Spain	2000	Regional PR	3.02	2.48	88.00%	1
Sweden	1998	Regional PR	4.53	4.29	61.03%	2
Switzerland	1999	Regional PR	5.62	5.16	47.50%	3
United Kingdom	2001	SM plurality	3.12	2.16	87.86%	1
Average			4.21	3.72	69.71%	1.90

Notes:
* These measures exclude independent candidates. In mixed systems, the effective number of elective parties was calculated as the weighted average of the effective number of parties in the two components of the ballot. In mixed systems list votes were used to calculate the effective number of elective parties.
** The Casa delle Libertà and L'Ulivo coalitions are treated as parties for the purposes of these calculations.
Sources: see Appendix.

the party systems generated by most recent elections in CEE and Western Europe respectively (as of 1 July 2001). Though there are a number of important outliers in both tables, the means are strikingly similar. The average effective number of elective parties in the CEE states was 5.37 as against a 4.21 average in Western Europe. The average effective number of parliamentary parties was 4.08, compared to 3.72 in the West.[8] Eastern European party systems are, ten years on from the communist transitions, slightly larger than those of the West, but the overall patterns are similar, and the difference between the size of the resultant party systems is not statistically significant.

Another way of assessing party systems is to examine their 'shape' (rather than their size). A good measure of this is the combined seat share of the two largest parties, which gives an indication of the extent to which the country in question approximates a two-party system. The average for this measure was 62.23 per cent in the CEE states and 69.71 per cent in the Western European parliaments. A second indicator of the shape of parliamentary party systems is the number of parties required to form a majority; the average on this measure is 2.15 in CEE and 1.90 in Western Europe. Again neither of these differences are statistically significant.[10] Compared with the established democracies of Western Europe, Central and Eastern European party systems tend to be slightly larger and less strongly dominated by a small number of core parties, but the convergence in overall outcomes between the two halves of the continent is more pronounced than their divergence.

But behind these broad similarities lie some interesting variations between East and West. The *difference* between the effective number of elective parties and the effective number of parliamentary parties is a good indication of the extent to which the electoral system is shaping the party system. In their original analysis of the effective number of parties in 15 Western European states, Laakso and Taagepera found that between 1945 and 1976 there were only 21 elections where the difference between the two figures was greater than 0.6.[11] Recalculations based on their data indicate that in these same 15 states the average difference between the measures was 0.3 ten years after the end of the Second World War when Western European party systems were re-formed. At the millennium, the average difference among the 20 Western European countries studied here was 0.50. By contrast, ten years after the fall of communism in Central and Eastern Europe, the average difference between the effective number of elective parties and the effective number of parliamentary parties was 1.29 - more than two-and-a-half times that found in the West, and four times that found in Western Europe at a comparable point in the process of party system development.[12] Moreover, the mean difference between the two figures in the West and East in 2001 was significant at the .001 level. Though outcomes may be broadly similar in East and West, electoral systems are having a much more restrictive effect on the size of party systems in the post-communist states than in their Western European counterparts.

Accounting for East-West Differences

Numerous studies of the effect of electoral systems on the size of party systems have found that the most consistently important determinant of the tendency of an electoral system to restrict the size of the party system is constituency design; smaller constituency size (or 'district magnitude') tends to be linked to smaller average party system size.[13] Yet established 'Western' democracies make up the majority of states that have been included in the analyses on which these findings are based, and it is not clear that the same relationship between constituency magnitude and party system size holds in Central and Eastern Europe.

Several studies of the effects of electoral systems in post-communist Europe have found that where party systems are not nationally integrated and/or not well institutionalised, small constituency size can lead to a proliferation in the number of parties represented in parliament, as it encourages candidacies by locally-based parties and independents.[14]

The type of mixed system most common in Central and Eastern Europe has a similar effect. Unlike in Germany and Italy, where the list-PR upper tier is used to compensate for the disproportionalities generated by the distribution of single-member seats, all the CEE mixed systems are, with the exception of Albania and the partial exception of Hungary, of the parallel type; there is no connection between the two components when it comes to seat distribution.[15] The consequence of this is that different types of parties tend to be successful in the single-member and PR components, leading to an overall increase in the number of successful parties when the results from the two halves of the system are combined.[16] Though mixed systems have traditionally been thought of as compromises between single-member and PR laws, they have often not operated in this way in post-communist Europe; nor have single-member systems consistently worked to reduce the size of party systems.

Nevertheless, the overall size of constituencies on CEE is similar to that in Western Europe, as can be seen from a comparison of Tables 3 and 4. The median size of constituencies in the primary or lower tier of the 20 Central and East European systems is 6.39 (the mean is 18.58, which falls to 6.70 if we remove the two large single-constituency systems of Moldova and Slovakia). In Western Europe the corresponding median is 7.60 (the mean is 14.82, or 7.71 without the single-constituency system of the Netherlands). The CCE systems do therefore have slightly smaller average sized constituencies than those in the Western portion of the continent, but the difference is not great, and it can largely be accounted for by the fact that there are so many mixed systems in the East. If we examine trends within system types, we find that the median size of lower-tier PR constituencies in CEE is 10.09 and the mean

Table 3: Constituency Design in the Most Recent Elections in Central and Eastern Eastern Europe

Country	Number of Lower-tier Constituencies	Number of Upper-tier Constituencies*	Size of Chamber	Average Number of Seats per Lower-Tier Constituency**
Two-vote systems				
Armenia	75	1 (a,p,56)	131	1.00
Georgia	85	1 (a,p,150)	235	1.00
Hungary	176	20 (a,p,< = 152) + 1 (r)	386	1.00
Lithuania	71	1 (a,p,70)	141	1.00
Macedonia	85	1 (a,p,35)	120	1.00
Russia	225	1 (a,p,225)	450	1.00
Ukraine	225	1 (a,p,225)	450	1.00
Average	134.57	4.00	273.29	1.00
List-PR systems				
Bosnia and Herzegovina	8	1 (r)	42	5.25
Bulgaria	31	None	240	7.74
Croatia	10	None	151	14.00
Czech Republic	8	1 (r)	200	25.00
Estonia	11	1 (r)	101	9.18
Latvia	5	None	100	20.00
Moldova	1	None	101	101.00
Poland	52	1 (r + a,p,69)	460	7.52
Romania	42	1 (r)	345	7.79
Slovakia	1	None	150	150.00

table (*cont.*)

Country	Number of Lower-tier Constituencies	Number of Upper-tier Constituencies*	Size of Chamber	Average Number of Seats per Lower-Tier Constituency**
Slovenia	8	1 (r)	90	11.00
Yugoslavia	27	None	138	5.11
Average	17.00	0.50	176.5	30.30 (11.26***)
Other systems				
Albania[18]	115	1 (a,p,40)	155	1.00
Average for all	63.05	0.70	209.30	18.58 (6.70***)

Notes:

* An 'r' indicates that the seats are remainders; an 'a' indicates that they are additional. When the additional seats are distributed so as to compensate for disproportionality the 'a' is followed by a 'c'; when they are used to magnify it the 'a' is followed by an 'm'. A 'p' indicates that the upper-tier seats are distributed through a parallel (independent) mechanism. These letters are followed, when applicable, by the number of additional seats.

** These figures exclude seats reserved for minorities, etc.

*** The figures in brackets exclude the single-seat systems of Moldova and Slovakia.

Sources: see Appendix.

Table 4: Constituency Design in the Most Recent Elections in Western Europe

Country	Number of Lower-tier Constituencies	Number of Upper-tier Constituencies*	Size of Chamber	Average Number of Seats per Lower-Tier Constituency**
Two-vote systems				
Germany	328	16 (a,c,341)	669	1.00
Italy	475	26 (a,c,155)	630	1.00
Average	401.50	21.00	649.50	1.00
List-PR systems				
Austria	9	2 (r)	183	20.33
Belgium	20	9 (r)	150	7.50

table (*cont.*)

Country	Number of Lower-tier Constituencies	Number of Upper-tier Constituencies*	Size of Chamber	Average Number of Seats per Lower-Tier Constituency**
Cyprus	6	1 (r)	80	13.33
Denmark	17	1 (a,c,40)	179	8.18
Finland	15	None	200	13.33
Greece	56	1 (a,m,12)	300	5.36
Iceland	8	1 (a,c,13)	63	6.25
Luxembourg	4	None	60	15.00
Netherlands	1	None	150	150.00
Norway	19	None	165	8.68
Portugal	22	None	230	10.45
Spain	53	None	350	6.60
Sweden	29	1 (a,c,39)	349	10.69
Switzerland	26	None	200	7.69
Average	*20.36*	*1.14*	*189.93*	*20.24*
				(10.26)
Other systems				
France	577	None	577	1.00
Ireland	41	None	166	4.05
Malta	65	None	13	5.00
United Kingdom	659	None	659	1.00
Average	*335.5*	—	*353.75*	*2.76*
Average for all	*121.50*	*(2.90)*	*268.65*	*14.82*
				*(7.71**)*

Notes:

* An 'r' indicates that the seats are remainders; an 'a' indicates that they are additional. When the additional seats are distributed so as to compensate for disproportionality the 'a' is followed by a 'c'; when they are used to magnify it the 'a' is followed by an 'm'. A 'p' indicates that the upper-tier seats are distributed through a parallel (independent) mechanism. These letters are followed, when applicable, by the number of additional seats.

** The figures in brackets exclude the single-seat system of the Netherlands.

Sources: see Appendix.

is 11.26 when Moldova and Slovakia are removed from the dataset. This is only marginally larger than the corresponding median of 9.57 and mean of 10.26 for Western Europe without the Netherlands.

In both East and West exactly half of the list PR systems have upper tiers, though as previously noted, these are more often or not distributed without reference to the lower tier in CEE, whereas in Western Europe they tend to be pooled remainders or compensatory seats. All three types of upper tier increase the effective number of parties, and their precise effects can be expected to depend in practice more on how they interact with the political system in question than on the manner of seat distribution which they prescribe.[17] What is clear is that there is not a great difference in constituency design between CEE and Western Europe, and there is little indication that the slightly smaller average constituency size in the East can account for the greater reductive effect of the post-communist electoral systems.

The principal mechanism through which electoral parties are being excluded from parliament in the CEE states is the formal threshold of representation - the number or percentage of votes above which a party must poll in order to be eligible to win seats. Whereas in Western Europe thresholds are used sparingly, and usually only to limit participation in second-tier seat distribution, thresholds are very commonly employed in list proportional systems in CEE to exclude parties that fail to achieve a certain minimum percentage of the national vote (compare Tables 5 and 6). As indicated in Tables 5 and 6, an average lower-tier threshold of 4.25 per cent for single parties in the East compares with only 1.23 per cent in the West, and many of the Eastern European electoral systems have higher thresholds still for coalitions. The regional difference is largely a function of the fact that thresholds are used to exclude parties in the lower or only tier of 17 out of 20 CEE systems but only 6 out of 20 Western European systems. But even if we restrict the comparison to those systems that incorporate lower-tier thresholds, the average was 5.00 in the East and 3.28 in the West. More CEE states impose thresholds, and those they impose tend to be higher than those found in Western Europe.[19]

Table 5: List Thresholds in the Most Recent Elections in
Central and Eastern Europe*

Country	List Threshold at the Last Election*
Albania	None for lower-tier distribution; 2% for upper-tier distribution
Armenia	5%
Bosnia and Herzegovina	None
Bulgaria	4%
Croatia	5%
Czech Republic	5% for a party; 7% for a coalition of two parties, 9% for a coalition of three parties, 11% for a coalition of four or more parties
Estonia	None for lower-tier distribution; 5% threshold for upper-tier distribution
Georgia	7%
Hungary	5% for a party, 10% for a coalition of two parties; 15% for a coalition of three or more parties
Latvia	5%
Lithuania	5%; 7% for coalitions
Macedonia	5%
Moldova	6%
Poland	5% for a party and 8% for a coalition in lower-tier distribution; 7% for upper-tier distribution
Romania	5% (+ 3% for the second party in a coalition and 1% for each additional party, up to a maximum of 10%)
Russia	5%
Slovakia	5% for a party or each party within a coalition
Slovenia	4%
Ukraine	4%
FR Yugoslavia	5% (at constituency-level)
Average (single-party threshold for lower-tier seat distribution)	4.25%

Note: * Only thresholds for list PR systems were coded, as the concept cannot be so readily transferred to either STV or the two-round system, and it does not apply to first-past-the-post elections.

Sources: see Appendix.

Table 6: List Thresholds in the Most Recent Elections in Western Europe*

Country	List Threshold at the Last Election
Austria	None in lower tier; one constituency seat *or* 4% of the national vote is required for participation in upper-tier seat allocation
Belgium	None in lower tier; 33% of the quota in at least one constituency is required for upper-tier seat allocation
Cyprus	None in lower tier; 1 constituency seat *or* 1.8% of valid votes required to be eligible for first seat in upper-tier distribution (10% for coalitions of 2 parties; 20% for coalitions of more than 2 parties); 3.6% is required for a second seat
Denmark	None in lower tier; one constituency seat *or* at least the average vote in at least two regions *or* 2% of the national vote is required to participate in upper-tier seat allocation
Finland	None
France	N/A
Germany	5% *or* three SM constituency seats
Greece	3% and candidates nominated in at least 3/4 of all constituencies
Iceland	None
Ireland	N/A
Italy	4%
Luxembourg	None
Malta	N/A
Netherlands	0.67%
Norway	None
Portugal	None
Spain	3% (at constituency level)
Sweden	Constituencies: 12% in lower-tier *or* 4% at national level; upper tier: 4%
Switzerland	None
United Kingdom	N/A
Average (single-party threshold for lower-tier seat distribution)	1.23%

Note: * Only thresholds for list PR systems were coded, as the concept cannot be so readily transferred to either STV or the two-round system, and it does not apply to first-past-the-post elections.

Sources: see Appendix.

Also noteworthy is the fact that these thresholds have risen over time. There have been increases in Georgia, Hungary, Latvia, Lithuania, Moldova, Poland, Romania, and Slovenia; and in the Czech and Slovak republics though the single-party thresholds have not changed, these have been supplemented by higher thresholds for coalitions (see Table 5).[20] By contrast, there are very few instances of a threshold having been lowered during the post-communist period. Albania lowered its threshold for upper-tier seat allocation from four per cent to two per cent prior to the 1997 elections, and a 2.5 per cent threshold in the Slovenian elections of 1990 (before Slovenia became an independent state) was subsequently abolished, before being re-introduced at the level of four per cent for the 2000 elections, yet these are the only cases of reduction.

Olga Shvetsova notes that legal thresholds have a greater effect in the context of post-communism than they otherwise would because uncertainty and lack of information on the part of voters, generated by inexperience, by the large number of parties on offer, and by the volatility of many of the party systems in the region, cause co-ordination problems for voters, making it difficult for them to vote strategically so as to ensure that their choice is one that has a realistic chance of clearing the threshold.[21] Not only are formal thresholds relatively high in and rising in CEE, but they also have a stronger impact on party system size than equivalent thresholds would have in established democracies.

A final difference between East and West that is worth pausing on is the varying 'reach' of party systems in the two parts of Europe. The party systems in some CEE states do not dominate political competition as they do in the West, where it is rare for political independents to be elected to parliament. While no independents were elected through the PR systems of CEE, and only one independent was elected from a single-member constituency in Hungary, the situation in some of the mixed systems in the former Soviet systems is rather different. In Russia 112 of the 225 single-member seats in the 1999 elections were won by non-partisans, and in Ukraine 116 such candidates won single-member seats in the 1998 elections. In both cases these numbers represent about half of all the single-member seats available for election and approximately a quarter of the entire parliament. It is fair to say that political competition is not completely 'partified' in these states, and that analysis of the party system alone neglects important aspects of the electoral dynamic.

Interpreting East-West Differences

Comparisons of the extent to which electoral systems restrict electoral party systems have demonstrated that Central and Eastern European electoral systems are doing far more 'work' than their Western counterparts. Similar overall party system configurations are being achieved from different inputs and through rather different mechanisms. Whereas decades of competition account for the relatively consolidated party systems in the West, consolidation is achieved in the East by use of 'artificial' devices such as thresholds which discourage small parties and encourage coalition formation.

It is understandable that the effective number of elective parties should be relatively high in new democracies. When competition has not yet developed into predictable patterns, uncertainty of electoral outcomes is high, and it makes more sense for aspirant politicians to try their luck. Moreover, individual parties are often not yet well enough institutionalised to maintain the loyalty of their members, which results in party system fluidity as parties split and regroup with relatively high frequency.[22] A more challenging question is why the new democracies have introduced electoral systems that reduce the size of their party systems to such an extent that they are able to achieve party systems of similar size to those in Western Europe.

A number of possible explanations might be advanced to account for this. A functionalist explanation would hold that contemporary democracies 'require' party systems of a certain size, and that the CEE electoral systems have been designed so as to deliver that outcome. The problem with this explanatory approach is that it does not provide a satisfactory account of the causal processes involved and the role of agency in generating the observed effect. A more plausible explanation is that the strong reductive impact of the CEE electoral systems reflects efforts by successful new parties to consolidate their strength by blocking potential competitors. This strategy is successful because social sectors represented by the excluded parties tend to be less well organised than their Western counterparts.

A second question is why so many of the CEE states have chosen the formal threshold as their tool of choice. Arend Lijphart notes that: 'Low magnitudes have the same effect as high thresholds: both limit proportionality and the opportunities for small parties to win seats [. . .] thresholds and district magnitudes can be seen as two sides of the same coin'.[23] Given that electoral system designers in Central and Eastern Europe could have chosen either to reduce the average size of constituencies or to impose formal thresholds in order to restrict the size of their party systems, why did they choose the latter route? The answer to this question is undoubtedly complex. Recent developments in CEE must be seen in the broader context of developments elsewhere. The use of formal electoral thresholds has increased dramatically in recent years, especially in third wave democracies in Africa and to a lesser extent in Latin America.[24] Taagepera and Shugart attribute their popularity to their success in Germany,[25] but there are also several other possible motives for this choice of electoral institution.

Use of a threshold rather than manipulation of constituency magnitude has advantages. It is relatively easy to predict how a threshold will work on the basis of previous election results, whereas the consequences of redistricting may be more difficult to determine. Predictability may be seen as an especial advantage in the context of democratisation, where unpredictable rules can foster the multiplication of parties who decide to try their luck in the electoral lottery. Predictability also enhances the ability of sitting legislators to bargain effectively over proposals for electoral reform. A corollary of this is that thresholds are a transparent mechanism that parties and voters alike can readily comprehend. The perceived fairness of this type of device may make it more appealing than districting decisions which can seem arbitrary at best or biased at worst.

Furthermore, reduction of constituency size poses certain problems in CEE. In several of the newly independent states electoral designers have been wary of introducing regional constituencies lest this has a fragmenting effect on already weak central state structures. This has been an issue in the PR systems of Bosnia and Herzegovina, Moldova, and Slovakia, and in the PR component of the mixed system in Ukraine. The thresholds employed in CEE, by contrast, generally apply to state-wide vote shares.[26] This means that they will tend to help integrate the party system at the national level and weed out small regionalist parties. In new states - which make up 15 of the 20 CEE cases considered here - national integration may well be a political priority during the early stages of democratic consolidation, even though such efforts can sometimes have negative consequences for regionally-concentrated ethnic minorities (such as the ethnic Hungarians in Slovakia who suffered in 1998 from the Slovak single constituency and high thresholds for parties and coalitions).

Finally, a significant reduction in constituency magnitude can come up against considerable problems of political acceptability in the Central and Eastern European context. Though reduction in average constituency size has in some cases been attempted as a means of excluding small parties from representation and thereby benefiting larger political organisations, it has not always been seen as being consistent with democratic principles. In 1996 Slobodan Milosevic's Socialist Party of Serbia enraged the democratic opposition by reducing the average size of PR districts in Yugoslavia from 36 to 10 in a move that was widely perceived as authoritarian.[27] A similar move was attempted in 2000 by the Czech Civic Democratic Party, but it was ruled unconstitutional by the Constitutional Court on the grounds that it did not conform to the spirit of proportional representation which was required by the Czech basic law.[28]

The use of an electoral threshold does, however, also have several disadvantages. One of the negative consequences of its transparency is that a threshold yields results that clearly show how many votes have been wasted. Though the proportion of wasted votes is typically considerably higher in plurality systems where the successful candidate will often win as little as 30 per cent of the vote, it would be necessary to aggregate all the individual constituency vote totals in order to demonstrate this. The proportion of wasted votes in a list PR system is far more readily calculated. This figure has been as high as 50 per cent in the Russian list vote of 1995 and 62 per cent in the Georgian list vote the same year, generating allegations that the elections in question were not legitimate. It is for this reason that some Central and Eastern European electoral laws have special provisions to deal with extreme outcomes. In Lithuania, for example, if fewer than 60 per cent of the valid vote goes to parties which clear the five per cent threshold on the list ballot, the threshold is reduced. In the Czech Republic a reduction is effected if fewer than two parties or coalitions obtain seats under the normal procedures.

A second disadvantage of formal barriers to electoral success is the 'threshold effect' they generate by imposing a sharp all-or-nothing cut-off. If parties clear the threshold they are guaranteed a certain minimum number of seats, often in excess of the threshold proportion because they will also win the seats that would otherwise have gone to the parties that fell short of the electoral hurdle. In the Georgian election of 1999, for instance, three parties cleared what was by now a seven per cent threshold, together polling 74.01 per cent of the vote. This meant that the weakest of the three - Industry Will Save Georgia - won 14 list seats on the basis of 7.08 per cent of the vote, whereas the Georgian Labour Party won no list seats because it gained only 6.69 per cent of the electorate's favour. High success premiums such as this may in some cases have serious consequences both for those who win them and for those who just fail. The sudden changes in political fortunes which result may give the appearance that thresholds are a somewhat arbitrary and ruthless device. Small constituency magnitude, by contrast, provides each party numerous chances to win seats, and it is likely that small but solid parties will manage to win at least one or two seats and thereby maintain token representation.[29]

Though there is undoubtedly no 'best' electoral system for emerging democracies, the choices made by electoral engineers reveal much about the political, social and institutional context in which they operate. Despite superficial similarities between the results generated by electoral systems in Eastern and Western Europe, the processes underlying these results are quite different. And despite - or perhaps because of - the high degree of uncertainty surrounding elections in the East, electoral institutions have a greater impact on political outcomes than they do in the established democracies of the West. This confirms the need for more research on the processes that subtend institutional choice and a better understanding of how these processes are linked to historical trajectories of political development.

Appendix: Data Sources

Data on electoral laws and results were taken from the following sources:
Database on Central and Eastern European Elections: Results and Legislation at
    www.essex.ac.uk/elections
International Foundation for Electoral Systems Election Guide at www.ifes.org
Elections Around the World database at www.electionworld.org
International Parliamentary Union Parline database at www.ipu.org
Parties and Elections in Europe database at www-public.rz.uni-duesseldorf.de
    /~nordsiew/

Alan Siaroff, *Comparative Party Systems: An Analysis of Parliamentary Elections since 1945* (New York and London: Garland Publishing, 2000).

Olga Shvetsova, 'A Survey of Post-Communist Electoral Institutions: 1990-1998', *Electoral Studies* 18/3 (1999), pp. 397-409.

These data were in some cases supplemented by other sources, including: Armenia: Website of the Armenian electoral commission at www.elections.am

Bosnia and Herzegovina: Website of the OSCE Mission in Bosnia and Herzegovina website at www.oscebih.org

Georgia: 'Georgia Parliamentary Elections, 31 October and 14 November 1999: Final Report' OSCE Office for Democratic Institutions and Human Rights, Warsaw, 7 February 2000.

Italy: Italian Ministry of the Interior website at http://cedweb.mininterno.it:8890/

Macedonia: Nova Makedonia 21 October, 1998, p. 5.

Yugoslavia: Yugoslav Ministry of Statistics website at www.gov.yu

Notes

[1] In the absence of clear criteria for determining the 'systematicity' of party configurations, the term 'party system' will be used in this paper to refer to the sum total of parties that are electorally active in a given country at a given time.

[2] Seymour Martin Lipset and Stein Rokkan, 'Cleavage Structures, Party Systems and Voter Alignments', in Seymour M. Lipset and Stein Rokkan (eds.), *Party Systems and Voter Alignments: Cross-National Perspectives* (New York: The Free Press, 1967), pp. 1-64; Stein Rokkan, *Citizens, Elections, Parties: Approaches to the Comparative Study of the Process of Development* (Oslo: Universitetsforlaget, 1970); Andrew McLaren Carstairs, *A Short History of Electoral Systems in Western Europe* (London: George Allen and Unwin, 1980).

[3] Maurizio Cotta, 'Structuring the New Party Systems after the Dictatorship: Coalitions, Alliances, Fusions and Splits During the Transition and Post-Transition Phase', in Geoffrey Pridham and Paul G. Lewis (eds.) *Stabilising Fragile Democracies: Comparing New Party Systems in Southern and Eastern Europe* (London and New York: Routledge, 1996); Herbert Kitschelt, Zdenka Mansfeldova, Radoslaw Markowski and Gabor Toka, *Post-Communist Party Systems: Competition, Representation and Inter-Party Cooperation* (Cambridge: Cambridge University Press, 1999); Paul Lewis, *Political Parties in Post-Communist Eastern Europe* (London and New York: Routledge, 2000).

[4] See the appendix for a list of data sources.

[5] See André Blais and Louis Massicotte, 'Mixed Electoral Systems: An Overview', *Representation* 3/4 (1996), pp. 15-18; Sarah Birch, 'The Effects of Mixed Electoral Systems in Eastern Europe', Paper presented at the 30th Annual Conference of the University Association for Contemporary European Studies, Budapest 7-9 April,

2000; Matthew Soberg Shugart and Martin P. Wattenberg (eds.), *Mixed-Member Electoral Systems: The Best of Both Worlds* (Oxford: Oxford University Press, 2001).

[6] Guy S. Goodwin-Gill, *Free and Fair Elections: International Law and Practice* (Geneva: Inter-Parliamentary Union, 1994).

[7] Though outside Europe, the events surrounding the 2000 US presidential race provide a good illustration of this phenomenon. The legal fiasco over the election outcome would have been far less likely to have occurred in most CEE states, and had it occurred, the results of the election would in all probability not have been recognised as legitimate by most 'Western' powers.

[8] The effective number of parties, designed as a measure of the number of parties that 'count' in an electoral system', is defined as one divided by the sum of squares of the fractional vote (or seat) shares of all the parties competing in (or successful in) the election (see Markku Laakso and Rein Taagepera 'Effective Number of Parties: A Measure with Application to Western Europe', Comparative Political Studies 12/3, (1979); Rein Taagepera and Matthew Soberg Shugart, *Seats and Votes: The Effects and Determinants of Electoral Systems* (New Haven and London: Yale University Press, 1989). Independents were excluded from these calculations. Where data were incomplete, Taagepera's method of bounds was used to perform the calculations (see Rein Taagepera, 'Effective Number of Parties for Incomplete Data', *Electoral Studies*, 16/2, (1997), pp. 145-51). The resulting figures have margins of error ranging from .01 to .05. The precise margins for each figure are indicated in the table in brackets where they are .01 or greater.

[9] The 50% PR/50% SM split in the German system is approximate, as the size of the parliament varies from term to term according to the number of extra compensatory seats (überhangmandate) that are created through the list seat distribution mechanism.

[10] The same is true of the seat share of the largest party, which conveys the same information as Taagepera's proposed measure of N-infinity, the inverse of the fractional seat share of the largest party (see 'Supplementing the Effective Number of Parties', *Electoral Studies*, 18 (1999), pp. 497-504).

[11] Laakso and Taagepera, 'Effective number of parties'.

[12] These differences indicate that the parallel between post-World War Two developments in Western Europe and post-Cold War developments in the East may not be an appropriate one, but as the Second World War is often taken to be a starting point in the study of Western European electoral system developments, the contrast has been retained for illustrative purposes.

[13] See, for instance, Douglas Rae, *The Political Consequences of Electoral Laws*, (2nd ed. New Haven and London: Yale University Press, 1971); Taagepera and Shugart, *Seats and Votes*; and Gary W. Cox, *Making Votes Count: Strategic Coordination in*

the World's Electoral Systems (Cambridge: Cambridge University Press, 1997).

14 Sarah Birch, 'Elections and Representation in Post-Communist Eastern Europe', in Hans-Dieter Klingemann and Kenneth Newton (eds.), *Elections in Central and Eastern Europe: The First Wave* (Berlin: Sigma, 2000), 13-35; Robert G. Moser, 'Electoral Systems and the Number of Parties in Post-Communist States', *World Politics*, 51/3 (1999), 359-84; Robert G. Moser, *Unexpected Outcomes: Electoral Systems, Political Parties and Representation in Russia* (Pittsburgh: University of Pittsburgh Press, 2001); Olga Shvetsova, 'A Survey of Post-Communist Electoral Institutions: 1990-1998', *Electoral Studies* 18/3 (1999), pp. 397-409.

15 The Albanian system is similar to that employed in Germany between 1949 and 1956; voters choose candidates in single-member constituencies only, and their party choices are then aggregated at the national level and used to distribute seats proportionally. This system is in many ways akin to a two-tier PR system. Hungary has a three-tier system in which there is one single-member seat tier, one parallel PR tier, and one compensatory PR tier.

16 Birch, 'Electoral systems and party system stability'.

17 It is notoriously difficult to quantify the role of upper tiers; Taagepera and Shugart incorporate them into their measure of 'effective magnitude' but in so doing they are obliged to make a number of questionable assumptions about the interactions between the tiers (see *Seats and Votes*). Cox (*Making Votes Count*, p. 215) finds that upper tiers have a considerable positive impact on the effective number of parties, but all his cases are of the compensatory variety. Katz finds that the distribution of upper-tier seats based on remainders has rather different effects from the distribution of additional upper-tier seats (see Richard Katz, *Democracy and Elections* (Oxford and New York: Oxford University Press, 1997), p. 136).

18 Although Albania is often classified as a 'mixed' system, voters only make one choice; it is therefore best to think of it as a single-member system with a compensatory upper-tier.

19 These figures actually under-estimate the extent of the difference, as they are based on thresholds for single-parties only, whereas higher barriers apply to coalitions in many CEE states (see Table 5).

20 Shvetsova, 'A survey of post-communist'.

21 Shvetsova, 'A survey of post-communist'; Cox, *Making Votes Count*, p. 107.

22 Sarah Birch, 'Electoral Systems and Party System Stability in Post-Communist Europe', Paper prepared for presentation at the 97th annual meeting of the American Political Science Association, San Francisco, 30 August - 2 September, 2001.

23 Arend Lijphart, *Electoral Systems and Party Systems: A Study of Twenty-Seven Democracies, 1945-1990* (Oxford: Oxford University Press, 1994), p. 12.

[24] Mark P. Jones, 'A Guide to the Electoral Systems of the Americas', *Electoral Studies*, 14/1 (1995), pp. 5-21; Shaheen Mozaffar, 'Electoral Systems and Their Political Effects in Africa: A Preliminary Analysis', *Representation* 34/3-4, (1997), pp. 148-56.

[25] Taagepera & Shugart, *Making Votes Count*, p. 37.

[26] The exception in this case set is the five per cent constituency-level threshold employed in the Yugoslav elections of September 2000.

[27] Slobodanka Nedovic, 'Democratic Electoral Systems', paper presented at the Second Meeting of the New Serbia Forum, Budapest, 1-2 February, 2000; Laslo Sekelj, 'Parties and Elections: The Federal Republic of Yugoslavia - Change Without Transformation', *Europe-Asia Studies* 52/1 (2000), pp. 57-75.

[28] Keith Crawford, 'A System of Disproportional Representation: The Proposed Electoral Law for the Czech Republic', *Representation* 38/1 (2001), pp. 46-58.

[29] This is evident from comparison between the single-member and list components of mixed systems; in virtually all cases more parties have won seats in single-member districts than on lists (see Birch, 'Electoral systems and party system stability in post-communist Europe').

Frances Millard
Party Development and the Polish Presidential Election of October 2000

ABSTRACT

The decisive victory of incumbent president, Aleksander Kwaśniewski in the year 2000 was generally expected, given his high popularity ratings and the absence of an effective challenger. However, comparative analysis with previous Polish presidential elections shows that although the electoral process has long been routinised and the legitimacy of the victor assured, the effects have been highly disruptive for the political parties and (partly in consequence) for the political institutions. The lack of synchronisation of presidential and parliamentary elections disrupts the normal processes of parliamentary government. It raises the spectre of uneasy cohabitation of president and prime minister. In 2000 the effects on the parties were particularly profound. Both Solidarity and the Freedom Union 'learnt lessons' from their past experience, but they proved inappropriate ones. The election further consolidated the social democratic Left, while accelerating the disintegration of the Right and generating the reshaping of the Centre.

In October 2000 the incumbent Polish president, Aleksander Kwaśniewski, won the third post-communist direct presidential election with a decisive victory on the first ballot. His success was generally expected, and the campaign itself was largely uninteresting. Nevertheless, this election was important in two - if perhaps somewhat contradictory respects.

On the one hand, the clear routinisation and sheer normality of the election process offered further testimony to Poland's successful road to democracy. Yet on the other, the election itself had profound institutional implications. In regards to the party system it further consolidated the social democratic Left while accelerating the disintegration of both the Right and Centre. In terms of executive power, Kwaśniewski's victory meant a further year of uneasy cohabitation of prime minister and president. This paper examines the election of 2000 first in the context of previous presidential elections, then reviews the election campaign, and finally analyses its effects on the institutional development of Polish democracy and its party system.

Presidential elections in Poland have not coincided with parliamentary elections since the resignation of President Wojciech Jaruzelski in 1990 and the institution of direct elections at that time. This is unusual in Europe, though not unknown. France currently provides the major example of this type of political discontinuity, although the position there will change somewhat with the reduction in the length of the presidential term from seven to five years. Slovakia replaced indirect election by parliament with direct presidential elections in 1999, shortly after the parliamentary elections of November 1998 brought the anti-Mečiar opposition to power. The new arrangements stemmed from a hiatus when no president could be elected, as parliament repeatedly failed to muster the necessary majority to provide a successor to Michal Kovac. In 1999 the Slovak victor Rudolf Schuster was the candidate of the governing coalition and no disjuncture resulted; but he did not always prove a compliant partner. In Poland, however, the holding of direct elections at five-year intervals, with parliament elected every four years (or less), has thus far shaken the political parties and proved highly disruptive to the party system. It has also meant two periods of cohabitation, of the Left government with President Lech Wałęsa from 1993-95 and of the Right with President Kwaśniewski after 1997.

The Elections of 1990 and 1995

In 1990 there was no 'party system' to shock or disrupt, but that election too could be seen as a spur to party development. Jaruzelski's presidency was a product of the 1989 Round Table agreement between the then ruling communist party and Solidarity. As communists lost power in Central Europe and beyond the arrangement was increasingly seen as an anachronism. Pressure from Solidarity's Wałęsa for fresh presidential elections bore fruit in a constitutional amendment for direct elections and Jaruzelski's immediate resignation. Solidarity's inability to unite fully behind Wałęsa inaugurated a process of fragmentation and change within the Solidarity movement still unresolved in 2000. Solidarity first split into two groups during the 'war at the top' of spring 1990, the larger group supporting Wałęsa and the smaller endorsing the incumbent prime minister Tadeusz Mazowiecki. In the first round of the two-ballot majoritarian system in November the population also delivered a resounding negative judgement on the first phase of Poland's programme of economic transformation: Wałęsa came first and the eccentric expatriate populist Stan Tymiński, previously unknown, came second (see Table 1). At the same time the candidates for the successor parties, Cimoszewicz for the new Alliance of the Democratic Left (*Sojusz Lewicy Demokratycznej*, SLD) and Bartoszcze for the Polish Peasant Party (*Polskie Stronnictwo Ludowe*, PSL) established a benchmark of core support on which to build.

Table 1: The 1990 Presidential election, first ballot

	Votes	Per cent
Lech Wałęsa (Solidarity, POC et al.)	6,569,889	39.96
Stan Tymiński (Independent)	3,797,605	23.10
Tadeusz Mazowiecki (Solidarity, UD)	2,973,264	18.08
Włodzimierz Cimoszewicz (SLD)	1,514,025	9.21
Roman Bartoszcze (PSL)	1,176,175	7.15
Leszek Moczulski (KPN)	411,516	2.50

Source: Państwowa Komisja Wyborcza, from http://www.essex.ac.uk/elections

Wałęsa won the second round convincingly on 9 December with 74.3 per cent of the vote. The political establishment was horrified at Tymiński's strong showing and mobilised in support of the Solidarity candidate. However, Mazowiecki's followers then formalised their Democratic Union (*Unia Demokratyczna*) as a new political party in opposition to the president. Other small groups that had emerged to support Wałęsa also tried to position themselves for the expected parliamentary election; they included the Civic Accord (POC), the Liberal Democratic Congress (KLD), the Christian National Union (ZChN), and the Solidarity Peasant Party (PL).

Wałęsa himself neither joined nor promoted any of these new Solidarity-'parties'. This meant that he was unable to act as an anchor point for future political developments, leaving him with no political base for his presidency and generating further splits in the Solidarity movement. It also paved the way for the intensive fragmentation of parliament with Poland's first fully competitive parliamentary election in 1991. The manifest political disarray and confusion took its toll with the entry into parliament of deputies under 29 labels, with large numbers of local groupings as well as some ten incipient political parties.

By the 1995 presidential election the situation had changed considerably. The difficulties of government formation after 1991 led to the premature dissolution of parliament and fresh elections in September 1993. Due largely to new electoral thresholds designed to combat the earlier fragmentation, most Solidarity parties failed to enter parliament, while the top-up national list further exaggerated the gains of the winners. The resulting coalition of the Democratic Left Alliance with the Peasant Party was not a harmonious one, and it was beset by presidential obstructionism. Throughout 1995 Wałęsa remained in conflict with the government, making extensive use of the presidential veto and referrals to the Constitutional Tribunal to slow or block significant elements of the government's legislative programme.

In the 1995 presidential election Aleksander Kwaśniewski was the leader and unchallenged candidate of the SLD, but the other political parties revealed their basic weakness throughout the campaign and were in turn further weakened by it. Internal party divisions over candidate selection were salient from the early months of 1995, not least because President Wałęsa's extraordinary unpopularity left no figure around which Solidarity-parties could unite. Only the SLD maintained its unity, mobilised its regional and local structures, and fought a professional campaign on Kwaśniewski's behalf. Indeed, from spring 1995 onwards the contest was effectively viewed as a challenge for a place in the second round against Kwaśniewski.

The tiny Non-party Reform Bloc (BBWR) and two offshoots, along with the Solidarity trade union executive, supported Wałęsa. Former Prime Minister Waldemar Pawlak won the Peasant Party's (PSL) nomination, if by a humiliatingly narrow margin. The Democratic Union had showed some survival instinct following the 1993 debacle by uniting with the Liberal Democrats

(KLD) to form the Freedom Union (*Unia Wolności*) in April 1994. Now it seemed to undo itself by selecting Jacek Kuroń as its presidential candidate. Kuroń was an extremely popular politician, but he was too secular for the party's Catholic elements and too 'leftist' for its economic liberals. The UW failed to mobilise on Kuroń's behalf. The leadership of the Labour Union (*Unia Pracy*, UP) favoured Kuroń but its party delegates preferred the Ombudsman, Tadeusz Zieliński, who also gained the endorsement of the new Pensioners' Party (KPEiR).

In Cracow a 'stop Kwaśniewski' movement within the UW sought cross-party support, and some UW members reportedly worked secretly for Hanna Gronkiewicz-Waltz, director of the National Bank. The Christian Nationalists (ZChN) officially endorsed her; but several prominent ZChN members worked openly for the president. Indeed, as the opinion polls reported a shift of support to Wałęsa, the ZChN effectively abandoned Gronkiewicz-Waltz.

In principle the Solidarity-parties of the self-styled right committed themselves to a common candidate. In practice they remained fractious and fragmented, and several well-publicised conciliation meetings came to nought. The ZChN endorsed the Catholic banker. Other small parties and groupings hostile to Wałęsa supported Jan Olszewski, prime minister of a minority coalition for five months in 1992 until his defeat on a confidence vote over the 'lustration affair' (see below). These included Olszewski's own Movement for the Republic (*Ruch dla Rzeczpospolitej*, RdR), Rural Solidarity and the Centre Accord (*Porozumienie Centrum*, PC).

During the campaign Wałęsa clearly benefited from his incumbency. He was a known, if erratic quantity in the sea of right-wing candidates and little known Independents; and he was an effective campaigner, playing skilfully on anti-communist and Solidarity-nostalgia themes. As the polls registered his rise, the feeling gained currency that only Wałęsa could defeat Kwaśniewski. With a turnout of 64.79 per cent, the result on 5 November was decisive. As expected, Kwaśniewski and Wałęsa took the lion's share of the vote, 68.22 per cent, with little between them (see Table 2) and Kuroń a distant third. Olszewski did rather better than expected and Pawlak far worse. This was described as the 'logic of polarisation', with voters behaving in the first round as though it were already the decisive choice.

Table 2: Results of the November 1995 presidential election

candidate party/support	1st ballot (%)	2nd ballot (%)
Aleksander Kwaśniewski (SLD)	35.11	51.72
Lech Wałęsa (Indep/Solidarity)	33.11	48.28
Jacek Kuroń (UW)	9.22	
Jan Olszewski (RdR/PC)	6.86	
Waldemar Pawlak (PSL)	4.31	
Tadeusz Zieliński (Indep/UP/PPEiR)	3.53	
Hanna Gronkiewicz-Waltz (Indep/ZChN)	2.76	
Janusz Korwin-Mikke (UPR)	2.40	
Andrzej Lepper (Samoobrona)	1.32	
Jan Pietrzak (Independent)	1.12	
Tadeusz Koźluk (Independent)	0.15	
Kazimierz Piotrowicz (Independent)	44	0.07
Leszek Bubel (Independent)	0.04	

Source: Państwowa Komisja Wyborcza, from http://www.essex.ac.uk/elections

The poor showing of their candidates and their consequent lack of bargaining power threw the losing political parties into disarray over the second round. The Labour Union and the Centre Accord remained hostile to both candidates. The Peasant Party, despite its coalition partnership with the SLD, declared its 'neutrality'. The Freedom Union immediately endorsed Wałęsa. The Church also swung its weight solidly behind Wałęsa.

The campaign intensified in the interval between the two ballots, with mutual accusations of various irregularities. Opinion polls showed the candidates running neck-and-neck,[1] but in the event Kwaśniewski's victory was assured.

Turnout on 19 November was 68.23 per cent, higher than in the first round, with Kwaśniewski winning by a margin of some three per cent (see Table 2). Historical-symbolic divisions clearly played a major role in the presidential election, but they told only part of the story. Certainly there was little difference between the two candidates' programmatic aims of continuing 'reform' and accession to NATO and the EU. The main differences lay in their professed moral values - Wałęsa associated with Catholicism and Kwaśniewski with secular humanism[2] - and in personality and style. Kwaśniewski also benefited from the perceived welfare-orientation of the SLD-PSL coalition. In the event, however, Kwaśniewski benefited from his association with a popular government, his youth, and his eloquence; he convinced more people of his ability to protect social welfare, while rejecting old-style communist authoritarian practices.

If the presidential election did not precisely recreate the old divisions between 'communism' and Solidarity, it divided society into 'post-Solidarity' traditionalism and 'post-communist' social democracy. The two major centre parties, the PSL and UW, fared badly; and they were further squeezed as attention shifted to the extra-parliamentary right. The Labour Union (UP) had few potential allies and it suffered serious internal divisions.[3] The polarization of the political scene gathered momentum as preparations began immediately for the 1997 parliamentary elections.

Following his defeat Wałęsa himself sought a new role as the patron of 'post-Solidarity' forces stretching from the Freedom Union to the tiny, fragmented 'pocket parties' of the nationalist right. These expectations foundered on now-familiar rocks of personal self-aggrandisement and petty disputes, the person of Wałęsa himself, and the hostility of smaller parties to the UW. Indeed, Jan Olszewski's new party, the Movement for Rebuilding Poland (*Ruch Odbudowy Polski*, ROP) gained support for a broad platform of Christian patriotism, anti-communism and social justice.

In the event ROP fell victim to the determination of the Solidarity trade union to serve as the linchpin of right-wing unity. Solidarity Election Action (*Akcja Wyborcza Solidarność*, AWS), was born officially on 8 June 1996 as an alliance of Solidarity with some twenty small right-wing parties. It immediately made its presence felt in the polls, reaching 27 per cent and equalling SLD support in July.[4] Its leader Marian Krzaklewski, undercut ROP by stressing his own nationalist-clerical credentials, including his opposition to abortion and the sale of land to foreigners, and the dangers of untrammelled liberalism. At its height AWS brought together some 39 parties, organisations, groups and associations.[5]

In September 1997 the polarisation that had characterised the presidential election appeared confirmed. AWS won the third free parliamentary election with 33.8 per cent of the vote, while the incumbent SLD increased its share to 27.1 per cent. The UW performed respectably, but the PSL vote nearly halved in comparison with 1993. Olszewski's ROP managed to scrape into parliament, but the Labour Union did not cross the threshold.

The AWS negotiated a coalition agreement with the Freedom Union, with AWS's unknown Jerzy Buzek as premier. Given the small parliamentary presence of the PSL and ROP, the UW was the only possible partner. However, the UW was anathema for many elements of AWS, and internal tensions rent the coalition from the outset. Nor did the AWS hide its antipathy to the president. Wałęsa's hostility to the SLD-PSL coalition was now matched by the AWS-UW coalition's hostility to Kwaśniewski.

As with Wałęsa, a key factor in government-presidential relations after 1997 was the presidential election of the year 2000. In Wałęsa's case the obvious strategy had been to emphasise the great divide between Solidarity and the (ex)communists. A co-operative president bridging the gulf would not appeal to the still salient anti-communism of the Right; nor would he necessarily attract voters for whom the division was increasingly irrelevant. However, Wałęsa's negative approach to the SLD-PSL coalition was indiscriminate scatterfire, and instead of nurturing his closest allies, he successively alienated them. In the end Wałęsa's electoral appeal was based less on public approbation than on the recognition that no one else could defeat Kwaśniewski.

In Kwaśniewski's case in 2000 the potential challenger was Solidarity trade union and AWS leader Marian Krzaklewski, whose presidential ambitions were an open secret from 1997. Krzaklewski refused to take a government post after 1997 and Buzek seemed little more than the leader's puppet. Given its own tensions - between the coalition partners and within AWS itself - the government could well have used President Kwaśniewski as a positive asset. Instead Buzek sought first to ostracise and then to neutralise the president. Historical enmities clearly played a role, but they were kept to the fore by personal attacks on Kwaśniewski from the government, from AWS and from Krzaklewski.

This antagonistic stance helped keep in line the most anti-communist, nationalist and clerical elements of AWS. Yet Krzaklewski's strategy of confrontation, like that of Wałęsa, yielded no initial success and for similar reasons: Wałęsa had offered no positive leadership strategy, and Krzaklewski, regarded as the power behind the government throne, shared Buzek's reputation for lack of leadership and ineffectual decision-making. The government's popularity plunged to unprecedently low levels in summer 1999[6] in an atmosphere of renewed social protest and widespread perception of failed health and pension reforms. As Buzek's standing continued to fall,[7] so did that of AWS; but that of the SLD rose.[8]

The Presidential Election of 2000: The Prelude

Twelve candidates contested the election, former prime minister Jan Olszewski having withdrawn in its final days. Of these, four could be regarded as serious contenders: Aleksander Kwaśniewski himself was now nominally a non-party candidate. Still, he benefited greatly from the full support of the SLD leadership and party apparatus. To this was added that of the extra-parliamentary Labour Union (UP), whose 'pro-presidential' group had emerged triumphant, with many founding members from Solidarity, including erstwhile leader Ryszard Bugaj, leaving the party. Marian Krzaklewski led both the Solidarity trade union and AWS. When the then-governing coalition fell apart in June 2000, AWS became the sole party of Jerzy Buzek's minority government.

The third candidate was the self-styled 'citizens' candidate', Andrzej Olechowski, a wealthy businessman who made much of his non-party label. Olechowski's previous forays into politics had not been notably successful. He was briefly Minister of Finance in Jan Olszewski's short-lived government in 1992. Then he had been closely associated with the failed Non-Party Reform Bloc (BBWR) initiated by President Wałęsa in summer 1993; and he had for a time been Foreign Minister - as President Wałęsa's nominee - in the social democrat-peasant coalition after 1993. In 1997 he had left a small AWS-linked grouping because of AWS's feeble support for European integration, although he continued to speak out on major issues.

The fourth major contender was Jarosław Kalinowski, who had replaced Pawlak as leader of the Polish Peasant Party (PSL) after the 1993 parliamentary election. Conspicuous by its absence was the candidate of the Freedom Union (UW), which decided not to contest the election, fearing the dissipation of its voters and a repeat of its poor performance in 1995.

Throughout summer 2000 opinion polls had correctly suggested the irrelevance of the other eight candidates, most of whom had also stood in 1995. Andrzej Lepper, leader of the protest-oriented peasant movement Self-Defence (*SamoObrona*), hoped to make serious inroads into Kalinowski's prospective rural vote. Janusz Korwin-Mikke of the Union of Political Realism (*Unia*

Polityki Realnej) was an eccentric fixture of the political scene with his rabid anti-state, extreme laisser-faire views. Lech Wałęsa was attempting a dramatic comeback from the political wilderness, but his new Christian Democratic Party was barely registering in the polls and he had no organisational base. Jan Łopuszański had left the Christian Nationalists (ZChN) and hoped to lay the ground for leadership of a putative anti-European Union political force. Dariusz Grabowski sought a renewal in different guise of elements of the moribund Confederation for Independent Poland (KPN). Piotr Ikonowicz in theory offered a radical left-wing alternative with a party behind him (the tiny Polish Socialist Party, PPS), but found no echo to his rallying cries. Bogdan Pawlowski and General Tadeusz Wilecki may be dismissed outright as authoritarian-minded attention-seekers.

Aleksander Kwaśniewski looked impregnable for months preceding the election. Following AWS's victory in 1997, Kwaśniewski achieved sensational ratings for his presidential role, rising to 80 per cent in September 1998.[9] Despite some fluctuations, positive assessments of his presidency generally remained very high.[10] These ratings were partly a product of the significant unpopularity of the-then AWS coalition with the liberal centrist Freedom Union (November 1997-June 2000), but they created a dilemma for AWS. Marian Krzaklewski had made clear his presidential ambitions, but the obvious strength of the incumbent and Krzaklewski's own consistently low polling ratings of c. 4-6 per cent from mid-1999 made him reluctant to stand, yet powerful enough within AWS to prevent an alternative candidate. For months the pusillanimous Krzaklewski dithered, finally pushed into declaring his candidacy by elements within Solidarity and the AWS Social Movement (*Ruch Społeczny*, RS-AWS), conceived as the trade union's political arm and as the 'party of power'. Only in May 2000 did Krzaklewski become the official candidate of AWS. By this time other right-wing candidates had thrown their hats into the ring, including Andrzej Olechowski, emerging in opinion polls as the main challenger to the president. In June the UW withdrew from the fractious governing coalition, leaving a minority government and raising the spectre of early parliamentary elections.

During the early summer aspiring candidates were gathering (a minimum of 100,000) signatures to support their registration. At the same time another type of political spectacle was also being played out, namely the lustration of the candidates. Lustration was the term used to describe the screening of high posts to reveal those who had co-operated with the communist security services. It had been a contentious issue since the first direct presidential election in 1990. The issuing of a dubious list of alleged 'collaborators' had brought down Olszewski's government in June 1992 and the issue had formed part of AWS's platform before a law was finally passed in 1997, though as a weakened version of previous proposals. Under the law candidates for elected office (and other high-ranking officials) must submit an affidavit stating or denying a history of such co-operation with communist authorities. No penalty attached to an affidavit affirming collaboration, though proponents of lustration clearly believed that confession would taint a candidate in the public's eyes. Of the presidential contenders, only Olechowski acknowledged co-operation with the security services, in his case in respect to economic intelligence. The Spokesman for the Public Interest investigated negative affidavits, and if appropriate, served as the effective prosecutor in the Lustration Court. With two significant exceptions the presidential candidates were rapidly found to be honourable men who had told the truth.

The exceptions, to the amazement and bafflement of many, were former president Lech Wałęsa and the current incumbent Aleksander Kwaśniewski. In both cases the Public Interest Spokesman questioned the veracity of their affidavits and the Court announced that it would summon witnesses. In Kwaśniewski's case, it would also investigate newly received documents from the Bureau of Polish Security (*Urząd Ochrony Polski*, UOP) to clarify whether a secret collaborator 'Alek' could be linked, as UOP suggested, to the president. Both men were finally vindicated, despite protests from the Spokesman, but the spectacle was an unedifying one, with renewed arguments about the obvious politicisation of the lustration process and its civil liberties implications.

This, then, was the political context: The incumbent Kwaśniewski was in a commanding lead; the natural challenger Krzaklewski was indissolubly associated with an unpopular minority government and suspect 'dirty tricks' in the lustration process; a third force had emerged in the elegant personage of Olechowski; and a pack of other contenders was snapping in the wings. For most of the minor challengers the aim was political visibility through free broadcasting time with a view to the forthcoming parliamentary elections in

2001. For Krzaklewski and Olechowski the main task was to come second, with enough combined erosion of Kwaśniewski's lead to ensure a second round.

Krzaklewski clearly hoped to emulate Wałęsa's 1995 first-round performance, when the-then President had risen from the depths of unpopularity to enter the second round exactly two per cent behind Kwaśniewski. Although Wałęsa lost narrowly in the second round, Krzaklewski aimed to succeed this time with a similar 'two-camp' strategy, a gladiatorial contest between the president, the (undoubted) leader of the Left and himself, the (*soi-disant*) leader of the Right. Olechowski sought the dark horse role He aimed to make a virtue of necessity in the absence of a political base. He was rational, pragmatic and non-confrontational, with a calm charm offensive seeking to serve as a centrist magnet, attracting voters from Kwaśniewski and Krzaklewski, as well as UW voters with no candidate of their own and no other obvious choice. Kalinowski never seriously challenged for second place, but he had important pockets of support which he needed to confirm, as well as to broaden his own narrow rural political base, under threat from the activist Andrzej Lepper.

The Campaign

The presidential election campaign was once again not issue-based, but candidate-based. In a winner-take-all presidential contest, there is inevitably stress on the personalities involved. In addition the president, though potentially influential,[11] had seen his powers reduced by the 1997 Constitution; these powers were largely negative in content, unlike those of say the U.S. or French presidents. Kwaśniewski had met with no response to his legislative initiatives since 1997, though he made effective use of the veto. A number of candidates, including the president, stressed the difficulties of achieving their policy aims in this variant of semi-presidentialism.

With few exceptions, then, policies were blurred during the campaign, and image was all. Kwaśniewski and Krzaklewski pledged in their different ways to continue the path of reform, including integration with the European Union, and stressed their respective positive achievements. Olechowski and Wałęsa also took this line, with Olechowski claiming single-handedly to have 'broken down the door to NATO[12] and Wałęsa seeking to prevent his own work from 'going to waste'. While Kalinowski was lukewarm to reform, stressing the harmful role played by excessively liberal policies and confessing to a lack of Euro-enthusiasm,[13] Korwin-Mikke saw too little reform, with the government consumed by greater bureaucracy and nepotism than in communist times. Other candidates, including SamoObrona Lepper, stressed Poland's deterioration, decline and despair. Anti-European sentiments were much in evidence, though Jan Łopuszański was the only candidate making his anti-EU stance the centrepiece of his platform.

Education, law and order, the need to combat unemployment and to improve the health care system were common themes, but there were no substantive policy debates. One sphere where the candidates divided was over the AWS law on so-called property enfranchisement (*uwłaszczenie*), recently vetoed by Kwaśniewski. This was seen as a massive vote-winner by Krzaklewski and AWS (it was also supported by Kalinowski and Grabowski). A Krzaklewski election leaflet stressed that such a law would 'give millions of flats to their tenants, plots of land to former state farm workers, the right to land of tenant farmers; the right to the land on which our homes stand; and vouchers giving millions a share in the profits of privatisation.' In contrast Kwaśniewski's veto had derided the law as legally flawed, socially unjust and economically illiterate, while Olechowski condemned it as 'pure populism'.

The leading candidates criss-crossed the country attracting significant numbers to their rallies, but television was deemed vital to the image-making process, and the serious candidates made use of advertising agencies to ensure the professionalism of their broadcasts.[14] The television campaign format still bore the hallmarks of a new democracy, scrupulously maintaining the requirements of absolute balance. Excruciating back-to-back slots provided about two minutes for each candidate in an order determined by lot. Those of the leading contenders were glitzy, slick productions; none of the broadcasts overly strained their viewers' intellects. In separate programmes panels of journalists also questioned candidates individually on successive evenings but without sparkle or depth. Educational programmes assumed a surreal quality, with academics engaged in interesting, animated discussions of the election without mentioning any candidate by name.

The campaign was uneventful in its first stages. Kwaśniewski's campaign stressed his experience, competence and professionalism. Olechowski claimed the same attributes, while adding his independence. Krzaklewski was less central to his own broadcasts, but his campaign strategists sought to present him as an educated, sympathetic family man caring deeply about his fellows.

The use of what the Poles call 'electoral sausage' was also observed, not least in Nysa, the town chosen for a September mock election because of its alleged representativeness. The prime minister took sausages to Nysa when he opened a new hospital and announced a new higher vocational school and the retention of a threatened army unit.[15] The Nysa result gave Kwaśniewski a clear first-round win with 53.66 per cent, but a surprising second-place for Krzaklewski with 17.52 per cent (Olechowski got 15.71 per cent and Kalinowski 3.87 per cent). AWS portrayed the Nysa result as the signal for the opposition to unite around Krzaklewski as the acknowledged leader of the right.[16]

At the same time, in the last week of September, the campaign took a new turn with a Krzaklewski television broadcast starring not the candidate but his opponent Kwaśniewski in the leading role. One film clip of an official visit by President Kwaśniewski to the Ukraine to pay homage to Polish victims of Stalinism showed the president clearly unsteady on his feet. The broadcast emphasised a public insobriety that made Kwaśniewski unworthy of high office (his supporters claimed his stagger, exaggerated by slowing down the film, was the effect of medication). The second clip from a visit to Kalisz two years earlier showed the president's entourage descending from a helicopter. Marek Siwiec, a local parliamentary deputy and head of the president's National Security Office, made the sign of the cross; then, encouraged by the president, he kissed the ground in a gesture reminiscent of Pope John Paul II. Because of its official dimension the Kharkov film was more serious than Kalisz, which was a flippant, if distasteful moment among friends. Yet it was Kalisz that created a storm of protest and moral outrage, as bishops fulminated and local AWS politicians declared the president *persona non grata* in their towns. The broadcast was shown repeatedly, and opinion polls registered a sharp drop in Kwaśniewski's support. For the first time a second round seemed possible. Moreover, Krzaklewski also secured the withdrawal and support of former prime minister Jan Olszewski and the endorsement of the national-clerical Radio Maryja.

Table 4: Support for Leading Candidates by Polling Organisation 2-5/10/00 (%)

	OBW	PBS	OBOP	CBOS	PBS2
Kwaśniewski	49.5	51.6	55	55	57
Krzaklewski	16.5	11.6	9	7	12
Olechowski	16.0	14.6	17	13	17
Kalinowski	8.0	7.2	7	6	5

Sources: *Zycie*, 4 October 2000, *Rzeczpospolita*, 5 October 2000, *Rzeczpospolita*, 6 October 2000.

Nonetheless in most polls published in the days before the election (see Table 4) Kwaśniewski's loss was not Krzaklewski's gain and the latter remained firmly in third place. Although the AWS leader had gained ground in the course of the campaign, the 'two-camp' strategy did not drain votes from Olechowski and may even have strengthened him. Kwaśniewski meanwhile intensified his campaign but did not alter his non-confrontational stance. He later commented that up to the Kalisz broadcast his supporters had been 'falling asleep'. It caused a 'revitalization, renewed interest and a new urgency' to his own campaign, with the president now venturing into areas such as Przemyśl not generally noted for their enthusiasm for his candidacy.[17]

The Results

On 8 October 17,789,231 voters of the potential electorate of 29,122,304 went to the polls (see Table 5). The turnout of 61.08 per cent was relatively high by Polish standards, though lower than in 1995. Kwaśniewski's early lead had been reduced during the campaign, but remained sufficiently high to secure his re-election without a second round. He did not gain much in comparison with the second round of 1995, but with 53.9 per cent of the vote the president won in every province, albeit lacking an overall majority in six. Kwaśniewski did especially well in western areas, where the SLD was consistently strong. Olechowski came second in twelve provinces, with Krzaklewski second in three and Kalinowski in one (Lublin). The Solidarity leader's best performance came in the southeastern corner (Podkarpackie province), where he gained 26.64 per cent of the vote.

How can we account for this easy victory? Despite his flaws, the president was undoubtedly an attractive candidate. His performance in office had been consistently highly evaluated. His pragmatism and his obvious preference for avoiding conflict were sufficient to command respect, if not deep affection. The Kalisz/Kharkov affect was not irrelevant, but did not constitute a major haemorrhage, and it also served to galvanise his campaign. His policies were couched in general terms (education, law and order), but they were undoubtedly relevant. Although nominally a non-party candidate, he had the support of the powerful, well organised apparatus of the social democrats.

Table 5: Results of the Presidential Election of 8 October 2000

Candidate	Party/support	Vote	% vote
Aleksander Kwaśniewski	SLD/UP	9485224	53.90
Andrzej Olechowski	Independent	3044141	17.30
Marian Krzaklewski	AWS	2739621	15.57
Jarosław Kalinowski	PSL	1047949	5.95
Andrzej Lepper	SamoObrona	537570	3.05
Janusz Korwin-Mikke	UPR	252499	1.43
Lech Wałęsa	ChDRP	178590	1.00
Jan Łopuszański	Polskie Porozumienie	139682	0.79
Dariusz Grabowski	Konwencja Polska	89002	0.51
Piotr Ikonowicz	PPS	38672	0.22
Tadeusz Wilecki	Stronnictwo Narodowe	28805	0.16
Bogdan Pawlowski	Independent	17164	0.10

Source: Państwowa Komisja Wyborcza, from http://www.essex.ac.uk/elections

Equally important, there was no candidate of genuine stature to challenge him. Andrzej Olechowski was efficient, elegant, and articulate, but his wealth and abstract approach served to distance him from ordinary citizens. Asked in one party broadcast what he would say to an unemployed person, he replied in effect that he would carefully explain the systemic causes of unemployment. His lack of political base also told; and he never appeared to constitute a clear alternative either to Kwaśniewski or to Krzaklewski. Still, his overall performance was impressive. According to exit polls Olechowski took almost two-thirds of the UW electorate, and even one-quarter of previous ROP (Olszewski) voters.[18] Marian Krzaklewski, in contrast, laboured under serious handicaps. He was disliked by large numbers. He was associated with an unpopular government seen to have bungled fundamental areas of reform such as health and pensions, yet he had consistently refused to take a government post. AWS was visibly divided, yet he had done nothing to unite it nor to resolve its ambivalent relationship with the trade union. He also misjudged the popular mood, both in his emphasis on the continued salience of historic divisions and in assuming that the new property law would be a major vote-winner. In the event Olechowski's performance also showed that lustration confessions would not necessarily prove harmful. In reaching out to Olszewski's supporters and those associated with Radio Maryja rather than to the centre, Krzaklewski was adding little to his support while potentially alienating those anxious about anti-communist fundamentalism. Indeed, Krzaklewski took only half the 1997 AWS vote. The peasant leader Kalinowski fought a good campaign, but he was too closely associated with his peasant constituency and had not long been seen as a politician of national standing.

The exit polls proved highly accurate and so provide a clear view of the profile of Polish voters' support for leading candidates, if no surprises (see Table 6). As in previous elections electors did not divide along demographic lines; indeed, Kwaśniewski's support represented a rough mirror of the population at large. Krzaklewski clearly did better among older voters and worse among younger ones. Olechowski was attractive to highly educated voters but not to the less educated.

Table 6: Electorates of top-placed candidates in 2000 (%)

	Kwaśniewski	Krzaklewski	Olechowski
Women	52.8	54.0	52.0
Men	47.2	46.0	48.0
age 18-24	15.8	10.2	18.9
age 25-39	26.7	23.0	31.3
age 40-59	40.9	38.5	38.4
age 60+	16.6	28.2	11.4
elementary education	13.0	15.8	6.6
vocational education	26.5	23.6	16.6
secondary education	45.2	40.3	47.2
higher education	15.2	20.2	29.6

Source: PBS exit poll data from Rzeczpospolita, 10 October 2000.

On 23 December 2000 Aleksander Kwaśniewski again took the presidential oath and began his second and final term of office. In the 2000 presidential election the best candidate won. Kwaśniewski had been tested in office. He had the professionalism, education and presence valued by the population as presidential attributes. Many of these features had been present in 1995, but Krzaklewski lacked the advantages and political skill of the-then incumbent Wałęsa. If the election result was clear-cut, however, its implications were not.

The Implications of the Presidential Election of 2000

Most parties (and many observers) now began to assume that Buzek's minority government would not survive to a full term, though much would depend on its ability to win Freedom Union support for the budget.[19] Even without a premature election, the parliamentary election would still be held in autumn 2001 at the latest. The SLD's position was very strong, with 51 per cent almost reaching the level of Kwaśniewski's support in a November poll.[20] Prospects for further consolidation of the Left were also promising. The Labour Union (UP) had supported the president and quickly reached agreement on an electoral coalition and principles of its location on the SLD's parliamentary list. Other groups formerly associated with the SLD, including the main pensioners' party, also began discussions about their role in the forthcoming elections.

For AWS the result was a catastrophe. In 1995 the Solidarity trade union and the numerous small right-wing parties associated with it had faced the shock of defeat, but Wałęsa had run a close race and they appeared to have a large electorate ready for mobilisation. In 2000 the party system again seemed to have suffered a reverse blow, with serious threat of destabilisation on the right of the political spectrum. AWS reeled under the blow of Krzaklewski's ignominious performance and the loss of over one million voters since 1997. Buzek's government also faced new rumblings of discontent from Solidarity miners and the rapid escalation of nurses' protests. Despite pressure from three of the four parties which made up AWS, both the Solidarity trade union and the AWS Social Movement (RS) continued to regard Krzaklewski as 'the only leader of the Right', and for almost three months Krzaklewski showed no inclination to resign.

The issue was not simply one of AWS leadership, however, but also of its structure. Krzaklewski had made no progress with his desire for a single, unified party. Of the four major party constituents of AWS the Conservative-Liberal Party (SK-L), the Christian Democrats (PPChD), and the Christian-National Union (ZChN) favoured a coalition of four equal parties. The Solidarity union and the 'party of power' the AWS Social Movement (RS), itself not immune from internal divisions, endorsed a united political party whose 'intermediate stage' would be a federation of the parties forming AWS. Despite attempts to mediate by Prime Minister Buzek and the Catholic Church, the decisive break-up of AWS looked the most likely development, as the SKL and PPChD formed their own 'AWS Federation' under Speaker of the Sejm Maciej Płażyński and suspended their participation in the AWS parliamentary club.

On 23 December, however, the patient was declared saved and ready for rehabilitation when leading AWS politicians achieved a compromise. 'The medicine of struggle was bitter, with numerous negative side-effects', said SKL leader Rokita; but the path is clear for recovery'.[21] Buzek would be leader and Płażyński deputy leader of the renewed AWS, with Krzaklewski agreeing to submit his resignation as soon as the constituent elements had ratified the agreement. A new unified AWS party would be created within six months of the parliamentary elections. Meanwhile the decision-making structures were altered to reduce the importance of the leader and to increase the role of the three disaffected parties.

The Freedom Union (UW)'s position was also difficult and it too undertook a programme of 'renewal'. Its support had fallen after its withdrawal from government, its failure to field a candidate was rapidly acknowledged as a mistake, and Balcerowicz's leadership was openly called into question. Olechowski had enjoyed good relations with the UW, as well as with the SKL, the most economically liberal wing of AWS and the most favourably disposed to the AWS-UW coalition. After the election Olechowski sought to exploit his election performance to exert influence on the reshaping of the centre-right. At first he rejected the notion of a new party[22] but appealed to the UW and SKL to cooperate with him to coordinate 'the political representation of the centre'.[23] Balcerowicz issued a cautious welcome, but SKL leader Jan Rokita replied that SKL wanted to 'repair AWS, not to demolish it'.[24] SKL's participation in the 'new' AWS structure seemed to thwart Olechowski's strategy of crossing party lines by dividing AWS and generating a new political centre.

In December the UW itself elected Bronisław Geremek as its new leader following Balcerowicz's departure to direct the National Bank. The UW conference also showed the continuing UD-Liberal divisions when it largely excluded its liberal wing from its newly elected executive organs. Neither the UW nor its original constituents the Democratic Union and the Liberal Democrats had chosen leaders known for their charisma, and the medievalist Professor Geremek, political gamesmaster and 'Polish Machiavelli', was no exception. Geremek was viewed as having less than enthusiastic attitudes to Olechowski, though the Congress (if coolly) 'welcomed' Olechowski's offer of co-operation and continuing discussions.

By January the situation had developed further, with Olechowski securing the defection of Maciej Płażyski from AWS and Donald Tusk from the UW to form the Civic Platform (*Platforma Obywatelska*) under the 'three tenors'. Many former liberals, including former prime minister Krzysztof Bielecki and the president of Warsaw Paweł Piskorski, followed Tusk into the PO, along with some other well known popular figures. As the PO rose in the polls, so the UW's support slipped below the electoral threshold of 5 per cent. The successful wooing of most of the SKL from AWS gave the *Platforma* high hopes of exceeding Olechowski's presidential performance in the forthcoming autumn parliamentary elections.

By spring AWS had fractured into four: part to *Platforma*; part to a new anti-corruption, law and order grouping under the brothers Kaczyński; part to a regrouping of the Catholic nationalists under Radio Maryja's auspices; with most of the remainder forming Right AWS (*AWS Prawica*, AWSP) under Jerzy Buzek. The hopes for a unified right, so strong in 1996, had crumbled to ashes five years later.

Thus as in 1995, the aftermath of the election of 2000 proved a bitter experience for all parties save the SLD, whose own new unified party format had proved itself in its electoral baptism. The election provided a catalyst for the emergence of new political formations of the right and centre. Although the PSL avoided immediate upheaval, it too remained anxious about the presence of Andrzej Lepper on its flank. Lepper's brand of direct-action populism had some support in the small towns, as well as in the countryside; and he was poised to benefit from an atmosphere of growing social pessimism.

Conclusion

The winner-take-all nature of presidential elections proved disruptive to party-system consolidation in Poland. The lack of coincidence of the timing of presidential and parliamentary elections did not aid Polish democratic development. Elections were routine, free, fair and conducted with impeccable administrative efficiency. However, presidential elections distracted political actors from the main and still urgent business of law-making in the context of system transformation. Conclusions drawn from analogies with previous experience were applied without regard to changing circumstances, as when Krzaklewski tried to imitate Wałęsa's strategy for gaining the presidency and when the UW failed to support Olechowski's candidature. With each election the personalism of presidential elections served as a destabilising mechanism for the parties as well as hindering the formation of loyal party electorates.

Notes

[1] Results from the leading polling organisations were published in *Rzeczpospolita*, 15 November 1995; *Rzeczpospolita*, 16 November 1995; *Rzeczpospolita*, 17 November 1995.

[2] On the particular significance of the religious factor see Radosław Markowski, 'Społeczne a polityczne podziały społeczeństwa polskiego' in L. Kolarska-Bobińska and R. Markowski (eds), *Prognozy i Wybory*, Warsaw (Wydawnictwo Sejmowe), 1997, pp. 31-68.

[3] See for example Janusz Tomidajewicz, 'Miejsce i taktyka Unii Pracy po wyborach prezydenckich', *Przegląd Społeczny* no. 1-2, 1996, pp. 125-41.

[4] PBS poll, *Rzeczpospolita*, 27 September 1996.

[5] For details of the constituent elements see Leszek Graniszewski, 'Akcja Wyborcza Solidarność-sojusz prawicy demokratycznej' in Stanisław Gebethner (ed.), *Wybory '97. Partie i programy wyborcze* (Warsaw, Elipsa, 1997), pp. 64-72. A number are also included in the useful compendium of party documents: Krystyna Paszkiewicz (ed.), *Polskie Partie Polityczne. Charakterystyki, dokumenty* (Wrocław, Hector, 1996).

[6] PBS data, reported in *Rzeczpospolita*, 21 September 1999.

[7] By October 58% disapproved of the prime minister's performance; CBOS data in *Rzeczpospolita*, 22 October 1999.

[8] SLD hovered around the 40% mark by the autumn; see PBS data in *Rzeczpospolita*, 20 July 1999, 23 August 1999, 20 September 1999; Pentor data in *Wprost*, 17 October 1999.
[9] CBOS data in 'Tydzień w kraju', *Polityka*, 17 October 1998.
[10] PBS polls in January 2000 found 70% approving and about 15% disapproving of Kwaśniewski's presidency; *Rzeczpospolita*, 14 February 2000; CBOS polls gave Kwaśniewski a popularity rating of 78% in February; 'Tydzień w kraju, *Polityka*, 12 February 2000.
[11] See Frances Millard, 'Presidents and Democratization in Poland: The Roles of Lech Wałęsa and Aleksander Kwaśniewski in Building a New Polity', *The Journal of Communist Studies and Transition Politics*, 16, 5, September 2000, pp. 39-62.
[12] TVP Election Broadcast, 24 September 2000.
[13] Jerzy Kubrak, 'Zielony to ładny kolor (Interview with Jarosław Kalinowski)', *Zycie*, 4 October 2000.
[14] Filip Frydrykiewicz and Kazimierz Groblewski, 'Najwięcej wydali najważniejsi', *Rzeczpospolita*, 17 October 2000.
[15] Marcin Dominik Zdort, 'Lista przebojów Krzaklewskiego', *Rzeczpospolita*, 6 October 2000.
[16] Wojciech Walendziak, quoted in *Zycie Warszawy*, 25 October 2000.
[17] Jerzy Baczyński, Mariusz Janicki, and Wiesław Władyka, 'Zostawcie to mnie' (Interview with Aleksander Kwaśniewski), *Polityka*, 14 October 2000.
[18] PBS exit poll data in *Rzeczpospolita*, 9 October 2000.
[19] The president could dissolve parliament only in tightly defined circumstances; these included a failure to pass the budget within three months of its presentation to parliament.
[20] PBS data in *Rzeczpospolita*, 17 November 2000.
[21] Quoted in *Rzeczpospolita*, 27 December 2000.
[22] Janina Paradowska, 'Nie potrzeba koguta' (Interview with Andrzej Olechowski), *Polityka*, 21 October 2000.
[23] Małgorzata Subotić 'Pomysł na parlamentarną reprezentację', *Rzeczpospolita*, 14-15 October 2000.
[24] Bernadeta Waszkielewicz, 'A może federacja', *Rzeczpospolita* 241, 14-15 October 2000.

Françoise Boucek
The Structure and Dynamics of Intra-Party Politics in Europe

ABSTRACT

Despite sketchy evidence, little comparative data, and evolving public expectations, patterns of intra-party behaviour in East Europe show signs of converging with those of West European political parties. This chapter first analyses the conceptual meanings of party coherence, factionalism, and voters' perceptions and expectations of party unity. It questions whether transition to democracy in late twentieth century Eastern Europe created exceptional conditions in the way that parties organise their internal affairs, thereby creating different incentive structures from those of political parties in advanced industrial democracies. Secondly, different institutions such as electoral systems, procedural legislative devices, and intra-party decisional arrangements are examined to assess how they shape intra-party behaviour. Thirdly, the effects on party cohesion of electoral systems are analysed in detail through case studies. These are single-member plurality rule in the UK, preferential voting in multi-seat districts in pre-1991 Italy, the single non-transferable vote in multi-seat constituencies in pre-1994 Japan, and mixed member systems in Eastern Europe and in post-reform Italy and Japan. Because intra-party actors are rational they adapt their behaviour to the institutional environment in which they compete. Hence, differentiated patterns of intra-party behaviour have developed under different institutional regimes in Europe.

Introduction

There are signs of convergence in the way political parties In Eastern and Western Europe structure their internal politics. But because many East European parties and party systems are still undergoing a process of consolidation, there is only sketchy evidence that patterns of intra-party behaviour are converging and the imbalance of empirical data between democracies in Western and Eastern Europe impedes conclusive generalisations.

The primary goal of political parties is to contest and win elections in order to control executive power. In the established democracies of Western Europe party labels are important because voters 'tend to vote for parties rather than people in legislative elections precisely because, when they vote, they feel that they are helping to choose a government'.[1] Party cohesion and party unity are perceived as necessary to the delivery of efficient government and most social research suggests that group cohesion is a good predictor of performance. But expectations of party unity are not as strongly developed among East European electorates. In many of the new democracies of East Central Europe parties are still weakly institutionalised and party brand names are not well established. Parties are prone to splinters and politicians with weak party identification are often motivated by individual or mass preferences rather than by party preferences. However, cohesion is still a valuable asset for office-seeking parties in Eastern Europe which have learned that disunity damages the brand name and hinders competition. And analysts have noted that in the more established democracies parties of government have become more cohesive than opposition parties.[2]

However, parties are not unitary actors but collections of individuals or coalitions of sub-party groups with common but also divergent preferences and interests and with competing claims on party resources. Consequently, parties face a management dilemma: that is, balancing the claims of party elites, of the rank-and-file and of party members against those of the electorate. And to carry out many of their organisational functions political parties are under less pressure to seek unity than they are in their inter-party electoral or parliamentary functions. Nevertheless, parties need to manage their diversity efficiently to preserve the value of the brand name. Indeed, it can be instrumental for party managers to give representation to the party's plurality of interests rather than to dampen competition between intra-party elements or to conceal dissent and resist fragmentation. Allowing party factions to exist and to be formally represented in the decision-making process can solve co-ordination problems and cut transaction costs inside the host party, thus preventing exit.[3]

The pull of political parties towards cohesion or towards fragmentation and factionalism is determined by contextual factors such as the circumstances and conditions prevailing during party formation but also by institutional factors which structure the internal and external environments in which parties compete. Institutions shape intra-party behaviour because they affect the motivations and expectations of politicians, party members, and voters and thus create incentives for strategic behaviour. Among these institutions are electoral rules for running inter-party and intra-party contests, procedures for selecting candidates for public office and for party posts, for dividing the spoils of office and party resources, for passing government legislation in parliament, and so on.

This article begins by exploring the conceptual meanings of party coherence and factionalism and analyses their impact on public perceptions. It asks whether transition to democracy created unique conditions in late twentieth century Eastern Europe in terms of how intra-party politics are structured. The focus then shifts to institutions by looking at two essential areas of party activity: that is, the nomination of candidates for public and party offices and the legislative process, to assess how different electoral systems and legislative devices impact on party cohesion. The effect of intra-party rules on party cohesion is also considered by examining two factionalised parties - the former Christian Democrats in Italy (DC) and the Liberal Democrats in Japan (LDP).

Party Competition and Party Unity

To maximise their chances of winning office, European parties seek to present themselves as coherent entities between which voters can make clear-cut choices of alternative governments. A party is a 'team seeking to control the governing apparatus by gaining office in a duly constituted election'.[4] It is 'a group whose members propose to act in concert in the competitive struggle for political power'.[5] In other words, winning office is a collective effort involving teamwork and co-operation among members.

However, where competition is framed in terms of individual candidates rather than in terms of partisan affiliations[6] (in the USA, for instance, where congressional representatives are seen as the agents of their districts or states) group cohesion is less essential to winning votes and expectations differ. Moreover, because American primary elections involve intra-party competition, the notion of party (at congressional, presidential, and state levels) is much looser and fragmented than it is in Europe. Hence, candidate-focused American parties face fewer pressures to portray themselves as coherent organisations and as united campaign teams than their counterparts in European parliamentary systems where general elections are partisan contests and where party unity matters a great deal to voters.

In Europe general elections are seen as opportunities for choosing governments and party unity is considered essential for party fitness for office and therefore for electoral success. For instance, in Britain, electoral analysts frequently assume that to be perceived as less united than a competitor is damaging for political parties.[7] Correlating perceptions of party disunity (and unity) with measures of party popularity for the Conservative and Labour parties between 1965-1997, confirms this assumption.[8] For the Conservatives, perceptions of unity and disunity used to be slightly better predictors of support than for Labour, but in both cases the two variables are strongly correlated. Forty-six per cent of the variation in Conservative support is explained by public perceptions of unity and fifty-three per cent by perceptions of disunity, as opposed to thirty-six per cent and forty per cent respectively for Labour.

Although historically Labour was perceived as much more factionalised and disunited than the Conservatives this began to change in the late 1980s when Labour leader Neil Kinnock succeeded in taming Labour's extreme left. Historical patterns were reversed in the early 1990s when the Conservatives came to be seen as very disunited because of their disagreement over the various issues of European integration. Hence, in Britain, government parties seek to behave as cohesive entities because party popularity is related to positive party image. And since in people's minds factionalism implies conflict, disunity, and a withdrawal of consent, office-seeking parties seek to conceal their factionalism. Displays of factionalism damage the brand name, the party's electoral prospects, government performance, and office tenure. To present a *façade* of unity has become critical to winning office at Westminster and in many West European democracies.

> 'Parties are cohesive, and remain the significant unit of analysis, with respect to their vote-getting preoccupations and 'the electoral party' (not the nominating or candidate-proposing party) provides the optimal standpoint for considering the party as a non-divisible unit'.[9]

But since parties are not unitary actors but collections of individuals and aggregates of sub-party groups of individuals who compete for power, they face conflicting pressures inside the organisation. Sub-party motivations can harm collective objectives and make coherence and party unity difficult to achieve even during election campaigns. This is especially true for parties competing under electoral systems that involve intra-party competition.

Coherence, Factionalism, and Party Formation

Twenty years ago, party coherence was defined by Kenneth Janda as the 'degree of congruence in the attitudes and behavior of party members', and Janda asserted that studies of political parties tended to examine coherence in terms of 'cohesion' and 'factionalism'.[10] In a cross-national survey, he operationalised coherence by coding parties according to six variables: legislative cohesion, factionalism based on ideology, on issues, on leadership, on strategy and tactics, and on party purges. However, Janda concluded that all types of factionalism were interrelated (for instance, a party with ideological factions also tended to have leadership factions).

Eighteenth-century British philosopher David Hume had divided factions into 'personal' and 'real' and sub-divided real factions into factions 'from *interest*, from *principle*, and from *affection*'. Hume denounced factions for being 'directly contrary to that of laws' and stated that 'factions subvert government and render laws impotent';[11] he was particularly critical of factions of *principle*. But Hume's categories are difficult to apply to modern political parties. Likewise, Richard Rose's differentiation between factions and tendencies is hard to operationalise and to apply empirically because the distinction between the two concepts is blurred and the definition of a tendency is time-bound.[12] Rose defines tendencies as 'stable sets of attitudes rather than stable groups of politicians', which are less organised and less permanent than factions. However, since Rose does not provide any criteria for measuring stability and permanence, it is difficult to discriminate between factions and tendencies.

Because there is strength in numbers, intra-party actors (especially inside 'big tent' parties) which share common interests and attitudes or which unite in a common cause may decide formally to set up a sub-party group to maximise welfare or achieve particular objectives. The aim might be to change some policy, to remove the party leader, to trigger a constitutional change (such as electoral reform) or an intra-party rule change. The fact that such a sub-group disbands after having achieved its aim does not make the group unstable. Short-lived, perhaps; efficient, quite probably; but not unstable. In other words, there is nothing inherently wrong with calling it a faction.

Temporary but organised factions regularly emerge in American politics. The Progressive Party (or Bull Moose Party) was a splinter faction of the Republican Party assembled by Roosevelt after he lost the Republican nomination for the White House in 1912 to William Taft, which cost the GOP the presidential election. The splinter group disbanded in 1916 when Roosevelt, along with many Progressives, decided to rejoin the GOP. Congressional bipartisan factions form occasionally when groups of Republican and Democrat legislators feel the need to moderate the policy stances of party leaders.[13] However, because politicians' careers and re-election prospects do not depend on party loyalty or on maximising access to party resources, policy-based factions rarely become institutionalised inside American parties - unlike those of the former Christian Democrats in Italy (DC) and the Liberal Democrats in Japan (LDP), a point to which we shall return.

Commenting on factionalism in East Europe, Paul Lewis points out the difficulty of defining factionalism in precise terms because 'the general context of party formation and organisational flux in Eastern Europe created a significant overlap between the different categories'.[14] For instance, factionalism inside the Polish Democratic Union is linked to a lack of organisational consolidation and to the importance of the parliamentary arena. And in the early parliamentary parties of the Czech and Slovak Republics factions tended to be the result of party disarray and fragile party systems rather than the products of stable intra-party organisation.[15] In contrast, in the Hungarian and Russian legislatures, factions are not intra-party groups but rather cross-party groups of legislators or *fraktions*: that is, a group of parliamentarians who by coalescing receive special privileges and resources within the legislative chamber.

> Issue and strategy-led factionalism can be seen to be as much a common element in modern party politics as are personal rivalry and competition on an individual basis within the newly opened political arena.[16]

In sum, factionalism can be described as a process of group formation within a larger group, or in the case of political parties, the de-concentration of a party into smaller units. And efforts to narrow down the meaning of factionalism by setting categories and typologies are frustrated by problems of overlap and by arbitrary thresholds separating the different categories. Consequently, the general definition of a faction proposed by Zariski in 1967 still remains, to my mind, the most useful guide because it stresses the collective motivations of actors who decide to form a separate bloc within a political party.

> 'Any intra-party combination, clique, or grouping whose members share a sense of common identity and common purpose and are organized to act collectively - as a distinct bloc within the party - to achieve their goals'.[17]

It is interesting to explore what motivates actors inside a political party to form sub-party groupings or to join factions instead of trying to classify such groups on the basis of issues, leadership or power, since all these elements are connected anyway. After all, members of a faction are bound to be united by some kind of common endeavour: otherwise why form a separate group? They are also bound to have a leader who represents their interests within the larger unit and who is able to bargain with other group leaders to maximise the welfare of the sub-group. And if the members of the sub-group fail to increase their power by forming a separate bloc they are likely to disband or to join another sub-group. As Gordon Tullock explains:

> Parties characteristically are not only fighting for control, but within each party there are a number of cliques fighting for control of the party, and there are sub-cliques fighting for control of cliques, and individuals trying to get control of the sub-cliques.[18]

Duverger asserted that parties are 'profoundly influenced by their origins'[19] and Panebianco stressed the relationship between a party's genesis and its 'institutionalisation': that is, the way the organisation 'solidifies'.[20] Factionalism is often associated with division during early phases of nation-building and during party development. Historically, faction and party meant the same thing and were used interchangeably in Madison's *Federalist*, for instance, and also by David Hume. The Jeffersonian and Federalist factions gave structure to the nascent American party system, as did Whigs and Tories with their respective factions in eighteenth century Britain. Factions inside Communist parties in Central and Eastern Europe represented the early components of post-Communist party systems and played a constructive role during the transition to democracy.[21]

Factions can solve political co-ordination problems during the early phases of democratisation by helping minority groups of voters with diverse social interests, tastes and shades of opinion coalesce and form a 'broad church' party. During a party's formative phase factions often represent different communities of interest and subcultures, distinct cleavages (political, socio-economic, ethnic or geographic), or separate ideologies. When different factions, political movements, or parties coalesce, the number of contestants to which seats are allocated is reduced. This can produce a more concentrated party system and help create integrated parties strong enough to govern on their own.

After the creation of Italy's First Republic in 1946, the new Christian Democratic Party (DC) brought together a variety of groups. These included the Milan *Guelfo Movimento*, the pre-fascist party Popular Party (*Popolari*), various Catholic student and trade union associations, and networks of parish priests, influential intellectuals, academics, and ex-Resistance members.[22] Keen to retain their identity, many of these groups came to represent the early factional alignments inside the DC such as *Cronache Sociali*, *Forze Sociali*, and *Parola Nueva*. While the DC was large enough to remain the dominant party of government for four decades, it adopted an incentive structure that encouraged factions to multiply. But in the long term, institutionalised factionalism created collective action dilemmas for the DC and inertia and 'public bads' for Italy (irresponsible and unstable governments which produced large deficits and invited political corruption).

Parties are often the products of coalitions of different political groupings. The French Socialist Party (PS), formed in 1971 by François Mitterrand was a merger of various left-wing parties and clubs born in the 1960s,[23] and non-institutionalised factions (sometimes called *courants*) have been a recurring feature of the PS. The initial factional configuration within Japan's Liberal Democratic Party (LDP) was based on the eight distinct leadership groups that came together in 1955 from the Liberal Party and from the Democratic Party. Similarly, in Canada, the initial leadership groupings contained in the federal Liberal Party represented separate elements that coalesced after Confederation (including pre-Confederation splinter parties and reform groups such as the *Clear Grits* of Upper Canada and the *Rouges* of Lower Canada). Hence, factionalism is a rational way of integrating within a single party the contradictions and cleavages present in heterogeneous societies. And in settled democracies, the organisation of a party into factions can be the product of merger agreements between elites from separate political parties. They form a coalition to increase their collective power but are also keen to maintain their separate identities within an integrated party and to maximise their intra-party power.

Hence, factions help structure the expression of heterogeneous beliefs within a merged party, and factions can solidify the party, thus giving structure to nascent party systems during transitional regimes or during the early phases of democratisation. Dissident groups like the Workers' Defence Committee in Poland and Charter '77 in Czechoslovakia which emerged during the 1970s eventually organised as political parties: that is, Solidarity and Civic Forum respectively. After anti-communism disappeared as the glue that bound 'refuseniks' together and after new political institutions were established in Eastern Europe, ideological differences within parties became more apparent. The risk of splits increased when the ideological orientations and contradictions contained within these broad party formations became more transparent (for instance, between social democratic, Christian, liberal, and market-oriented conservative forces). And when politicians' individual motivations began to supersede the collective motivation for party, ideological divergences provoked defections. Dissident MPs inside the Hungarian Democratic Forum split and became independents while a new far right party - the Hungarian Justice and Life Party - was formed.[24] Similarly, in Spain, the ruling *Unión de Centro Democrático* (UDC), dominant during the 1977-1982 transition to democracy, was eventually pulled apart by inner disagreements and the party split after its leader Adolfo Suárez resigned in January 1981. In sum, factions and factional splits are part and parcel of the consolidation of party systems.

But factions can become significant and active players in their own right (inside political systems and inside parties). In emerging party systems where bases of party support are unstable, where parties are insufficiently organised or too small, and where party identification and party loyalty among legislators is weak, factions can play a constructive role. For instance, in the Hungarian and Russian parliaments, parliamentary 'factions' usually encompass several parties which join together to co-ordinate their legislative activities and to maximise their access to parliamentary resources, while retaining their separate identities *vis-à-vis* the voters. Even so, in Hungary factions inside governing parties tend to be more disciplined than in the parties of the Russian Duma[25] where problems related to size, high levels of non-partisanship, and a general lack of experience with democracy may be at play. However, preliminary evidence from Russia and Ukraine suggests that party systems are developing at a much faster rate than previously suggested.[26] Despite the large number of parties present, a majority of citizens in the two countries identify with one party or another and share with party leaders attitudes and views of the political system.

As long as these parliamentary factions reach a minimum size (ten members in the Hungarian parliament, for instance), parliamentary parties and independent MPs can establish standing groups of legislators to solve co-ordination problems in the legislature (such as setting up committees). But when legislatures rationalise and party systems stabilise such cross-party factions tend to consolidate or disappear, allowing broader and more stable political parties to emerge. Because of their larger size and greater sense of identity these parties are able to resist fragmentation, particularly if they adopt institutions designed to represent the diversity of opinion within the organisation. Consequently, like-minded politicians are likely to form separate intra-party groups to express different opinions. Party sub-groups are now a common feature of party organisation in the more firmly established democracies of East Europe. The Czech Republic is a case in point; a recent survey showed that 61 per cent of Czech MPs recognised that there were sub-groups or currents within their parliamentary party.[27]

In sum, factionalism can represent a coming together of members of different movements, different political formations, and different ideological groups to maximise political power and influence during the early phases of party formation. Non-partisan factionalism has been a feature of developing democracies with weak party identities and unstable and fragmented party systems. This form of factionalism can offer a rational way for politicians from diverse parties to organise their parliamentary activities more efficiently. But factionalism can also be a party feature whereby members holding different preferences from those of the larger group decide to form separate groups to gain bargaining power. They might want to maximise their influence on the party leadership or to increase their claims on the party's power, but by choosing to remain inside the party they retain the opportunity to negotiate, transact and compromise. As long as it does not become excessive, intra-party factionalism can solve co-ordination problems and can reduce transaction costs through a rational allocation of power resources. It can democratise intra-party relations by introducing internal 'checks and balances' to empower members and protect minorities.

While 'factionalism is a fact of life within most political parties',[28] it can grow and become a permanent feature of party organisation. If institutions and actors do not put a high value on party unity and/or if parties adopt rules that guarantee representation and devolve decision-making to component groups, factionalism may grow. Such mechanisms for inclusion can act as barriers to exit and help keep a party together. However, they can also create collective action dilemmas and decisional stalemate inside a party. When power is divided in too many ways and the number of factions becomes excessive there is a risk of inertia.

The Impact of Institutions on Intra-Party Politics

The institutional regime under which a party competes is an even more powerful shaper of intra-party politics than the context of a party's genesis. Institutions such as electoral systems, presidentialism, parliamentary procedures, and intra-party decisional arrangements create incentives for politicians to either compete or to co-operate with party colleagues. Hence, they have a direct influence on party structure and on intra-party dynamics. For instance, electoral systems that foster intra-party competition between candidates, notably the Single Non Transferable Vote (SNTV), the Single Transferable Vote (STV) and systems of Proportional Representation (PR) with preference voting, have the potential to divide parties into competing groups. This can complicate party management and might encourage politicians to cultivate the personal vote. But since such incentives are absent from electoral systems based on Single Member Plurality rule (SMP) parties competing under SMP tend to be cohesive and partisan oriented (see sections three and four below).

In presidential systems people have different and generally lower expectations of party cohesion than in parliamentary systems. In the US separate executive and legislative powers and non-concurrent elections for the presidency and for each of the two chambers of Congress (and for state governorships and state legislatures) tend to produce non-coincidental majorities as well as rolling and cross-cutting memberships in the different centres of party power. While these 'checks and balances' reduce the likelihood of strong government they also lessen the scope for imposing party discipline. Moreover, the widespread use of primary elections to nominate candidates for public office, including the presidency, introduces a strong element of intra-party competition in many American electoral contests. Primaries usually lead to party conventions to select the winner among several intra-party finalists and different parties use different rules for selecting the winner.[29] American parties are thus loose and disconnected organisations able to absorb dissent within their own ranks.

In France, apparent disenchantment with *co habitation*[30] prompted a referendum to reduce the presidential term from seven to five years, which set presidential contests to coincide with elections to the Chamber of Deputies for the first time in the spring of 2002. This change effectively removes one of few 'checks and balances' of the French constitution and it increases the likelihood of strong government and disciplined parties since the president and the prime minister and government are more likely to belong to the same party or party bloc. This increases the stakes for MPs from the parliamentary majority parties who will be deterred from expressing dissent and it may prevent different shades of opinion being represented within the presidential majority party.

In European parliamentary democracies, the executive relies directly on the legislature for its survival, which means that internal dissent can be very costly for office-seeking parties and particularly for governing parties ruling alone. Consequently, such parties have strong incentives to impose legislative discipline on their MPs. And because legislators in parliamentary systems are at the mercy of the executive for their career advancement (and of local associations for their selection) they are inevitably more compliant than their American counterparts. The careers of legislators in the American Congress are not tied to the majority or minority status of their party in different jurisdictions and different legislative coalitions are assembled for each bill. In sum, in parliamentary systems, there are strong incentives for politicians to co-operate with partisans in the electoral, parliamentary and governing arenas.

Other constitutional features such as federalism, bicameralism, and corporatism impact on intra-party politics by tending to cross-cut and reduce partisanship. Dispersing power away from national parties narrows the scope for intra-party conflict. Under Germany's federal system much political power is devolved to the *länder,* which also wield much influence in the legislative process at the federal level through the *Bundesrat*, as more than half of all bills require formal approval in this upper chamber. This produces parties that are federations of more or less independent and powerful *Land* organisations where land interests often override party interests. The American federal system produces national parties that are more like associations of state parties. And Confederation in Canada has led to the creation of provincial party organisations that are separate and autonomous from their federal counterparts. By devolving power to lower tiers of government in substantive policy areas such as health, welfare, education, culture, and taxation, federalism reduces the scope for policy disagreement inside national parties.

Consensus-building mechanisms as used in many Northern European democracies can have the same effect because government policies are often formulated outside parliament by consulting 'social partners' or by giving local authorities more say in government decisions. This also applies to some political systems marked by ethnic, linguistic, and regional cleavages such as Belgium where sub-national authorities have jurisdiction over sensitive issues that can strongly divide parties (especially issues related to sovereignty, self-determination, regional disparities, and so on).

However, electoral systems have the most direct impact on intra-party politics because they affect the number of parties in competition and produce differentiated levels of partisanship and of intra-party competition. These factors create incentives or disincentives to exit for actors inside political parties. According to Duverger, electoral systems have a direct effect on the number of parties competing in a party system. The single-member plurality (SMP) system has a reductive effect on the number of parties and favours the two-party system. Because citizens are rational they vote strategically (choosing the most preferred of two parties to avoid wasting one's vote on a candidate with little chance of winning even if s/he matches the voter's own preferences). And since parties are also rational and want to maximise their share of the spoils of power, they remain separate, thus compressing the number of viable government parties towards two and producing single-party governments with strong partisan politics. In contrast, the simple majority system with run-offs and election procedures based on proportionality favour multi-partism and tend to produce coalition governments where partisanship is more muted and intra-party competition more common.

Electoral systems structure party competition. SMP consolidates parties while proportionality systems fragment them. In terms of campaign styles and party cohesion, we can say that SMP used to elect members of the British House of Commons, for instance, stands at one end of the spectrum. Plurality rule in single-member constituencies encourages candidates to build collective reputations under their party's recognisable brand name and to co-operate in legislatures. At the other end of the spectrum are hyper representative systems with high district magnitude and low or no thresholds of representation (as well as primary elections), which promote competition between co-partisans. These electoral systems often encourage candidates to build reputations based on private-goods in order to win personal votes. And under coalition governments (the norm under non-SMP systems), dynamics encourage more strategic and self-centred behaviour by legislators than under SMP. Very representative systems include the multiple preference list system in multi-seat districts used in Italy until 1991 and SNTV used in Japan before electoral reform was passed in 1994. The old system was a plurality system of single non-transferable (and non-list) vote in multi-seat districts of between three to five members.

In terms of intra-party constraints and opportunities, we can say that, depending on their particular features, the mixed member electoral systems or list proportional systems chosen by many East European democracies[31] stand in between the two previously mentioned electoral systems. Because there have been few general elections in each of the new East European democracies and some countries have already altered their electoral systems it is not possible to single out clear intra-party effects yet and it is too early to detect trends. Moreover, the differentiated effects generated by the various features of MMS make systematic comparison across counties difficult. But in countries that have abandoned electoral systems involving intra-party competition for mixed-member majoritarian systems (such as Japan and Italy) it is possible to observe how intra-party behaviour has changed (although the complete realignment of political forces after electoral reform in Italy makes comparison across time difficult). In the remainder of this article, I shall investigate in greater depth, and through recourse to case-studies, processes of sub-party politics under different institutional settings.

High exit costs under single member plurality rule: Britain

By narrowing the field of competition down to two large dominant governing parties SMP consolidates parties.[32] In Britain, SMP has produced two large integrated parties of the Left and Right which alternate in government (albeit irregularly) and form single-party governments held responsible to parliament and to voters. The logic of two-party competition under the Westminster 'responsible party' model acts as a disincentive to exit. As mentioned above, under single-party government, parties need to be cohesive to gain power and to stay in power and politicians face high exit costs if they wish to leave the party they belong to.

As Fig. 1 demonstrates, in post-war Britain, SMP has had a strong reductive effect on the number of parliamentary parties. This effect can be measured by using the index of 'relative reduction in parties' (RRP) suggested by Taagepera and Shugart.[33] The RRP index is expressed as the difference between the effective number of electoral parties (N_v) and the effective number of parliamentary parties (N_s)[34] or as a ratio or percentage difference:

$$\frac{Nv - Ns}{Nv} * 100$$

The index has an upper limit of 1 (100%) and can take slightly negative values in the rare cases where N_s exceed N_v. The RRP index captures the reductive effect of the electoral law on the party system by showing the extent to which different electoral systems can set barriers to entry. The higher these barriers are, the costlier it is for politicians to start new parties or to defect from existing parties.

For the post-war period the average relative reduction in the number of parties in Britain is 20 per cent. But it has increased significantly since the mid-1970s and it reached a maximum of 34.5 per cent in 1997. In 1951, Britain had a near-perfect two-party system when Labour and the Conservatives shared 97 per cent of the popular vote and N_v and N_s almost coincided (see Figure 1). But the mechanical effect of SMP restricts party competition considerably and raises high barriers to entry for third parties with geographically dispersed support. And with a growth in third party support since the mid-1970s, there has been a widening gap between N_v and N_s. Britain now has a three-party system in terms of votes but a two-party system in terms of seats. Vote shares of 25 per cent and 23 per cent for the Liberal-SDP Alliance in 1983 and 1987 translated into puny seat shares (at below 4 per cent). In 1983, electoral support for Labour was barely 2 per cent above that of the Alliance and yet this 2 per cent difference in support translated into a 186-seat difference in the House of Commons.

Under SMP general elections are centred on parties rather than candidates and to compete and maximise their parliamentary seats national parties build

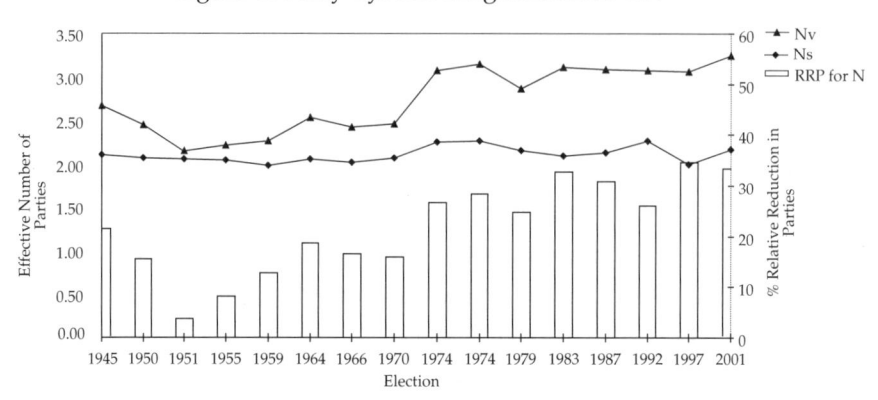

Figure 1: Party System Fragmentation UK

policy reputations based on collective goods. Under SMP there is no intra-party competition for votes since each of the competing parties nominates a single candidate in each constituency. Since candidates are under no pressure to maximise their advantage over party colleagues in each constituency, there are no strong incentives for them to cultivate the personal vote. While party headquarters get involved in candidate selection (by 'vetting' candidates or parachuting favourites into safe seats) it is generally the prerogative of local party associations to nominate a single candidate in each constituency. And the threat of de-selection acts as a deterrent against dissent.

However, in the nineteenth century British MPs did build personal reputations. The 1832 Reform Act, which created a variety of district magnitudes,[35] led to patterns of competition that were more candidate and patronage oriented. Local questions tended to influence legislative politics and the sectional single-issue groups that selected MPs often dictated their behaviour.[36] But under the Reform Act of 1867 single-seat constituencies were established and the party gaining a majority or at least a plurality of the vote won the seat. Thereafter, legislative politics became more partisan-oriented and legislative parties became more cohesive, especially after the secret vote was introduced in the House of Commons, which made MPs less accountable to party sectional groups. After the First World War, the development of a national, programmatic, two-party system secured parliamentary tenure for governments and general elections transformed from the choice of local constituency representatives into the choice of a national ministerial team.[37]

In Britain the logic of two-party competition and adversarial politics generated by SMP creates strong incentives for intra-party co-operation. High barriers to entry make defection very costly for politicians from the two major parties and create high 'start-up' costs for dissenters and independents wanting to set up new parties. The defection in 1981 of senior left-of-centre politicians from the Labour Party (the so-called 'Gang of Four') opposed to the leadership of Michael Foot cost the Labour Party and its defectors dearly. By forming the Social Democratic Party (SDP) with nineteen other Labour MPs, the 'Gang of Four' split the non-Conservative vote, enabling the Conservatives to be re-elected with a landslide in 1983, despite achieving a share of the popular vote slightly lower than in 1979. Labour gained a dismal 27.6 per cent share of the vote.

High exit costs tend to keep discontented MPs from defecting because their chances of gaining seats as members of fringe parties or as independents are limited. At the general election in 1997, 1678 candidates stood for fringe parties or under an independent label,[38] while the Referendum Party, opposed to Britain's EU membership, presented candidates in most constituencies, but failed to gain any seats. Consequently, institutional constraints make party defections and splits rare in Britain and when they happen they become highly publicised events usually involving individual MPs crossing the floor between Labour, the Conservatives or the Liberal Democrats. Parties (with much media reinforcement) try to make political capital out of defections from rival parties, and this reinforces the public's negative perceptions of what are effectively minor displays of party disunity.

When the Conservatives became very unpopular in the mid-1990s after almost eighteen years in power, the disincentives to defect eroded, at least for many Conservative MPs pessimistic about their chances of re-election. The prospect of defeat prompted four disenchanted Conservative politicians to defect and join other parties.[39] In relative terms, these defections were very costly to the Conservative Party because at that time John Major's government had a wafer-thin majority in the House of Commons and the Conservatives were being torn apart by internal battles over Europe.

If there are strongly divergent preferences inside parties competing under SMP it might become difficult for the leadership to manage dissent, especially for governing parties with narrow majorities, because dissenters gain more bargaining power as the probability of their votes becoming decisive to the survival of the government increases. This can force the party leader (and Prime Minister in the case of a government party) to use threats in order to extract compliance from party members. But to remain credible, threats of party expulsions, confidence votes, and prime ministerial resignations must be used sparingly. During his term in office, Prime Minister John Major found himself in situations of having to exercise such threats to deter Euro sceptic MPs from voting against the government.

But there are few safety valves for divided parties under the Westminster model. The Prime Minister's powerful but eroded institutional resources were set against the growing strategic resources of rebel MPs during the lengthy passage of the Maastricht bill in the House of Commons in 1991-92. The rebels' pivotal power increased after the 1992 general election when the Conservatives' majority was reduced to twenty-one seats. The 1992-97 parliament was marked by regular confrontations between a faction of rebel MPs and Prime Minister John Major who engaged in frequent games of 'dare' to extract commitment from rebels.[40] The Conservative government was effectively put in a minority position in November 1994 when, having exhausted his political resources, the Prime Minister decided to disown eight rebels who voted against the government on the European (Finance) bill.

Although there are issues (such as joining the Euro in Britain) that occasionally divide parties very strongly, SMP generally produces cohesive and concentrated legislative parties. In Britain, SMP has reprocessed electoral and legislative multi-partism into a duopoly of party government with the Conservatives and Labour alternating in power. And the Westminster 'responsible party' model based on a pattern of two-party competition has not only re-directed MPs' loyalties away from local interests and towards party politics,[41] but it has also generated expectations of legislative cohesion among voters and politicians. This model has created cohesive parliamentary parties and produced collegial decision making in cabinet.

As Table 1 confirms, legislative cohesion had become the norm by the early 20th century,[42] with partisan voting in the House of Commons increasing significantly after the adoption of SMP. Party voting or party unity scores (see column 3) are votes on which a majority of Conservatives voting cast their votes on one side of an issue and a majority of Liberals or Labour on the other side. Scores for party voting and party cohesion have been very high since the middle of the twentieth century. Party cohesion is the absolute difference between the percentage of a party voting for an issue and the percentage voting against it. Hence, if every Conservative voted 'yes' on a particular vote while 75 per cent of Labour voted 'no' and 25 per cent voted 'yes', the party cohesion score for the Conservatives would be one hundred points (100-0), and for Labour fifty points (75-25). It would also constitute a party unity vote (a majority of Conservatives voting on one side and a majority of Labour on the other).

To achieve such high levels of cohesion British parties enforce loyalty on their MPs through procedural devices such as the no confidence vote and the whipping system. This term borrowed from the hunting field simply means that

Table 1: Party Cohesion in the British House of Commons
1836-1945 (% of all Divisions)

Year	Party	Party Voting	Index of Cohesion
1836	Liberals	40	61.1
	Conservatives	56	73.9
1850	Liberals	37	61.7
	Conservatives	45	65.3
1860	Liberals	25	59.8
	Conservatives	31	57.3
1871	Liberals	55	71.7
	Conservatives	61	76.2
1881	Liberals	66	82.0
	Conservatives	71	82.9
1883	Liberals	51	Data unavailable
	Conservatives	64	Data unavailable
1890	Liberals	64	Data unavailable
	Conservatives	87	Data unavailable
1894	Liberals	81	86.9
	Conservatives	91	94.1
1899	Liberals	76	84.3
	Conservatives	91	94.2
1903	Liberals	88	Data unavailable
	Conservatives	83	Data unavailable
1906*	Liberals	88.2	93.9
	Conservatives	80.4	89.8
	Labour	80.4	88.4
1908*	Liberals	97.9	95.0
	Conservatives	78.7	88.4
	Labour	87.2	92.8
1924	Liberals	62	77.6
	Conservatives	77	86.1
	Labour	83	89.1
1924-1928	Liberals	49.3	71.5
	Conservatives	96,6	97.7
	Labour	97.3	98.3
1945*	Conservatives	95.9	99.0
	Labour	100	99.9

* The results of the years shown with an asterisk are based on sampling on a basis of 1 division in 10.
Source: E. Ozbudun, 'Party Cohesion in Western Democracies: A Causal Analysis', in Eckstein H. and Gurr E. (eds.), *Comparative Politics* Series No. 01-006 Vol. 1 (Beverly Hills, Sage Publications: 1970), pp. 303-88.

parties rely on 'whipped divisions' to get their bills passed.[43] At the turn of the twentieth century when the Liberals and the Conservatives were the main contenders for office, the Liberals were putting their whips on more than 90 per cent of divisions and the Conservatives on 85 per cent.[44] Except for Tariff Reform and Irish Home Rule, local associations gave up control over their members' voting decisions and specialised in mobilising the vote. Consequently, there was a significant decline in the number of government defeats. Thus, while the second half of the nineteenth century (1847-1905) featured 301 government defeats on 'whipped' votes, the following 67 years (1905-72) witnessed only 34 defeats. Although the 1972-78 period saw 50 government defeats, there were only 14 during the eighteen years of Conservative rule.[45]

> Party discipline became more and more exacting; each party, whilst permitting some leeway in speech, imposed Prussian conformity in the division lobbies.[46]

By the middle of the twentieth century the model of 'responsible' single-party government had become so normalised in Britain that 'governments being defeated by their own followers became virtually impossible'.[47] Samuel Beer even argued that 'there was no longer any point in measuring party cohesion'.[48] An international survey covering 1950-62 showed complete legislative cohesion in Britain with Labour and the Conservatives scoring 100 on the estimated index of cohesion.[49] Until the 1970s, the number of divisions witnessing dissenting votes was less than 5 per cent for most parliaments except for the 1959-64 Conservative parliament that featured a 12 per cent rate of dissent (but mostly due to dissenting votes on the Resale Price bill).

It is important to note that in the British House of Commons legislative dissent tends to be concentrated on relatively few issues (such as devolution or Europe). Claims that the 1974-79 Labour government experienced unprecedented levels of backbench revolts against government policy were exaggerated.[50] Half of the defeats imposed on that government concerned devolution bills for Scotland and Wales. Surveys based on aggregate data that calculate the number of divisions in which government backbenchers cast dissenting votes as a proportion of *all* divisions (see Table 2) can exaggerate the extent and significance of legislative dissent.[51]

Table 2: Dissent by government backbenchers 1945-1997

Date	Governing Party	% of divisions seeing dissenting votes by government MPs
1974-79	Labour	20
1970-74	Conservative	19
1983-87	Conservative	17
1992-97	Conservative	13
1987-92	Conservative	13
1979-83	Conservative	13
1959-64	Conservative	12
1966-70	Labour	8
1974 (Feb.-Oct.)	Labour	7
1945-50	Labour	6
1950-51	Labour	2
1955-59	Conservative	1
1951-55	Conservative	1
1964-66	Labour	0.25

Source: P. Cowley, 'The Conservative Decline and Fall', in A. Geddes and J. Tonge (eds.), *Labour's Landslide: The British General Election of 1997* (Manchester: Manchester University Press, 1997).

When instances of dissent and government defeats are looked at individually, parliaments assumed to be notoriously rebellious seem much less so. Indeed, in 1992-97 when the Conservative government was perceived as very disunited, government backbenchers broke ranks on only 13 per cent of all divisions and Europe accounted for 60 per cent of all Conservative dissenting acts (all of them on the bill to approve the Maastricht Treaty.)[52] In other words, even the most rebellious Conservative MP in the notoriously divided 1992 parliament was apparently loyal in more than nine out of ten votes.

In sum, national parties in the UK are concentrated and cohesive because the rules under which they compete impose high exit costs on politicians. All legislators base their voting decisions on cost-benefit calculations factoring in considerations of career, re-election, seniority, and reputation. In the UK MPs are compliant because it is in their interests to comply. They are patronage recipients, not distributors of patronage. The party leader controls their career advancement and the party brand name provides them with campaign savings. If party policies deviate from manifesto pledges or with ideological commitments it is still possible for MPs to manifest their disagreement in less costly ways than through exit. Parliamentary devices such as 'early day motions', parliamentary questions, private members' bills, and adjournment debates enable MPs to express their views and to influence legislation without putting the party in danger.

British parties are built around a compelling consensus and sense of identity, and their cohesion is the product of the 'responsible party' model. This model encourages collective behaviour and saves on parties' transaction costs (particularly in terms of campaigns and legislative management). But the adversarial style of politics that it generates is increasingly at odds with growing third party support and 'de-ideologised' party politics. Auditors of democracy believe this model of party government has irretrievably broken down.

> The adversarial character of Commons proceedings reduces the policy choices of backbenchers in all parties from the potentially infinite variety associated with the Burkean idea that they act as trustees for their constituents to a basic dichotomy: either voting for or against the government ... Thus, executive and party cues coalesce into an adversarial style of decision-making, which simplistically reduces voting options to two mutually exclusive alternatives: voting for or against the government on partisan grounds.[53]

Intra-party competition under hyper-representative systems

In contrast, parties competing under systems based on proportional representation run the risk of becoming divided because multiple candidacies fragment the mobilisation of the party vote and can promote the formation of rival intra-party groups. Low entry thresholds also encourage minority parties to enter the fray, thus fractionalising party-systems. The preference vote and the single non-transferable vote in multi-seat constituencies (in use in Italy and Japan respectively until the early 1990s) promoted intra-party competition. These systems encouraged the personalisation of politics and the formation of internal leadership groups and factions within ruling parties. By giving factions control over candidate nomination and party list composition and by letting factions control decision-making and the distribution of patronage, Italy's Christian Democrats (DC) and Socialists (PSI) and Japan's Liberal Democrats (LDP) institutionalised factionalism within their organisations.

Preference voting in Italy

The mixed-member majoritarian electoral system adopted in Italy on August 4 1993 was designed with a strong SMP component to minimise problems associated with the previous system of proportionality with multiple preference voting which had already been reduced to a single preference after a referendum in 1991. Reformers were seeking to create a less fragmented party system and to eliminate the style of 'money politics' that was linked to intra-party competition under the old electoral system.

In 1945, preference voting had been seen as a safeguard against the accumulation of dictatorial power experienced under fascism. However, since there was no minimum threshold of representation to deter small parties from competing the Italian party system became fractionalised. As Figure 2 shows, PR with preference voting produced many electoral and parliamentary parties. The average RRP for the post-war period was just below 10 per cent. And in 1992, the entry of new regional and protest parties widened the field of competition considerably so that N_v more than doubled from 3.39 to 6.86.

Under the new mixed-member system voters have two votes to elect members of the Chamber of Deputies and one vote to elect senators. 75 per cent of deputies in the National Assembly and 74 per cent of senators are elected by plurality rule in single-member districts (SMDs) and there is a partial compensatory allocation for the remaining 25 per cent list tier seats.[54] But despite a 4 per cent national minimum threshold of representation there has not been a reduction in the number of parties competing for votes. Almost forty parties gained representation in the House of Representatives at the 2001 elections (although some parties only have one or two seats).

The party system remains fragmented mainly because political parties have adapted their strategies to the new (albeit complicated) rules. The new system provides powerful institutional incentives for parties to enter into pre-election coalitions, which simplifies government formation but increases uncertainty and voters' information costs. And the rules for allocating list seats (for each chamber) leave scope for party manipulation.[55] Briefly, in the SMDs, parties make electoral pacts with other parties by agreeing to withdraw candidates in some constituencies if their allies agree to withdraw their candidates in other constituencies thus allowing a single candidate to fight the seat on behalf of the inter-party bloc or cartel. This has produced a more bipolar pattern of competition, longer-lived governments, and three alternations in office (at the time of writing) between two large cartels - Olive Tree on the Left and House of Freedoms on the Right.

However, Italian voters do not necessarily know to which party the candidate representing the cartel belongs and this makes it impossible so far to measure each party's vote share in the SMDs.[56] The practice of allowing joint endorsement (whereby a candidate can be affiliated with more than one list and can carry the symbol of more than one party) complicates the voter's calculus and the computation of the *scorporo* or party votes for allocating the list seats.[57]

Under the old electoral system the dynamics of the preference vote exacerbated intra-party competition. Relatively large district magnitude ranging from one to thirty six members in 31 constituencies[58] (and a national distribution of remainders using the Imperiali quota) meant that nominees from large parties would end up competing against intra-party rivals within the same district. Candidates were elected to fill their party's shares of the seats in each constituency according to the individual preference votes cast by the party's voters in that constituency. For elections to the Italian National Assembly before 1991 each voter was allowed to cast three or four preference votes for different candidates on the same party list. And candidates who were awarded their party's seats were those who gathered the highest number of preference votes.

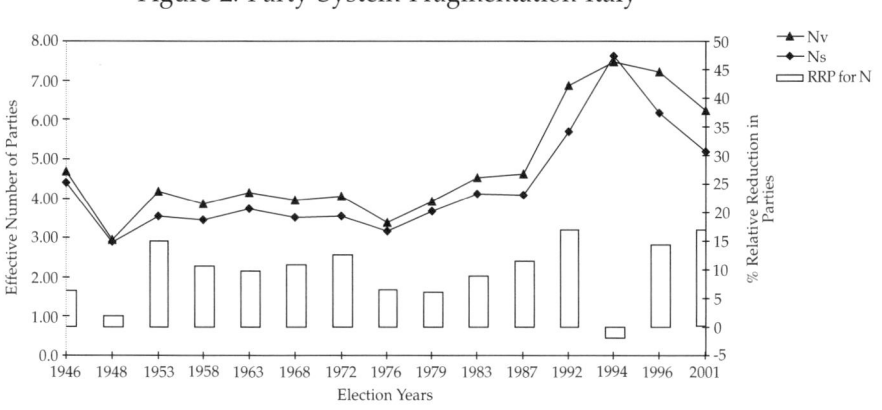

Figure 2: Party System Fragmentation Italy

But since the number of candidates a party nominated in each constituency tended to exceed the number of seats that party could reasonably expect to win, and given the narrowness of victories, candidates ended up competing against partisans for campaign endorsement and for list placement. Because a relatively small number of preference votes were sufficient to make the difference between winning and losing it was important for party nominees to maximise their advantage against intra-party rivals. Sometimes endorsement by a single collateral organisation or interest group or by one prominent politician who controlled local patronage could be enough to make the difference between victory and defeat.

Moreover, since only an average thirty per cent of Italian voters stated individual preferences for candidates[59] while the majority preferred to cast a simple party list vote, candidates from large parties needed to have their names near the top of the party list to stand a chance of being elected. And to press their claim to a favourable list position they would solicit the sponsorship of senior politicians and faction leaders within their own party. In the ruling DC and its coalition partner the PSI faction leaders and local chieftains tended to control the composition of lists and access to party resources (such as campaign funding, pork barrel projects, and so on). Hence, DC and PSI candidates had an incentive to affiliate with particular factions to maximise their election chances. In exchange they would demonstrate their allegiance and loyalty to their sponsors by voting for them at intra-party elections (during party congresses, for instance). Sponsorships enabled local DC and PSI chieftains to strengthen their personal power bases and to bolster the power of their individual faction inside the party. 'Like a party, each of the factions engages in the business of nominating its candidates, campaigning in elections, dispensing patronage, and competing to acquire political power in ways otherwise quite like political parties.'[60]

In sum, electoral systems that involve intra-party competition have the potential to fragment large parties and to produce candidate-centred contests that can become more like intra-party primaries. Open-list PR opens opportunities for party elites to manipulate list composition, but closed lists give the party leadership more control over nomination. Because partisans had to compete for nomination, for list placement, and for preference votes, they pursued endorsement and vote-maximisation strategies by cultivating personal ties with voters and faction leaders. Collective party behaviour inside the large DC and the PSI was hampered by the fact that their factions developed reputations based on private goods. (There were no factions inside the big Communist Party because candidate-rivalry during campaigns was forbidden). Relationships of exchange between politicians, voters, faction leaders, and local barons encouraged self-centred behaviour and the development of personal reputations. And since the DC (and the PSI after the mid-1960s) were continuously in power until 1992, opportunism produced large-scale corruption scandals within government. The 'Clean Hands' investigation by Milan magistrates in 1993-94 finally brought the Italian regime down and caused the ruling Christian Democrats to implode.

However, despite a high degree of intra-party competition and low thresholds of entry for party competition there were disincentives to exit for politicians within ruling parties. Since the DC and PSI were pivotal players in forming government coalitions (the DC from its formation in 1945 and the PSI after the early 1980s), utility-maximising politicians had nothing to gain by defecting even if they were dissatisfied with their party. Exit would have been irrational since it would have meant exclusion from the spoils of office and from a guaranteed share of party resources. Moreover, the DC and PSI adopted proportionality rules to distribute patronage among their factions. Consequently the DC experienced no factional defection during its forty-five years of uninterrupted rule (although in the early 1990s a few senior politicians, including former president Cossiga, split when it was clear that the game was up for the Christian Democrats).

Internal rules designed to accommodate factional demands constituted barriers to exit but created long-term decisional dilemmas inside the DC. While the DC already contained three factions at birth their number gradually increased[61] because the party adopted a proportional system for allocating power that encouraged factions to multiply. The spoils of office were usually divided among existing factions according to their strength on the various party organs and usually in proportion to the share of votes received by each faction at the party congress. These factional arrangements extended to the election of the Party Secretary (party leader) who was usually the head of the largest faction: that is, the faction gaining the greatest number of delegate votes at the biennial National Congress.

Before 1964, competition for seats on the party executive body, the National Council (NC), was based on the rival policy motions submitted to the national congress. Attached to each motion was a list of names of candidates who supported it and who ran as unofficial nominees for election to the NC. But a system of 'reinforced' majority gave four-fifths of NC seats (and seats on other party organs) to the group receiving a plurality of the preference votes cast by congress delegates. This gave disproportional power to the dominant faction or the majority factional bloc. Protest by minority factions led to the introduction in 1964 of two procedural changes, which required first that only motion-lists could be submitted. This meant that the motion-lists presented at the national congress formed the basis on which the party chose its majority platform and selected its majority leaders in the National Council. The second change required that motions be submitted to the Central Directorate *prior* to the convening of the provincial congresses, thus effectively forcing all nominees to the NC to attach themselves to one of the motion lists previously received by the Party Directorate.

Since delegates to the various party assemblies were elected by proportional representation among contending lists, this change of rules institutionalised factionalism from below. It created incentives for local activists to affiliate with a particular faction in order to be selected as delegates to attend sectional and regional assemblies. By the same token, it put pressure on factions to decentralise their operations and to compete directly at the local level. Factions began to recruit and campaign locally. In sum, these changes forced factions to become institutionalised since delegates from sectional assemblies to provincial assemblies, to the regional pre-congresses, and finally to the National Congress, were selected on the basis of motion-lists associated with different national factions.[62]

But factionalism also regulated the distribution of government spoils. Cabinet portfolios, ministerial posts, parliamentary appointments (posts of Speakers and committee chairs), and shares of government patronage were similarly allocated to each faction in proportion to its strength in the National Council. Precise rules for this calculation were even spelled out in the so-called *Manuale Cencelli*.[63] Government contracts (notably in construction and highway building works) were allocated along factional lines. Since faction leaders were guaranteed a share of office and party spoils on the basis of relatively small shares of intra-party support senior politicians had incentives to build local power bases, to split from existing factions, and to set up their own faction.

Consequently, the effective number of factions (that assigns weighted values to each faction's fractional share of support) increased significantly after 1964 (see Figure 3). I have adapted the indices developed by Taagepera and Shugart for calculating the effective number of electoral (N_v) and parliamentary parties (N_s) to the intra-party arena. Hence, factional strength is calculated according to the support received by each faction on the party National Council (from 1946-59) and at the party National Congress (from 1962-1989). Thus:

$$Nf = [1/(Vf_1^2 + Vf_2^2 + Vf_3^2 + \ldots + Vf_n^2)]$$

Where 'Nf' is the 'effective' number of factions. In short, Nf is measured by dividing one by the sum of the squared fractions of total votes held by each faction at the Party National Congress or on the National Council.

While the number of observable factions ranged from three (in 1947) to twelve (in 1982) the effective number of factions is slightly lower because factions with very small percentages of support become practically discounted in the weighting process. However, by 1982 collective action problems emerged in the hyper-fractionalised DC as individual factions gained blocking power. With so many factions in competition, inter-factional alliances became necessary to extract internal majorities and agree the party's programme, make internal decisions, and elect the party leader. But once factions arranged themselves into three equally powerful and pivotal inter-factional blocs at the 1982

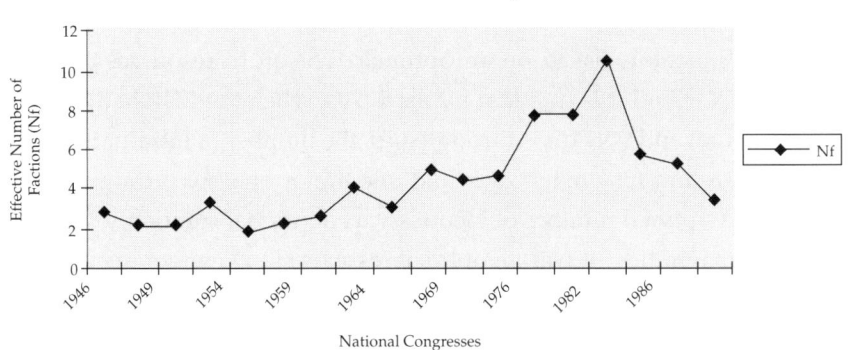

Figure 3: Effective Number of Factions in the Italian Christian Democratic Party 1946-89

congress 'cycling' became a problem and there was no mechanism to prevent factions from bolting from one factional alliance to join another. This created decisional stalemate and prevented the DC from reforming itself. The reform efforts of Party Secretaries (Zaccagnini during the 1970s and de Mita during the 1980s) were blocked by factional vetoes.

SNTV in Japan

Similar problems linked to intra-party competition affected politics in Japan and dynamics inside the ruling LDP. Instead of promoting collective goods policies, SNTV encouraged politicians to collect personal votes in exchange for clientelistic favours. In brief, Japanese voters had a single vote to elect between two to six candidates in each district but votes could not be pooled with those of intra-party colleagues or be transferred to lower scoring candidates within the same party. So to survive candidates needed a bloc of committed voters, and large parties such as the LDP, which presented multiple candidates in the same districts, needed to optimise their nomination and vote division strategies. It was important to avoid nominating too few or too many candidates (perhaps by not contesting the third or fourth seat in many of the bigger multi-seat districts). And it was equally important to limit the number of wasted votes by trying to apportion the LDP vote in each district equally enough so that all nominees could win. And this depended on the expected vote share matched against the district magnitude.[64] By targeting the narrowly based local vote, an LDP candidate could secure a seat with 15 per cent or less of the popular vote in the largest constituencies. And by helping candidates build personal reputations LDP factions were instrumental in targeting such vote.

It has been argued that there was a 'natural selection' in the size and number of LDP factions based on an optimal division of resources and spoils under SNTV.[65] And it is true that by the 1970s, when the LDP had optimised its nomination and vote division strategies, the number of intra-party factions stabilised around four major ones and one minor one. According to Masaru Khono, this optimal number of factions was a rational solution to variations in district magnitude. It was an optimal response to Duverger's 'mechanical' and 'psychological' rules.[66] The logic is that rational politicians will leave losing parties (or losing factions) that are under-represented, while rational voters will not waste their votes on losers and will not support candidates from parties or from factions that are under-represented.

To help them build their personal reputations under SNTV LDP candidates (like their DC counterparts) sought the backing of faction leaders with direct access to funds. Campaign finance was needed to bribe voters and to pay for innumerable gifts offered to constituents at weddings and funerals, and the clout of a national faction leader was indispensable to attract 'pork barrel' projects to the area. National faction leaders played a key role in raising large sums of money from economic interest groups to secure the 'pork' and therefore to boost the campaign of LDP candidates affiliated with their factions. Access to campaign resources motivated candidates to affiliate with a faction (before nomination and after election). Only a very small number of MPs did not belong to a faction. The election of the LDP leader and the apportioning of cabinet and party posts were also made along factional lines. And these arrangements led to the emergence of two factional alignments inside the LDP - the mainstream bloc, made up of factions supporting the party leader/Prime Minister and gaining the majority of government portfolios, and the non-mainstream bloc which manoeuvred to gain more stakes.

But by delegating campaign funding to its factions and by letting faction bosses arrange 'pork barrel' projects the LDP opened itself to opportunism and 'money politics'. Like the DC, the LDP became periodically embroiled in scandals of political corruption and electoral reform was introduced in 1994 to try and clean up 'money politics'. While electoral reform has stripped LDP factions of their traditional fund-raising function, factionalism remains an important feature of the LDP. After elections for the Lower House of the Diet in June 2000, the party still contained seven observable factions and 6.2 effective factions.[67] Realising that factionalism still structures relationships and the allocation of power LDP members began to affiliate in greater numbers again. The number of unaffiliated MPs dropped to 9 per cent in 2000 from 22 per cent in 1996, the first election held under the new electoral system. Factionalism still regulates the apportioning of cabinet posts and of top executive appointments and the selection of the party president. And membership of the 'mainstream' and 'non-mainstream' coalitions based on the configuration of factional alignments remains the building bloc of government formation.

Factionalism became widespread and institutionalised inside the DC and the LDP because the dynamics of intra-party competition under preference voting and under SNTV promoted party fragmentation and because intra-party proportionalism for dividing the spoils encouraged factions to become embedded. The faction became the building bloc in the formation of cabinets, the selection of candidates for public and party offices, the election of the party leader, and the organisation of intra-party life. When factions are recognised as legitimate organisational structures, more politicians are encouraged to set up their own factions to maximise their pay-offs. And if there is no mechanism to limit their proliferation factions multiply, and in the long run parties with a high tolerance of factionalism can become captives of their factions. Since factions focus on sub-party preferences, their presence hinders collective goals and invites opportunism, and when their operations are decentralised, accountability lines are blurred.

Intra-party implications under mixed electoral systems

In their search for the right balance between SMP and pure PR many post-communist democracies in Eastern Europe adopted mixed member electoral systems (MMS) to elect members of their national assemblies. MMS and its variants were seen as the best way of stabilising nascent party systems while simultaneously moving away from the majoritarian principle associated with the former Communist regime (although in Hungary it was more the outcome of brinkmanship and intense bargaining between political parties). In the early 1990s Italy and Japan swapped preference voting and SNVT for variants of MMS to correct flaws linked to intra-party competition under their old electoral systems.

Based on the German electoral system, MMS combines single-member districts (SSDs) with multi-member districts (MMDs) in various proportions. And there are many variations in other features of mixed-member systems across countries.[68] They include the number of ballots available to the voter, the percentage of seats set aside in the list tier, the magnitude of the list tier, whether the PR seats are allocated in a compensatory or in a parallel fashion, and whether there are run-offs in the plurality area. These features have differentiated effects on political parties' strategies and affect intra-party politics in different ways.

Since high thresholds of representation make entry more costly for new parties and since low thresholds create incentives for party splits, several East European countries have over the past decade made some adjustments to their electoral systems.[69] In several cases the minimum size of parliamentary parties has been raised in an effort to reward large parties and to reduce party system fragmentation. In the Czech Republic this has led to a reduction in the number of observable parties from ten to six between 1993-1996. But where such thresholds do not exist to deter small parties from entering the race, minor parties overcome their size problems by forming strategic coalitions with stronger contenders to enter the legislature. In Slovakia, the Party of the Democratic Left joined the Common Choice coalition with the Social Democratic Party, the Greens, and a Farmers' Party. The Movement for Democratic Slovakia brought together the Peasant Party of Slovakia and offered places on its list to candidates from the environmental Green Alternative. By contrast, in Poland the absence of a threshold requirement led to extreme party system fragmentation during the country's founding elections.

Since electoral reform was introduced in Italy and Japan, national elections have been significantly de-personalised because the majority of seats under the new systems are fought under SMP and nominal voting reduces the scope for intra-party competition. There are large components of single-seat districts - 75 per cent in Italy and 60 per cent in Japan. With less intra-party competition for party resources factions lose their *raison d'être* as channels for distributing campaign funding or for processing the exchange vote. Consequently LDP candidates have less of an incentive to affiliate with a faction for campaigning purposes although the factions remain the main channels for distributing patronage. There is only slight evidence that they play a smaller role in providing posts than prior to electoral reform.[70]

However, MMS is not free from party manipulation and from intra-party conflict since different strategies are required in the plurality SSD arena and in the list-tiers PR arena. In the latter, elections are by nature competitive and parties seek to differentiate themselves from their rivals to maximise their list seats. Proportionality-based systems tend to produce parties of national scope and coherent and disciplined parties that offer programmatic representation.[71] But under the majoritarian system in the SSDs parties are under pressure to co-operate and to form inter-party alliances or (in the case of the LDP cross-factional coalitions). And these alliances have intra-party implications.

When a party joins a cartel it puts its identity and coherence at stake and risks devaluing its brand name. The need for inter-party alliances in single-seat races forces parties to moderate their stances. But moderate strategies can create discontent among ideological sub-groups and among the grass-roots. If members of a particular faction or activists feel that joining a cartel is compromising ideological principles, they might be tempted to bolt (as PDL members did in Slovakia). New parties face a greater risk of defection because exit costs are lower than for members of well-established parties.

Other features of MMS can affect intra-party politics if they provide more scope for conflicts inside parties. Simultaneous candidacies in the different tiers (allowed in Italy, Japan and Hungary) can cause friction if a candidate contesting a seat in the PR tiers finds herself in competition with a partisan who is also contesting the plurality seat in the same district. Ballot structure also has intra-party implications and can create leader-follower conflicts. Under closed lists voters cannot express preferences for one candidate over party colleagues and therefore intra-party competition to seek the favour of voters is practically eliminated. But under open lists there is the possibility of altering the proposed lists by casting preferential votes (as in the Czech and Slovak Republics) and this can encourage a more personalised act of voting and motivate partisans to compete for personal votes.

Under closed lists intra-party conflict can emerge between leaders and followers over the rank-ordering of candidates. Czech party executives interfere in the composition of the regional lists, thus challenging the power of local and regional branches. Party headquarters commonly reshuffle and add names to party lists in the Christian Democratic Union and Czechoslovak People's Party (KDU-CSL) and in the Czech Social Democratic Party (CSSD), and preferential votes rarely alter original party rankings.[72] In Slovakia the veto power of party executives over local and regional nominations is so strong that challenges by local branches are rare. In Russia the PR element of the electoral system gives party leaders leverage over rank-and-file deputies, but the exceptional absence of regional lists discourages the formation of regional parties.

In sum, because MMS systems have gained popularity only recently there is limited evidence to assess their efficiency gains, particularly in the intra-party arena. But in as much as MMS is chosen for its ability to produce a stable and less fractionalised party system, we can expect that over time politicians competing under such systems will face more disincentives to exit as access to parliament and government becomes more restricted. And in Hungary, Poland and the Czech Republic where party systems seem to have stabilised much more quickly than expected,[73] party leaders have gained insurance against potential challenges; there is thus now less 'political tourism' and fewer party splits than in the past.

As MPs begin to identify with their party more strongly and as majority rule becomes established, legislative parties in East Europe are behaving more like their West European counterparts. Voting cohesion is high among Czech parliamentary parties, particularly those who have participated in coalition governments where members have more at stake. As in Western Europe, career advancement is linked to party loyalty. The Czech and Slovak parliaments have adopted traditional means (such as whips) to co-ordinate the passage of legislation. However, party sanctions against non-compliant MPs are still difficult to apply because disciplinary measures go against the grain of their constitutions. Sanctions remain strictly intra-party affairs.[74]

Conclusion

Different institutional regimes produce differentiated patterns of intra-party co-operation. Because electoral systems structure party competition they create different incentives for intra-party actors to either co-operate or to compete. SMP produces large but cohesive parties with clearly identifiable brand names and low campaign costs, which motivates politicians to co-operate and deter them from exit. The logic of two-party competition under plurality rule means that voters expect parties to behave as united actors and party leaders expect cohesion in the legislature and in cabinet. Hence, parties adopt procedural arrangements and design incentive structures that motivate collective behaviour, minimise independent action, and make exit very costly for politicians. But if parties become divided over a particular issue or programme SMP can put them into a strait-jacket.

Most parliamentary democracies in Europe use electoral systems involving variants of preference voting and proportional representation in multi-member constituencies, which tend to produce multiparty systems and coalition governments. Because solid party unity is not assumed for election victories, for cabinet formation, and for efficient government these systems generate different incentives for intra-party actors. Depending on their particular features, these systems encourage intra-party competition and create more costly campaigns for politicians in their search for personal votes. Because they fragment party systems electoral systems based on proportionality lower exit costs for politicians, particularly in democracies that are not yet well established.

Highly representative systems run the risk of fragmenting parties excessively, particularly when parties adopt institutional arrangements that maximise intra-party representation and devolve power to internal groups and factions. Excessive fragmentation can create cycling and instability leading to decisional stalemate if intra-party groups decide to use their veto power to block party decisions. To achieve electoral efficiency and minimise the risk of party fragmentation many democracies in Eastern Europe have adopted mixed-member electoral systems. While evidence is too sketchy to draw generalised conclusions yet, it appears that intra-party behaviour in the more established East European democracies such as the Czech Republic and Slovakia is beginning to converge with that found in Western Europe, and that western-derived theory remains appropriate to the analysis of developments further East.

Notes

[1] Michael Gallagher, Michael Laver, and Peter Mair (eds.), *Representative Government in Modern Europe*, 2nd edition (New York, St. Louis, San Francisco, Auckland, Bogota, Caracas, Lisbon, London, Madrid, Mexico City, Milan, Montreal, New Delhi, San Juan, Singapore, Sydney, Tokyo, Toronto: McGraw-Hill Inc., 1995).

[2] Petr Kopecky, *Parliaments in the Czech and Slovak Republics* (Aldershot, Burlington USA, Singapore, Sydney: Ashgate, 2002).

[3] Françoise Boucek, 'The growth and management of factionalism in long-lived dominant parties: comparing Britain, Italy, Canada, and Japan', The London School of Economics and Political Science: PhD thesis, 2001), pp. 302-314.

[4] Anthony Downs, *An Economic Theory of Democracy* (New York: Harper and Row, 1957), p. 25.

[5] Joseph A. Schumpeter, *Capitalism, Socialism and Democracy* (London and New York: Routledge, 1943), p. 283.

[6] Richard S. Katz and Robin Kolodny, 'Party Organisation as an Empty Vessel: Parties in American Politics', in R. Katz and P. Mair (eds.), *How Parties Organize: Change and Adaptation in Party Organizations in Western Democracies* (Sage Publications: London, Thousand Oaks, New Delhi, (1994).

[7] John Curtice and H. Semetko, 'Does it matter what the papers say? in A. Heath, R. Jowell and J. Curtice (eds.), *Labour's Last Chance? The 1992 Election and Beyond* (Aldershot: Dartmouth, 1994), pp. 43-64.

[8] Boucek, 'The growth and management of factionalism', pp. 85-9.

[9] Giovanni Sartori, *Parties and Party Systems: A Framework for Analysis*, Volume 1, (Cambridge: Cambridge University Press, 1976) pp. 85-6.

[10] Kenneth Janda, *Political Parties: A Cross National Survey* (The Free Press: New York, 1980).

[11] David Hume (1741), *Essays: moral, political and literary*, from edited version by Eugene F. Miller (Liberty *Classics,* Indianapolis) p. 55.

[12] Richard Rose, 'Parties, Factions, and Tendencies in Britain' *Political Studies* 12(1), February, 1964, pp. 33-46.

[13] Robin Kolodny, 'Moderate Party Factions in the U.S. House of Representatives', in John C. Green and Daniel M. Shea (eds.), *The State of the Parties: The Changing Role of Contemporary American Parties* (3rd ed.) (Lanham, Boulder, New York, Oxford: Rowman and Littlefield Publishers Inc., 1999).

[14] Paul Lewis, *Political Parties in Post-Communist Eastern Europe* (London and New York: Routledge, 2000).

[15] Peter Kopecky, *Parliaments in the Czech and Slovak Republics: Party Competition and Parliamentary Institutionalization* (Ashgate: Aldershot, Burlington USA, Singapore, Sydney, 2002).

[16] Paul Lewis, *Political Parties in Post-Communist Eastern Europe* (London and New York: Routledge, 2000), p. 119.

[17] Raphael Zariski, 'Party Factions and Comparative Politics: Some Preliminary Observations', *Midwest Journal of Political Science,* February 1960, pp. 372-90.

[18] Gordon Tullock, 'A Model of Social Interaction', in James F. Herndon and J.L. Berndl, *Mathematics Applications in Political Science* (University of Virginia, 1969), pp. 4-28.

[19] Maurice Duverger, *Political Parties: Their Organisation and Activity in the Modern State* (London: Methuen, 1964).

[20] Angelo Panebianco, *Political parties: organisation and power* (Cambridge, New York, New Rochelle, Melbourne, Sydney: Cambridge University Press, 1988).

[21] Richard Gillespie, Michael Waller, and L. Lopez-Nieto (eds.), 'Factional Politics and Democratisation', *Democratisation* special issue, 2(1), 1995.

22. Robert Leonardi and Douglas A. Wertman, *Italian Christian Democracy: The Politics of Dominance* (Basingstoke and London: Macmillan, 1989).
23. Frédéric Sawicki, 'The *Parti Socialiste*: From a Party of Activists to a Party of Government' in Pietro Ignazi and Colette Ysmal, *The Organisation of Political Parties in Southern Europe* (Westport: Connecticut, London: Paraeger, 1998).
24. László Szarvas, 'Parties and Party Factions in the Hungarian Parliament', *Journal of Communist Studies and Transition Politics*, 10(3), September, 1994, pp. 120-36.
25. A. Agh, 'From nomenclatura to clientura', in G. Pridham and P.G. Lewis (eds.) *Stabilizing Fragile Democracies* (London: Routledge, 1996).
26. Arthur H. Miller and Thomas F. Klobucar, 'The Development of Party Identification in Post-Soviet Societies', *American Journal of Political Science*, Vol. 24(4), October 2000, pp. 667-685.
27. Petr Kopecky, *Parliaments in the Czech and Slovak Republics* (Aldershot, Burlington USA, Singapore, Sydney: Ashgate, p. 174.
28. Harmel R., Heo U.K., Tan A. and Janda K. 'Performance, Leadership, Factions and Party Change: An Empirical Analysis', *West European Politics*, Vol. 18(1), 1995, pp. 1-33.
29. For instance, American Democrats follow plurality rule for choosing a presidential candidate at the national convention: that is, the candidate who gets the most votes in the state's primary gets all the state's votes at the national convention. But Republicans use a rule approximating proportional representation: that is, the votes at the national convention are divided in proportion to the votes the candidates received in the primary election.
30. *Cohabitation* refers to the situation whereby the President and the Prime Minister/government belong to different parties or party blocs.
31. See Sarah Birch in this volume.
32. However, Duverger's rule does not apply to party systems that contain strong regional parties such as Canada.
33. Taagepera R. and Shugart S., *Seats and Votes: The Effects and Determinants of Electoral Systems* (New Haven & London: Yale University Press, 1989), pp. 209-273. This index is not widely used although Dunleavy and Margetts have applied it to disaggregated data in a six-country survey. (See Patrick Dunleavy and Helen Margetts, 'Disaggregating Indices Of Democracy: Deviation From Proportionality And Relative Reduction In Parties', Paper presented at the *ECPR Annual Workshops*; University of Leiden, 2-8 April, 1993.)
34. N_v is measured as one divided by the sum of the squared fractions of the vote for each party: that is, $N_v = (1 / (V1^2 + V2^2 + \ldots Vn^2)$ and N_s is measured as one divided by the sum of the squared fractions of total seats held by each party: that is, $N_s = (1 / (S1^2 + S2^2 + \ldots Sn^2)$.

[35] Under the 1832 Reform Act there were 153 single-member constituencies, 240 double-member, seven three-member, and one four-member constituency.

[36] Hugh Berrington, 'MPs and their Constituents in Britain: The History of the Relationship' in Bogdanor V. (ed.) *Representatives of the People? Parliamentarians and Constituents in Western Democracies* (Gower: Cambridge, 1985).

[37] Alan Beattie, 'Ministerial Responsibility and the Theory of the British State', in R.A.W. Rhodes and P. Dunleavy eds. *Prime Ministers, Cabinet and Core Executive* (New York: St. Martin's Press, 1995), pp. 158-178.

[38] Pippa Norris, 'Anatomy of a Labour Landslide' in P. Norris and N. Gavin (eds.) *Britain votes 1997* (Oxford: Oxford University Press, 1997).

[39] Between October 1995 and February 1997, Alan Howarth defected to Labour, Emma Nicholson and Peter Thurman to the Liberal Democrats, and Sir John Gardiner to the Referendum Party.

[40] These interactions can be modelled as games of 'chicken'. Françoise Boucek, 'The growth and management of factionalism . . .', 2001: chapter 4.

[41] Garry Cox, *The Efficient Secret: The Cabinet and the Development of Political Parties in Victorian England* (Cambridge: Cambridge University Press, 1987).

[42] E. Ozbudum, 'Party Cohesion in Western Democracies: A Causal Analysis' in Eckstein H. and Gurr E. eds. *Comparative Politics* Series No. 01-006 Vol. 1 (Beverly Hills: Sage Publications, 1970).

[43] The whip today is a party management document that takes the form of a weekly communication setting out the Commons business for the week, notices of party political meetings, and a sheet with 'all party' notices (John Biffen, *Inside the House of Commons*: p. 81).

[44] Samuel H. Beer, *Modern British Politics: A Study of Parties and Pressure Groups* (London: Faber and Faber, 1965).

[45] Stuart Weir and David Beetham, *Political Power and Democratic Control in Britain*, The Democratic Audit of the United Kingdom (London and New York: Routledge, 1999) p. 380.

[46] Berrington, 1985, p. 26.

[47] Ozbudun (1970) as before, p. 318.

[48] Samuel Beer, 8 (1965), p. 350.

[49] Kenneth Janda, *Comparative Political Parties Data 1950-1962* (Ann Arbor: Inter-University Consortium for Political and Social Research, study 7534, 1979).

[50] Philip Norton, *Dissension in the House of Commons 1945-79* (Oxford: Clarendon Press, 1980).

[51] Philip Cowley and Philip Norton (1996b), *Are Conservative MPs Revolting?* (Hull: University Of Hull Centre for Legislative Studies).

[52] David Baker, Andrew Gamble, Stephen Ludlam and David Seawright, 'Backbenchers

with Attitude: A Seismic Study of the Conservative Party and Dissent on Europe', in Bowler S., D. Farrell, and R. Katz, eds. *Party Discipline and Parliamentary Government* (Ohio State University, 1999).

[53] Stuart Weir and David Beetham (1999), as before, pp. 375-6.

[54] These compensatory seats are allocated according to a list system of proportional representation. Hence, each voter has 2 votes: one for electing the candidate in the local *collegio* and the other for electing a candidate on the party list at the level of the regional *circoscrizione*.

[55] See particularly chapters 5 and 15 in Matthew Soberg Shugart and Martin P. Wattenberg, *Mixed-Member Electoral Systems: The Best of Both Worlds?* (New York: Oxford University Press, 2001). Richard Katz 'Reforming the Italian Electoral Law, 1993' pp. and Roberto D'Alimonte 'Mixed Electoral Rules, Partisan Realignment, and Party System Change in Italy'. See also D'Alimonte R. and P. Mair (1998) 'The Italian parliamentary elections of 1996 - Competition and Transition', *The European Journal of Political Research,* Special issue (August 1998).

[56] Under the new MMS it is so far not possible to calculate the 'effective number of parties' accurately because in the single-seat districts candidates are not identified by their party label but only as members of a particular cartel. Hence, only a partial calculation of Nv and Ns is possible: that is, for the 25 per cent list tiers. However, there are analysts working on the field trying to collect such data.

[57] Katz, *Reforming* ... pp. 115-117.

[58] The Valle d'Aosta constituency had a single-seat.

[59] David Hine, *Governing Italy: The Politics of Bargained Pluralism* (Oxford: Clarendon Press, 1993).

[60] Belloni F. and D. Beller, *Faction Politics: Political Parties and Factionalism in Comparative Perspectives* (Santa Barbara, Oxford: ABC-Clio Inc., 1978) p. 89.

[61] Article 87 in the party statutes actually banned factions or *correnti* from the DC.

[62] Robert Leonardi and Douglas A. Wertman, *Italian Christian Democracy: The Politics of Dominance* (Basingstoke and London: Macmillan, 1989), p. 137.

[63] Named after Massimo Cencelli, secretary in the personal office of DC leader Mariano Rumor, the manual assigned points to each government post. A full ministerial portfolio was worth the equivalent of three points but the presidency of the Council of Ministers was assigned only two points while a post of under-secretary of state was given one point. These points were distributed among all the DC factions on the basis of their respective strength in the party National Council but rules were not applied rigorously.

[64] Garry Cox, *Making Votes Count: Strategic Coordination in the World's Electoral Systems* (Cambridge University Press, 1997), pp. 238-50.

[65] Watanabe T. (1964) *Habatsu, Nihon Hoshuto No Bunseki* (Tokyo: Kobundo). Cited in

Masaru Kohno, *Japan's Postwar Party Politics* (Princeton NJ: Princeton University Press, 1997), pp. 108-9.

66 Masaru Kohno, *Japan's Postwar Party Politics* (Princeton NJ: Princeton University Press, 1997).

67 Françoise Boucek, pp. 285 and 294.

68 For an overview see Matthew Soberg Shugart and Martin P. Wattenberg, *Mixed-Member Electoral Systems: The Best of Both Worlds?* (New York: Oxford University Press, 2001), especially p. 20.

69 See Birch, 'Electoral systems and party systems'.

70 Garry Cox, 'Electoral Reform and the Fate of Factions: The Case of Japan's Liberal Democratic Party', *British Journal of Political Science*, 29, 1999, pp. 33-56.

71 Shugart and Wattenberg, p. 582.

72 Petr Kopecky, *Parliaments in the Czech and Slovak Republics* (Aldershot, Burlington USA, Singapore, Sydney: Ashgate, p. 196 and p. 61).

73 James Toole, 'Government formation and party system stabilization in East Central Europe', *Party Politics*, 6(4), 2000, pp. 441-461.

74 Petr Kopecký, as before.

Ingrid van Biezen and Petr Kopecký[1]
On the Predominance of State Money: Reassessing Party Financing in the New Democracies of Southern and Eastern Europe

ABSTRACT

This article looks at the patterns of party financing in the relatively recently established democracies of Southern and Eastern Europe, with a particular emphasis on the relative importance of the state and society as financial contributors to political parties. Our reassessment of the practice of party financing in these new democratic polities shows that public funding has become a critical source of income in all of the democracies considered here. However, the article also shows that the importance of public money does not unequivocally rule out the relevance of society. Rather than through membership subscriptions, however, society seems to have acquired a special relevance as an illicit source of party financing. We argue that money accrued from corrupt sources may nevertheless reinforce rather than counterbalance the parties' overall dependence on and orientation towards the state, especially since illicit financing tends to be most profitable for government parties in exploiting the spoils of office. We also argue that the predominance of state money may act to freeze the status quo of the party system and hence achieve a sense of stability that may otherwise be difficult to achieve in the context of relatively vulnerable party organisations and unstable party systems.

Introduction

The introduction of state subventions to political parties has clearly encouraged important changes in the way in which parties organise. The increasing financial dependence on the state as a single financier of party activity, for example, may result in a corresponding increase of power concentration within the party.[2] Moreover, for parties in the established Western democracies, it has been observed that changing patterns of party financing and particularly the increasing availability of public funds have served to strengthen their orientation towards the state while it has at the same time contributed to their shifting away from society.[3] Public funding also appears a generally widespread phenomenon in newly emerging democracies. In fact, precisely because parties in these countries have enjoyed the strong privilege to define the rules of the political game in a relatively unconstrained fashion while, at the same time, they experienced the social environment characterised by the erosion of mass participation similar to contemporary Europe, we may expect the state to dominate party finances even more - and society to be even less relevant - than in the case of established parties in the West.

This article explores patterns of party financing in four newly established democracies of Southern and Eastern Europe: Spain, Portugal, the Czech Republic and Hungary. Thus, in addition to focusing on new democracies *per se*, the article also offers an important cross-regional comparison. We may expect the tendencies common to newly emerged democracies to be even more strongly pronounced in Eastern Europe, which joined the family of democratic countries more than a decade after their Southern European counterparts. We focus on the practice of party financing, with a particular emphasis on the relative importance of the state and society as financial contributors to political parties. This is the subject of analysis in the first two sections of the article which analyse the legal side of state funding of political parties, one the one hand, and the societal funding, that is membership fees, private donations and illicit financing, on the other. The third section then looks at the impact of party finance on party organisations and explores the extent to which financing of parties may be geared towards electoral as opposed to organisational purposes in particular. The final section assesses the extent to which rules on party finances may be seen as protecting the privileges of established parties against the small parties and newcomers.

State Funding

Political parties in the established liberal democracies in Western Europe traditionally depended primarily on private contributions. Government financing of the political process, if at all, occurred mainly indirectly, and the introduction of direct state funding of parties has been a relatively recent phenomenon.[4] In the recently established democracies in Southern and Eastern Europe, by contrast, state subsidies to political parties have been widely available from the very beginning. Indeed, direct public funding of parties was normally introduced at an early stage of the democratisation process, and often without much debate on the role public money should play in the financing of political parties.[5]

Public financing of parties in all four countries analysed here is primarily party rather than candidate oriented, and resembles the general Western European tradition of public funding in this respect.[6] The Spanish, Portuguese and Czech regulations on party financing are in fact defined entirely in terms of party, whilst in Hungary state money for election expenses is in principle also available for individual candidates. In principle, the systems of direct funding of political parties, although different from each other in many details, all rest on three pillars: annual subventions for routine activities, subsidies for electoral expenditures, and subsidies to support the activities of the parliamentary groups.[7]

The first type of state subsidy that parties in all four countries receive is an annual sum of money in order to cover the parties' normal daily functioning, i.e. money for the maintenance of the party organisation or the payment of the party employees, and for extra-parliamentary activities with no direct electoral purpose more generally. We will refer to this type of money as *subventions for routine activities*, thereby distinguishing them from another important source of public subsidies that parties in all four countries receive, namely state money for the reimbursement of their election campaigns. To this latter type of public money, which is normally not an annual but a one-off subsidy for each election, we will refer to as *electoral subventions*. In this paper, we will concentrate on the subventions for national elections only.

While public subsidies for parties were introduced at a very early stage of the democratisation process in all four countries, the timing of the introduction of the different types has varied widely. In Spain, the introduction of electoral subventions preceded that of any other type of public subsidy to political parties. Electoral state subventions have been distributed since the first democratic elections of 1977, while subventions for routine activities were established somewhat later, i.e. in 1978.[8] In Hungary, both types of financial state support were introduced more or less simultaneously at what should be noted was a very early stage, i.e. before the first post-communist elections. The foundations for the system of public funding of the routine activities of parties was written down in the 1989 law on the operation and financial functioning of political parties.[9] The reimbursement of the cost of election campaigns was regulated similarly early and were included in the 1989 electoral law.[10] In order to compensate the anticipated costs of the 1990 elections, the sums of state support for these elections were agreed upon in the round table negotiations.[11]

In Portugal, laws or decrees on the state financing of parties were introduced shortly after the first democratic elections: in 1977.[12] These concerned annual routine subventions; electoral state subsidies were introduced only later, i.e. in 1993. In the Czech Republic (then Czechoslovakia), state financing of political parties was introduced prior to the 1990 elections, in a law on political parties, which entitled parties to an annual subvention formally designated to reimburse their electoral campaigns.

State subsidies are usually distributed in proportion to the number of seats and/or votes. In both Portugal and the Czech Republic the amounts of annual routine subventions are established by law. In Portugal, by law, all state subsidies are related in a fixed proportion to the national minimum wage. The amounts parties receive for routine activities are based on the number of votes in the national legislative elections.[13] Parties in the Czech Republic are entitled to subventions from the state according to a combination of the percentage of the vote in the national elections and the number of parliamentary deputies. The maximum of annual subventions allocated according to the percentage of the vote is 5 million Czech crowns.[14] In addition, parties receive half a million crowns per year for each parliamentary seat.[15]

In Spain and in Hungary, by contrast, the amount of state money is not predetermined by law but is decided anew annually by the government and included in the national budget. Since there is no law that establishes the amounts of state subsidies, Spanish and Hungarian governments potentially have more leverage to increase the public money for parties. Indeed, Spanish governments have been observed to make use of this possibility. While the annual growth of routine subsidies generally did not exceed the increase in the consumer price index,[16] there have been significant exceptions. Most notable was a 150 per cent raise in the 1987 budget. Several incidents, such as the costly NATO campaign of the PSOE in 1986 or, more illegitimately, the *Flick* case[17] can account for the decision to a significant raise of the routine subventions to political parties.[18]

What the Spanish and Hungarian laws do establish, however, is the method of distribution of state money once the amounts have been decided. In Hungary, 25 per cent of the state money for routine activities is to be distributed equally among all parties that have obtained a seat in parliament. The remaining 75 per cent is distributed on the basis of the votes for the parties or their candidates in the first round of the parliamentary elections. In Spain, state money is distributed between parties according to the number of both seats and votes obtained in the most recent elections for the lower chamber, by which the total designated sum is divided into three equal parts, of which one third is allocated according to the number of seats and the remaining two according to the total number of votes.[19]

As far as electoral subsidies are concerned, these are all based on the number of votes. The electoral state subsidies that were introduced with the 1995 law in the Czech Republic entitle parties to 90 Czech crowns per vote, which represents a significant increase from the 10 and 15 crowns which Czech parties obtained (in Czechoslovakia) for each vote after the 1990 and 1992 elections respectively. As in the Czech Republic, the 1993 Portuguese law on the financing of political parties and election campaigns introduced election subsidies as a new and additional source of public party financing, on the necessity of which all parties had agreed.[20] State subsidies for election expenditures in Portugal are again related to the legal minimum wage.[21] Of this amount, 20 per cent is distributed equally over the participating parties and candidates and the remaining 80 per cent is divided in proportion to the obtained electoral result.

Electoral subsidies in Spain are allocated on the basis of the percentage of votes and the number of deputies in the lower and upper chambers. Between

1977 and 2000, these amounts have increased from one million to almost 2.7 million pesetas for every seat obtained in either one of the two chambers, from 45 to 101 pesetas for every vote in the lower chamber elections and from 15 to 40 pesetas for every vote in the Senate elections.[22] In addition, the 1991 modification of the Spanish electoral law brought about an important change, in that it introduced state support for the costs of direct election mailing. Parties are entitled to a sum of money per voter in every electoral district in which they present their candidates.[23] These amounts in fact add up to quite considerable sums, with consequently soaring levels of state subventions (see below).

The third type of public money is the *subventions to the parliamentary groups*. These are normally regulated by the parliamentary standing orders, which generally establish that the groups receive an equal amount of money each, plus a fixed sum for every parliamentary deputy. The state subsidies for the parliamentary groups in Portugal's unicameral chamber consist of at least four times the annual minimum wage, plus one third of this amount - which was increased to half of this amount in 1993 - per deputy. The Hungarian parliamentary groups receive an amount of money equivalent to 20 times an MPs (basic) salary, plus a sum per individual MP, which amounts to 25 per cent of the basic salary per MP for a government party and to 50 per cent for opposition parties. The parliamentary fractions in the Czech lower chamber receive 20,000 crowns per month, plus 2.5 thousand crowns per deputy.[24] In Spain, similar general provisions apply to both the lower and upper chamber, although the fractions in the Senate receive considerably less than those in the Chamber of Deputies.

How important, then, is the state in practice for the financing of political parties, and how does the state compare with society in this respect? The first point to make is that public funding has always been likely to play a critical role in the financing of political parties in these new democracies because state subventions were introduced when most parties were still in incipient stages of party formation and usually lacked the organisational resources to generate their own income. Indeed, for most parties, membership subscriptions constitute only a secondary source of income. For the two major Portuguese parties, the Socialist Party (PS) and the Social Democratic Party (PSD), for example, state subsidies are the single most important source of income, on average contributing to more than 80 per cent of the parties' total income in the early 1990s. Only in the Communist Party (PCP) does the state seem to play a relatively minor role in financing the party. In the mid 1990s, the PCP claimed that state subsidies made up only some 8 per cent of the party's annual income.[25]

The state also plays a considerable role in the financing of Spanish parties, as can be seen from Table 1, which shows the financing of Spanish routine activities between 1988 and 1992. For the purpose of this analysis, the traditional distinction between membership fees and ad hoc private contributions from individuals and business organisations has been abandoned. Instead, these two types of donations have been combined into one category, i.e. sources of income from society, so as to arrive at a clearer picture of the relevance of society *vis-à-vis* the state for the financing of political parties. For Spanish parties, the state is not only clearly the single most important contributor to their total income, the amounts of state subventions have also attained such an elevated level - around an average of almost 80 per cent - as to make them virtually entirely dependent on public money. Societal financial resources, by contrast, including membership fees and private donations, are relatively unimportant. With time, moreover, the relevance of society seems to be diminishing, although the limited range of these figures warrants a careful interpretation of any possible trends.

The state plays an equally significant role in the financing of Spanish elections, as can be deduced from Table 2. This stands in contrast not only with Portugal, but also with other more recently established democracies, such as the post-communist Czech Republic, where the relevance of state contributions for campaign expenses is evident, but where private donations and fundraising activities also play a role (see below).[26] With an average contribution of almost 90 per cent of the parties' total income, the state seems in fact virtually the only significant financial contributor to the cost of Spanish election campaigns. The importance of society in this respect is even more marginal than for the financing of routine activities. In general, the parties' heavy financial reliance on the state, and thus their dependence on a good electoral performance, makes them quite vulnerable to changes in the behaviour of the electorate, which tends to be quite volatile in newly established democracies more generally.[27] The example of the Spanish Communist Party

Table 1: Financing Spanish Parties, 1988-1992

million pesetas

	State	Society	Other	Total
1988	5570.9	877.7	451.7	6900.3
1990	6740.1	1156.4	308.3	8204.8
1992	7745.0	1123.6	1062.5	9931.1

% of total income

	State	Society	Other	Total
1988	77.4	14.2	8.4	100
1990	83.7	12.8	3.5	100
1992	78.3	9.7	12.1	100.1
Mean	79.8	12.2	8.0	

Notes: Parties include the PSOE, AP/PP and PCE/IU. Bank loans are not included. 1$ = 126.7 pesetas (mid 1987) and 96.0 pesetas (mid 1992).

Source: I. van Biezen, 'Party Financing in New Democracies: Spain and Portugal', *Party Politics* 6(3) 2000, pp. 329-342.

Table 2: Financing Spanish Elections, 1986-1996

million pesetas

	State	Society	Other	Total
1986[a]	1627.1	3.0	399.4	2029.5
1989	2739.4	2.7	55.9	2798.0
1993	5859.6	114.6	1069.7	7043.9
1996	7235.4	3.8	408.3	7647.5

% of total income

	State	Society	Other	Total
1986[a]	80.2	0.1	19.7	100
1989	97.9	0.1	2.0	100
1993	83.2	1.6	15.2	100
1996	94.6	0	5.3	99.9
Mean	89.0	0.5	10.6	

[a] 1986 figures include only the PSOE and PCE/IU.

Notes: Parties include the PSOE, AP/PP and PCE/IU. Bank loans are not included. 1$ = 139.1 pesetas (mid 1986) and 128.2 pesetas (mid 1996).

Source: see Table 1.

is quite illustrative in this regard. The very poor result in the 1982 elections, when the vote for the party declined from almost 11 to only 4 per cent and the number of seats plummeted from 23 to 4, so drastically reduced the state subsidies that the PCE was brought to the verge of bankruptcy and was forced to sell many of its assets and property, including its headquarters in Madrid. Hence, although the dependence on the state was generally substantially lower for the Communist Party than for any of the other Spanish parties, the PCE clearly exhibits the potentially catastrophic consequences of this vulnerability that results from a party's financial dependence on the state.

The financial profile of the parties in post-communist Hungary also shows strong patterns of state dependence. Table 3 represents the sources of income of Hungarian parties for the period of the first legislatures (1990-1994) and the first two years of the second legislature (1995-1996). The role of the state stands out quite clearly as a crucial source of income. Also the irrelevance of other sources, and particularly the membership fees, is unmistakable, reaching a level of almost zero in the extreme case of FIDESZ. However, the bulky category of 'other' sources of income requires further analysis. In some cases, the (partly illegal) sale of party property and particularly real estate may account for part of these 'other' sources. What caused a serious political scandal, for example, was the fact that in 1993 the Hungarian Democratic Forum and FIDESZ sold their party headquarters which had been donated state property at the time of the transition.

Table 3: Financing Hungarian Parties, 1990-1996

million forint				
	State	Society	Other	Total
1990-94	4280.8	873.7	5132.9	*10287.4*
1995-96	2191.2	221.8	2535.1	*4948.1*
% of total income				
	State	Society	Other	Total
1990-94	41.6	8.5	49.9	*100*
1995-96	44.3	4.5	51.2	*100*
Mean	43.0	6.5	50.6	

Note: 1$ = 151 forint (August 1996)
Source: I. van Biezen, *Party Organization in New Democracies: Southern and Eastern Europe Compared* (PhD thesis, Leiden University, 2001).

While state funding is generally assumed to be of critical importance for parties in newly established democracies, the financial profile of parties in the Czech Republic reveals that this is not unequivocally the case. The figures presented in Table 4, represent a less clear-cut case of exclusive dependence on the state and negligible contributions from society. While the financial assistance from the state is of course still considerable, society seems to play an equally important part, primarily in the form of donations from individuals and business organisations.

Table 4: Financing Czech Parties, 1995-1996

million crowns

	State	Society	Other	Total
1995	82.3	76.7	115.0[a]	274.0
1996	544.2[b]	170.4	79.0	793.6

% of total income

	State	Society	Other	Total
1995	30.0	28.0	42.0[a]	100
1996	68.6[b]	21.5	10.0	100.1
Mean	49.3	24.8	26.0	

[a] for some parties, this figure includes the sum of several years
[b] total of annual and electoral subventions (ratio approximately 1:5)
Note: 1$ = 26.9 crowns (July 1996)
Source: see Table 3.

Furthermore, there appears to be substantial variation between parties, revealing a relatively higher importance of public money for newly established parties, such as the ODS and ODA than for the older parties (i.e. parties established prior to the transition), such as the Communist Party (KSČM) and the Christian Democrats (KDU-ČSL). Perhaps not quite unexpectedly given its large membership organisation, the KSČM stands out for the relatively large share of membership contributions, which are in fact the most important source of income to finance the party's routine activities. The membership is clearly as important for the KDU-ČSL: in one year alone (1994), for example, the party received about 7.44 million crowns from membership fees, while the state subsidy (reimbursement of electoral expenses for 1992 elections) amounted to about 17.8 million crowns.[28] For newly created parties, by contrast, membership fees do not have a similar relevance. Indeed, in all three of the newly established parties - ODS, ODA and ČSSD - do the membership fees contributes to a below average share of the total income.[29]

In general, older parties are relatively advantaged over newly established ones because they can rely on various types of organisational resources. Not only a large membership organisation may be financially beneficial, but also the maintenance of property clearly brings ensuing financial privileges, in that the sale of real estate and letting of buildings provides parties with an important additional source of income. This applies not only to the Communist Party, but also to the Social Democrats, for example, for which the ownership of its party headquarters stems from its pre-communist ancestor of the First Republic.[30] Moreover, established parties also tend to conduct least expensive electoral campaigns, because their large membership provides these parties with a stable electoral base that does not have to be mobilised through an expensive electoral campaign. For example, the cost of 1992 electoral campaign of KDU-ČSL amounted to about 17 million crowns, while the same campaign of ODA cost around 45 million crowns.[31]

On the other hand, the ODS and ODA have been capable of compensating for the lack of such profitable organisational legacies by collecting large sums of money from business sector. In general, the incumbent parties have clearly been more attractive to private financing from the business sector than the opposition parties, which mainly attract donations from individuals rather than business. This distinction between government and opposition parties also seems to tap into a fundamentally different mode of financing for parties such as the ODS and the ODA, on the one hand, and the ČSSD and KSČM, on the other.[32] The two Civic Democratic Parties represent a way of private financing close to the traditional cadre party, with a predominant dependence on relatively large sums of individual contributors. The Social Democrats and the Communists, by contrast, spread the financial burden over the largest possible number of members and supporters, instead of appealing to a few big private donors, which is a device once characteristic for the predominant mode of private financing of the classic mass party.[33]

Societal Funding

It should be clear from the above that a key element in a discrepancy between state and societal party funding is obviously the generally low levels of party membership. In Portugal and Spain, only 3.4 and 4.0 per cent of the national electorates are affiliated to a political party while the corresponding figures for the Czech Republic and Hungary are 3.9 and 2.2 per cent.[34] As a consequence, membership fees generally contribute to only a minor financial resource. In the post-communist democracies, the share of membership fees to the parties' total income on average amounts to just 5.6 per cent. For Southern European parties, the figure is somewhat higher, standing at an average of almost 9 per cent.[35] There are a few parties for which party members continue to matter in financial terms, however. Examples of such parties are primarily those with a longstanding organisational legacy, such as the Communist Party in Portugal (PCP), or the Czech Communist Party (KSČM). More generally, these parties prove to be financially quite self-sustaining, in that it is the membership organisation rather than the state that constitutes the most important source of income for the party. To a lesser extent, the same can be observed for the Spanish Communist Party and the Czech Christian Democrats.

However, it should be underlined that the role of society for the financing of political parties is not exclusively confined to party members paying their fees, but can - as we have already alluded to in the context of the Czech Republic - also include private donations. The relevance of societal funding is clearly apparent in Portugal, at least as far as the financing of elections is concerned. The pattern that emerges from Table 5 is similar to that of the Czech parties, in that it shows that the relative unimportance of society for the financing of political parties in new democracies should not be taken as inevitable. In fact, the trend is even substantially reinforced compared with the Czech case, in that for the financing of the 1995 elections, the state played indeed only a minor role. If anything, it was financial contributions from society - primarily the party membership in the case of the Communist Party, and private contributors in the case of the PSD and PS - that provided the bulk of the parties' income. What is also worth underlining here is that the PS and the PSD were the only two parties that received money from the business sector.[36] This suggests that the prospect of incumbency is an attractive if not crucial factor for private financing and thus confirms the observation made earlier in the context of the Czech Republic. In sum, while the state plays a noticeable role in the funding of the parties' routine activities, its importance is less evident in financing the elections as parties seem to have resources other than the state to rely on to finance their campaigns.

Table 5: Financing Portuguese Elections, 1995

	State	Society	Other	Total
million escudos	130.3	1235.0	231.2	1596.5
% of total income	8.2	77.4	14.5	100.1

Notes: 1$ = 145.7 escudos (mid 1995).
Source: see Table 1.

Other financial contributions emerging from society, such as those furnished by organised interests, are generally less important in all four countries. Corresponding to the reduced relevance of the membership organisation in the context of a new democracy, organised interests associations are usually not closely linked to political parties. To be sure, the balance sheets of the Communist Party and the Socialist Party in Spain reveal occasional financial transfers to and from the trade unions CCOO and UGT.[37] This underlines the close ideological and organisational linkages between these parties and their affiliated trade unions, but with time for both parties the relationship has lost much of its original strength.[38] Moreover, the financial contributions of the trade unions were only small in practice, and this type of party financing is practically irrelevant.

However, membership fees, declared private donations and contributions from organised interest associations are only a part of a broader category of societal funding, which should also include the obscure area of illicit financing. Indeed, for all four countries there is ample evidence that parties also receive considerable amounts of money from sources that seem to escape legal control. Despite the formally marginal role of private business for the financing of political parties, for example, considerable amounts of money have been obtained from corrupt sources and parties have accessed big donors through kickbacks and toll-gating. A subtle strategy has been imported to Portugal and Spain from France and Germany: front companies affiliated with a party have charged businesses and banks for false research papers, consultancy work or technical advice in exchange for favourable decisions. This type of plutocratic fundraising seems to have assumed extensive proportions - particularly in Spain, where it was first uncovered through the 'Filesa affair' and other scandals, which meanwhile have followed suit.[39]

Despite strict regulations controlling income from private contributions in order to counteract improper sources of income, Spanish and Portuguese parties have resorted on a large scale to patronage and clientelism[40] and especially the Spanish parties seem to have successfully tapped most techniques of political graft. Parties governing the nation, a region or a municipality have been engaged in classic examples of pork-barrel graft by peddling their influence and selling their decision-making power over sources of patronage: building companies, trash-collectors and other contractors pay kickbacks (commission fees) of 2 to 4 percent of the total value of a contract in return for many public works contracted with a government agency. For handling this 'compulsory political tax', middlemen who sell such political favours to business interests pocket part of the commission paid in return for the contract and hand over most of the money to the party in power. The Guerra, the Naseiro, the S.A.S, the Prenafeta and the Ceres affairs of the early 1990s divulged the details of these patterns of influence trafficking.[41]

Spain in particular is indeed notorious for its high levels of corruption. In fact, according to Heidenheimer's classification of 17 West European countries, Spain ranks together with Italy, Greece and Turkey as 'quite corrupt'; Portugal is only 'somewhat corrupt'.[42] The extent of corruption is of course, due to its very nature, difficult to assess, although it appears to have assumed more extensive proportions in Spain than in any of the other countries included in the present analysis. However, of the newly established democracies, it is also the Spanish case that tends to receive greater attention. Not only are cases of illegal financing more frequently under scrutiny in the Spanish press, the Spanish case appears also more frequently than Portugal in scholarly assessments on the practices in West Europe[43] as well as in Southern European comparisons.[44] The perception of the Spanish case as more corrupt might thus be partly biased. Although illicit party financing in Portugal does not seem to have assumed the extensive proportions prevalent in Italy and Spain, it has also for Portuguese parties increasingly become a *modus vivendi*[45] and the same might be argued for Eastern Europe.

The apparent pervasiveness of illicit party financing could explain the somewhat paradoxical situation that Spanish, but also Czech and Hungarian, parties frequently complain about the lack of financial resources and the consequent necessity to resort to large bank loans, which has caused a large number of parties to be in debt. One of the possible explanations for this discrepancy between the proclaimed insufficiency of the public subventions and the absence of fundraising efforts, is the inadequate control on party financing, as a result of which unauthorised private financing frequently compensates for the officially declared lack of income. The fundamental problem of political financing in new democracies is not so much the deficient regulations but seems to be the unwillingness of parties and politicians to abide by the rule of law. Although some improvements to the existing laws on party financing are conceivable, faulty laws are not the primary cause for the abundance of illicit financing.

In fact, the laws on party financing normally include stringent legal requirements for disclosure, as well as bans and limits on expenditures and on certain types of contributions, such as anonymous donations of the total of private contributions. However, parties have proven reluctant to disclose their financial accounts. In Spain, information on party financing was initially scarce and, particularly during the first years after the transition, party financing lacked practically all legal control.[46] In Portugal, the unlawful conduct in this respect was also common to all parties (de Sousa, 1983). In 1996, for example, three of the four parliamentary parties (the PS, PSD and CDS-PP) were penalised with a total fine of 2,784,000 escudos for infringements of the law.[47] The situation was very similar in the early stages of post-communist transformation in Hungary, and also in the Czech Republic where, in addition, the lack of legal provisions on party finances was a deliberate choice of policy-makers in order to extricate newly emerged parties, often dependent on financial aid from abroad, from disadvantages in competition with the materially secured Communist Party.

It should be noted that in the countries analysed here, illicit party financing has not caused similar disruptions to the political systems as in Italy, for example. However, media investigations as of the early 1990s unveiled the involvement of especially the Spanish Socialist Party (PSOE), but also others, in a series of corruption scandals. The ensuing public disapproval and judicial prosecutions proved a major discrediting factor for the Socialist government and significantly contributed to the ascendancy to power of the Partido Popular in 1996. Also in the post-communist context have practices of illicit financing increasingly been revealed. In fact, illicit financing was one of the major reasons for the resignation of Klaus' government in the Czech Republic in November 1997, and subsequent split of ODS. According to an external international audit, the Civic Democrats had indeed rigged its own accounts and failed to abide by donation disclosure laws, among others concealing donations from companies and individuals by using false names.

Similarly, the Czech television almost derailed the 1998 electoral campaign of CSSD when it broadcasted a document in which the party allegedly offered prominent state positions to a group of Czech-Swiss businessmen in exchange for campaign funds.[48] Although the party (and its leader) were later cleared of the allegations, another prominent Czech party - the ODA - had almost ceased to exist prior to the 1998 elections. The problems followed investigations into the usage of false names on donations to campaign funds from Virgin Islands, and after the press discovered the party's links with industry during the process of privatisation. The 2001 report of the Transparency International[49] in fact ranks the Czech Republic 47th on the world-wide Index of Corruption Perception, where the country placed 1st (Finland) is least corrupt. The Czech Republic is placed well below Spain (22nd) and Portugal (25th), but also below Hungary (31st). Indeed, in a regional comparison, the Czech Republic is placed in a second group (with Poland, Slovakia, Croatia and Bulgaria), which is perceived to be more corrupt than Hungary, which in turn belongs (with Estonia and Slovenia) to the group of least corrupt post-communist countries.

To be sure, the real amounts of money parties obtain from corrupt sources can of course not be easily quantified, neither by reviews of individual financial scandals nor by ranking the various scores on the perception of corruption in a country. The relative overall importance of society - including legitimate and illegitimate sources - for the funding of political is thus likely to be distorted. However, the same is necessarily true for the relevance of state money as the official subventions do not capture state support for parties in all its respects. In providing free radio and television broadcasting, reduced postal rates, or various types of tax exemptions, for example, the state indirectly provides parties with significant additional aid. In addition, there is often a less legitimate side of state support, i.e. patronage. In fact, it has been suggested that the wealth of unauthorised use of public resources and illegal party financing indicates that parties may be more inclined to turn to the state for additional resources on top of the official subsidies because of their already strongly developed formal linkage with the state.[50] More generally, and as Pasquino has also pointed out, a system of public funding may have a supplementary rather than substitutory effect on clientelistic forms of financing, and the abundance of illicit party financing in each of the four countries shows that this is indeed largely the case.[51]

Nevertheless, our data depict quite a clear trend: although the dependence on public money may not be unequivocally high among all parties and we should keep the distinction between new parties and parties with strong organisational legacies in mind, the state is indeed the predominant player in party financing. A comparison of the total amounts of state money furthermore shows that it is in fact in the Czech Republic that a relatively high priority is accorded to the funding of political parties. The Czech Republic ranks second if the amounts of money in real terms are compared between countries, and even occupies the first position if the relative amounts - i.e. the amounts per voter - are considered. In 1994-1996, political parties in Spain received 164 million dollars from the state, as against 51 million dollars in the Czech Republic in 1996, 24 million for Portugal in 1995 and 18 million in Hungary in 1996[52] - although it should be noted that the figure for Hungary is less easily comparable with the others.[53] In relative terms, parties in the Czech Republic receive the highest amounts of state reimbursement, consisting of 6.42 dollar per voter. Spain ranks second, with a compensation of 5.04 dollar for every voter, followed at a distance by Portugal with 2.71 and Hungary with 2.27 dollar per voter. The position of the Czech Republic ahead of the other countries is, therefore, a remarkable indication of the much higher priority of the state to the funding of political parties in this much newer democracy.

Party Finance and Party Organisations

Regarding this major trend of party financing, two further aspects are worth emphasising. The first relates to the financial balance of power between the extra-parliamentary organisation and the parliamentary group. While the complexity of this relationship precludes any detailed elaboration here,[54] in the context of this article it is worth underlining that it is the party central office (i.e. party executive and party bureaucracy) that is normally in financially the most beneficial position *vis-à-vis* the party in public office (i.e. parliamentary party and party in government). State subventions for routine expenditures significantly outweigh those for the parliamentary groups, e.g. by four times in Portugal to some 180 times in the Czech Republic. Changes in the allocation of state subvention to these two faces of party over time, moreover, appear to have favoured the extra-parliamentary party rather than showing any trend in an increased predominance of the party in public office.[55] All this suggests that these parties show a different organisational balance of power from that observed from their counterparts in the established West-European democracies, where organisational changes are generally seen to increase the dominance of the party in public office.[56]

Secondly, it is important to assess whether the primary focus for parties lies on their routine activities or on conducting election campaigns, i.e. whether parties in newly established democracies maintain an organisational or rather electoralist orientation. In order to arrive at a preliminary answer to this question, what will be looked into in more detail here are the different patterns of party expenditures, distinguishing between electoral and routine organisational activities, as well as the relative importance of the electoral versus routine state subventions. Regrettably, however, it is only for Spain that we possess figures over time regarding the pattern of party expenditures, which furthermore enable a distinction between routine expenditures and expenses on election campaigns.

The evidence for Spain suggests that expenditures on routine activities for the main parties (PSOE, AP/PP, PCE, IU, CiU and PNV) have almost doubled between 1988 and 1992 (see Table 6). A comparison of the routine expenses with the expenditures on electoral activities reveals that, on the whole, Spanish parties spend much more money on routine organisational activities than on election campaigns. The same seems to be true for Portuguese parties: the four major Portuguese parties (PCP, PS, PSD and CDS-PP) spent a total of 1,633 million escudos in the 1995 elections against 4,042 million escudos for routine purposes in 1997.[57] For Spain, moreover, the figures in Table 6 reveal that the aggregate campaign expenses seem to have increased at a much lower rate than those on organisational activities. Between 1988 and 1992, the total of routine expenditures increased with 72.4 per cent. The aggregate expenditures on election campaigns between 1986 and 1996, by contrast, increased with only some 25 per cent, over what was furthermore a much larger period. Perhaps surprisingly, therefore, in financial terms the limited evidence seems to reveal a primary focus on the routine activities of the extra-parliamentary party rather than any increasing electoralist orientation,[58] although the analytical distinction between these two types of activities may be somewhat blurred in practice.

Table 6: Party Expenditures, Spain, 1979-1996

	Routine Activities		Election Campaigns	
	total[a]	per voter[b]	total[a]	per voter[b]
1979			1,265[c]	
1982			3,200[c]	
1986			5,461	188
1988	8,510	290		
1989	15,023	508	5,026	170
1990	11,888	397		
1991	14,148	466		
1992	14,675	478		
1993			7,362	237
1996			6,829	213
Increase (%)	72.4	64.8	25.1[d]	13.3[d]

[a] total expenditures in million pesetas.
[b] cost per voter in pesetas.
[c] PSOE and AP/PP only; because of too many missing data - including the largest and governing party UCD - the cost per voter is not given for 1979 and 1982.
[d] increase between 1986-1996.
Notes: Parties include the PSOE, AP/PP, PCE, IU, CiU and PNV. 1$ = 66.1 pesetas (mid 1979) and 128.2 pesetas (mid 1996).
Source: I. van Biezen and K.H. Nassmacher, 'Political Finance in Southern Europe: Italy, Portugal and Spain', in K.H. Nassmacher (ed.), *Foundations for Democracy: Approaches to Comparative Political Finance - Essays in Honour of Herbert E. Alexander* (Baden-Baden: Nomos, 2001), pp. 131-154.

Also the state subventions show a similar balance in favour of routine activities: comparing the relative weight of the different types of state subsidies shows that in both Spain and Portugal subventions for routine activities are higher than those for electoral purposes. The ratio amounts to approximately 2.5 : 1 in the late 1980s in Spain, while the Portuguese case shows a particularly uneven allotment of state subventions, in which those for routine activities are about ten times higher than the election subsidies. On the other hand, however, for both countries it should be observed that, with time, the balance has changed clearly to the advantage of the subsidies for electoral purposes. While state subventions for routine activities in Spain grew by some 36 per cent between 1988 and 1992, the subsidies for electoral activities increased by more than 200 per cent between 1986 and 1996.[59] Also the modification of the system of party financing in Portugal in 1993 is indicative of an increasing electoralist orientation. Although the state subsidises election expenditures in much smaller sums than routine activities, the introduction of state reimbursement for electoral costs as a new source of public funding is in itself a revealing sign of a growing importance of electoral activities.

We should note that the prevalent orientation to electoral activities applies to an even greater effect to parties in the Czech Republic, where the state subsidies for routine activities are not nearly as important as those for electoral purposes. Whereas the total amount of routine subsidies clearly outweighs the electoral subventions in Portugal and Spain, in the Czech Republic the sum of state money for the costs of election campaigns is about five times higher than the state subsidies for routine activities. This indicates a much higher orientation towards electoral rather than non-electoral activities - a clear priority accorded by parties to maintain electoral basis rather than to cultivate an extensive party organisation. In this sense, it seems that the much anticipated relevance of electoral linkages and electoral success for parties in modern democracies works with an even greater effect in the most recently established democracy.

Incumbents versus newcomers

The final point we wish to explore, albeit briefly, is the extent to which the rules regulating public funding of political parties may be geared towards protecting the privileges of incumbent and established parties against the newcomers and extra-parliamentary opposition. If anything, this should be an indication of the extent to which parties in these new democracies can be seen as possessing some capacity to constrain choice and to manage the political and social environment for their own ends. In addition, given the general importance of the state for parties' survival in new democracies on one hand, and their vulnerability in electoral and individual organisational sense on the other hand, we may expect the rules governing public funding of political parties to be tailored precisely in the way as to facilitate the survival of those who (first) acquire power and office.

Indeed, state funding clearly disadvantages electorally smaller parties, although the legal thresholds vary between countries. The threshold for routine subventions in Hungary is established at a modest one per cent of the vote, as opposed to a more discriminating 3 per cent in the Czech Republic. In Spain, the threshold equals the electoral threshold, i.e. 3 per cent of the vote at the constituency level, as opposed to a more modest threshold in Portugal, set at only 50,000 votes, which equals about 0.6 per cent of the electorate. For electoral subventions, the threshold in Portugal is set at parties contesting the elections in at least 51 per cent of the constituencies and obtaining at least two per cent of the votes for electoral subsidies. Nevertheless, state money is distributed quite more proportionally to the number of votes. For example, for the 1995 election campaign, the two biggest parties (the PS and PSD) acquired 79.7 per cent of the campaign subsidies with 78.7 per cent of the vote.

A noticeable characteristic of the Spanish system of party financing, by contrast, is its significant bias in favour of the bigger parliamentary parties and parties with a regionally concentrated vote, which is especially noticeable in the distribution of electoral subventions. The method of allocation of state money for election expenditures in practice intensifies the particular disproportional tendencies of the electoral system: not the aggregate vote on the national level but only the votes in those electoral constituencies in which a party has obtained a parliamentary seat qualify for financial compensation. As a consequence, the PSOE and PP have collected between 82 and 89 per cent of the total of regular electoral subventions for the past four elections, with a combined 65 to 76 per cent of the vote.[60] Only the recent introduction of state money for the costs of direct mailing, for which a much lower threshold applies, somewhat counterbalances these disproportional tendencies.[61]

The skewed distribution of seats, and hence of state money, is even more pronounced for the Spanish Senate elections, due to the majoritarian system of seat allocation for this chamber. In the 1996 elections, for instance, *Izquierda Unida* did not succeed in acquiring a seat and thus was denied financial compensation, despite being the third largest party with approximately 6.8 million votes on the national level. Much smaller regional parties such as the Catalan CiU and Basque PNV, by contrast, which obtained roughly 1.5 million and 0.6 million votes respectively, did succeeded in acquiring representation in the upper chamber with eight and four senators respectively, and thus also secured electoral money from the state. For this reason, Gillespie has argued that the system of public funding in Spain has encouraged the cartelisation of parties and the party system.[62]

A similar trend is apparent in the Czech Republic, where recent (2000) proposed changes to electoral laws and laws governing party finances can be seen as a unmistakable tendency to adopt institutional devices that protect the privileges of established parties against potential newcomers. For example, the threshold for routine subventions is set to rise from 3% to 4% of vote which, together with the proposed overall increase (of about 100%!) for routine subventions, would dramatically increase the gap between the 'haves' and 'have nots' on the party political scene. Moreover, the numerous modifications to constitutional, electoral and parliamentary rules in the Czech Republic since 1992 show a rather consistent trend to establish and reinforce institutional rules where both party strength and the rule of majority play a crucial role.[63]

Conclusion

The central concern of this article has been the balance between public funding of political parties in new democracies and the monies that parties accrue from societal sources. Our evidence clearly shows that public funding has become a critical source of income in all of the new democracies considered here. In that sense, the new democracies of Southern and Eastern Europe do not buck the trend observed in many Western European countries; in fact, it is in some of these new democracies, like Spain, where the money from the state quite dramatically surpasses the money parties receive as a result of their own fundraising activities. This trend, we should note, goes in reality well beyond the figures we were able to present here. For the state resources do not consist of only direct subsidies for electoral and routine activities of parties, but also revolve around numerous indirect subsidies, such as salaries of staff working for political parties, access to media and, perhaps most importantly in new democracies, party patronage. At the same time, however, our findings show that the importance of public money does not necessarily rule out the relevance of society, as is testified by the importance of private donations - especially for the financing of elections - in the Czech Republic and Portugal for example.

We also wish to underline that the high financial dependence on the state outlined in this article seems to concur with an increasing electoral orientation of parties. To be sure, not all the evidence points unequivocally towards a neglect of the party organisation and the Spanish parties in particular seem to have been spending relatively larger amounts on their party organisations than on their electoral activities. However, in terms of the relative weight of state subventions for electoral purposes and routine organisational activities there is a clear tendency towards an increasing importance of the former in all countries. Especially the Czech system of funding shows a clear bias in favour of electoral activities and it is also the Czech state that distributes the highest amounts of money per voter. Hence, it seems that it is one of the most recently established democracies that a relatively high priority is accorded to the funding of political parties as such and where also an electoral orientation is most clearly visible.

As regards the discrepancy between state resources and private resources, the single most important explanatory factor seems to be the generally low levels of party membership, both individual and collective, observed in new democracies. Moreover, an additional factor which may be seen as equally important in explaining the apparent predominance of state funding is the fact that corruption, or illicit financing, has been a widespread phenomenon in these countries, largely unaccounted for by parties' official documents. Since the state has been far more susceptible to party manipulation in new democracies than in (the majority of) Western European countries, effective checks on abuses of power are lacking, and mechanisms of bureaucratic accountability are poorly developed. Indeed, corruption appears especially linked to modern democracies where political parties dependent on mass electorates had been established while the central state was generally weak[64] - a situation arguably relevant to all country cases we discussed here.

Of course, much of the evidence on illicit financing and obscure fundraising activities remains necessarily nebulous, and only further research can determine, where possible, the actual importance of such activities for the parties' overall income. Since it is much too soon to draw any ultimate conclusion in this regard, we wish to raise a few questions for further exploration instead. One such additional question is the extent to which it is parties as organisations that benefit from corruption, or rather the individuals that are associated with parties. The answer to that question will differ from one social context to another, but given the fact that parties as organisations appear generally weakly institutionalised in new democracies, and especially in Eastern Europe, the scope for personal enrichment may well be much higher than the potential to translate illegally obtained benefits to the resources geared towards the survival of the party organisation. Yet another under-researched question concerns the extent to which illicit financing comes - as we assumed in this article - primarily from concealed societal sources. At the same time, most of the documented corruption scandals in the countries studied here seem to suggest that the parties which actually take advantage of public resources are government parties, which exploit the distribution of office spoils to reward their supporters. In that sense, the money accrued from illicit financing may actually reinforce rather than counterbalance the overall financial state dependence of political parties. In this context, moreover, it is perhaps not surprising to see that public subsidies are defined entirely in terms of electoral success or parliamentary strength. In this way, public subsidies may act to freeze the status quo of the party system and hence achieve a sense of stability that may otherwise be difficult to achieve in the context of vulnerable party organisations and unstable party systems.

Notes

[1] Ingrid van Biezen, University of Birmingham, Petr Kopecký, University of Sheffield.
[2] Cf. A. Panebianco, *Political Parties: Organization and Power* (Cambridge: Cambridge University Press, 1988), p. 35.
[3] R.S. Katz and P. Mair, 'Changing Models of Party Organization and Party Democracy: the Emergence of the Cartel Party', *Party Politics*, 1(1) 1995, pp. 5-28. See also

O. Kirchheimer, 'The Transformation of West European Party Systems', in J. LaPalombara and M. Weiner (eds), *Political Parties and Political Development* (Princeton: Princeton University Press, 1966), pp. 177-200.

4 H.E. Alexander, 'Money and Politics: rethinking a Conceptual Framework', in H.E. Alexander (ed.), *Comparative Political Finance in the 1980s* (Cambridge: Cambridge University Press, 1989), pp. 9-23.

5 P. del Castillo, 'Financing of Spanish Political Parties', in Alexander, *Comparative Political Finance*, pp. 172-99.

6 K.H. Nassmacher, 'Comparing Party and Campaign Finances in Western Democracies', in A.B. Gunlicks (ed.), *Campaign and Party Finance in North America and Western Europe* (Boulder: Westview Press, 1993), pp. 233-67.

7 Some of the data and analysis here draws on I. van Biezen 'Party Financing in New Democracies: Spain and Portugal', *Party Politics,* 6(3) 2000, pp. 329-342. For more details see I. van Biezen, *Party Organization in New Democracies: Southern and Eastern Europe* Compared (PhD thesis, Leiden University, 2001).

8 The rules were first introduced in 1978 (Ley de Partidos Políticos, 54/1978) and are currently prescribed by the 1987 law on financing political parties (Ley Orgánica sobre Financiación de los Partidos Políticos 3/1987 - LOFPP).

9 Reprinted in G. Tóka, (ed.), *The 1990 Election to the Hungarian National Assembly: Analyses, Documents and Data* (Berlin: Sigma, 1995), pp. 135-42.

10 Reprinted in Tóka, *The 1990 Election.*

11 M. Szabó, 'The State of Political Institutions, Political Society and Civil Society in Hungary', in A. Bibič and G. Graziano (eds), *Civil Society, Political Society, Democracy* (Ljubljana: Slovenian Political Science Association, 1994), p. 272.

12 Lei 32/77-25 May. Currently, the financing of political parties in Portugal is regulated in the 1993 law (Lei 72/93, Financiamento dos Partidos Políticos e das Campanhas Eleitorais).

13 That is, parties receive 1/225 of the monthly minimum wage for every vote obtained in the most recent elections.

14 For the first 3 per cent of the vote, parties receive 3 million Czech crowns. To this amount a supplementary one thousand Czech crowns for every 0.1 per cent of the obtained votes is added up to 5 per cent of the vote.

15 The Czech system of state funding has been in effect since the 1996 elections (the law was modified in 1995). Between 1992 and 1996, party financing by the state was based on the 1990 and 1991 regulations, which granted parties 10 and 15 Czechoslovak crowns (for the 1990 and 1992 elections respectively) per vote for each of the three federal chambers. See P. Kopecký, *Parliaments in the Czech and Slovak Republics: Party Competition and Parliamentary Institutionalization* (Aldershot: Ashgate 2001).

16 del Castillo, 'Financing of Spanish'.
17 The Flick case involved allegations of illegal financial donations to the PSOE from the German SPD, transferred to the party by the Flick Corporation. The inquiry carried out by the Tribunal de Cuentas to investigate the accusations concluded that no formal evidence could be found that could substantiate such a financial exchange (see also below).
18 D. López Garrido, 'La Financiación de los Partidos Políticos: Diez Propuestas de Reforma', in *La Financiación de los Partidos Políticos* (Madrid: Centro de Estudios Constitucionales, 1994), pp. 65-72.
19 This system has been in effect since the adoption of the 1987 law. Prior to that, the system of party financing consisted of fixed amounts per seat and vote in each of the two chambers. The new system of allocation of state money not only abolished the amounts related to electoral and parliamentary size, it also rendered the seats and votes obtained in the Senate elections irrelevant for subsidising routine party activities. See van Biezen, 'Party Financing'; E. Álvarez Conde 'Algunas Propuestas sobre la Financiación de los Partidos Políticos', in *La Financiación de los Partidos Políticos* (Madrid: Centro de Estudios Constitucionales, 1994), pp. 13-36.
20 J.M. Meirim, *O Financiamento dos Partidos Políticos e das Campanhas Eleitorais* (Lisbon: Aequitas/Editorial Notícias, 1994).
21 The total sum of state money assigned for national legislative elections amounts to 2500 monthly minimum wages.
22 I. van Biezen and K.H. Nassmacher, 'Political Finance in Southern Europe: Italy, Portugal and Spain', in K.H. Nassmacher (ed.), *Foundations for Democracy: Approaches to Comparative Political Finance - Essays in Honour of Herbert E. Alexander* (Baden-Baden: Nomos, 2001), pp. 131-54.
23 Between 1993 and 2000, these amounts increased from 22 to 27 pesetas per voter. See van Biezen and Nassmacher, 'Political Finance'.
24 Kopecký, 'Parliaments in the'.
25 van Biezen, 'Party Financing'.
26 For the regional parties, a similarly high dependence on the state applies to the Catalan CiU. The Basque PNV, however, seems less dependent on the state and derives most of its income from donations to the party. See van Biezen, 'Party Financing'.
27 For example, J.J. Linz and J.R. Montero, 'The Party Systems of Spain: Old Cleavages and New Challenges, Estudio/Working Paper 138 (Madrid: Instituto Juan March de Estudios e Investigaciones, 1999); P. Mair, *Party System Change: Approaches and Interpretations* (Oxford: Clarendon Press, 1997); G. Tóka 'Party Appeals and Voter Loyalty in New Democracies', *Political Studies*, 46(3) 1998, pp. 589-610.
28 Kopecký, 'Parliaments in the'.

[29] See van Biezen, 'Party Organization'.
[30] Lidový Dům (House of the People) was the party headquarters of the Czechoslovak Social Democratic Party until it was confiscated by the Communist Party after its takeover in 1948. Because the ČSSD considers itself the legal successor of the First Republic Social Democrats, it also claimed to be the legitimate owner of Lidový Dům. The building was indeed returned to the ČSSD in the first months of the democratisation process, but in 1993 the ODS, ODA, KDU-ČSL government decided to nullify this decision on procedural grounds. The party accounts were first partially and later completely frozen, causing serious financial problems. See J. Vermeersch, De Rode Herinnering: Sociaal-demokraten in Praag (Leuven: Garant, 1994).
[31] Kopecký, 'Parliaments in the'.
[32] van Biezen, 'Party Organization'.
[33] See M. Duverger, *Political Parties: Their Organization and Activities in the Modern State* (London: Methuen, 1954).
[34] P. Mair and I. van Biezen, 'Party Membership in Twenty European Democracies, 1980-2000', *Party Politics,* 7(1) 2001, pp. 5-21.
[35] See van Biezen, 'Party Organization'.
[36] van Biezen, 'Party Financing'.
[37] van Biezen, 'Party Financing'.
[38] I. van Biezen, 'Building Party Organisations and the Relevance of Past Models: The Communist and Socialist Parties in Spain and Portugal', *West European Politics*, 21(2) 1998, pp. 32-62; R. Gillespie, 'The Break-up of the 'Socialist Family': Party-Union Relations in Spain, 1982-1989', *West European Politics*, 13(1) 1990, pp. 47-62.
[39] P. del Castillo, 'Problems in Spanish Party Financing', in Herbert E. Alexander and Rei Shiratori (eds), *Comparative Political Finance among the Democracies* (Boulder: Westview Press, 1994), pp. 97-104; V. Pujas and M. Rhodes, 'Party Finance and Political Scandal in Italy, Spain and France', *West European Politics,* 22(3) 1998, pp. 41-63.
[40] J. Cazorla, 'El Clientelismo de Partido en la España de Hoy: una Disfunción de la Democracia', *Revista de Estudios Políticos*, 87, 1995, pp. 35-52; F.F. Lopes, 'Partisanship and Political Clientelism in Portugal (1983-1993)', *South European Society and Politics* 2(3) 1997, pp. 27-51.
[41] See del Castillo, 'Problems in Spanish'; P. Heywood, 'Continuity and Change: Analysing Political Corruption in Modern Spain', in W. Little and E. Posada-Carbó (eds), *Political Corruption in Europe and Latin America* (London: Macmillan, 1996), pp. 115-36.
[42] A.J. Heidenheimer, 'The Topography of European Scandals and Corruption', *International Social Science Journal*, 149, 1996, pp. 337-47.

43. Y. Mény and M. Rhodes, 'Illicit Governance: Corruption, Scandal and Fraud', in M. Rhodes, P. Heywood and V. Wright (eds), *Developments in Western Europe* (Basingstoke: Macmillan, 1997), pp. 95-113.
44. For example Pujas and Rhodes, 'Party Finance'; for a recent exception see van Biezen and Nassmacher, 'Political Finance in'.
45. M.R. de Sousa, *Os Partidos Políticos no Direito Constitucional Portuês* (Braga: Livraria Cruz, 1983).
46. del Castillo, 'Financing of Spanish'.
47. For more details see van Biezen and Nassmacher, 'Political Finance'.
48. P. Kopecky and C. Mudde, 'The 1998 Czech Parliamentary and Senate Elections', *Electoral Studies*, 18(3) 1999, pp. 415-24.
49. See www.transparency.org.
50. See Katz and Mair, 'Changing Models'.
51. Pasquino, quoted in R.L. Blanco Valdés, 'La Problemática de la Financiación de los Partidos Políticos en España: Regulación Jurídica y Propuestas de Reforma', *Revista de Estudios Políticos*, 87, 1995, pp. 163-97; see also K.Z. Paltiel, 'The Impact of Election Expenses Legislation in Canada, Western Europe, and Israel', in H.E. Alexander (ed.), *Political Finance* (Beverly Hills: Sage, 1979), pp. 15-39.
52. These figures include the aggregate sum of state subventions to all parties with parliamentary representation for both routine and electoral activities. Only for Spain are the figures restricted to the psoe, pp, pce/iu, ciu, and pnv. For reasons of comparability, the PPP (purchasing power parities) rates of currency conversions rather than the simple currency exchange rates have been used. These conversion rates equalise the purchasing power of different currencies by eliminating the differences in price levels between countries.
53. From the Hungarian party accounts it cannot be determined with certainty whether the state subventions only include those for routine activities or also for election campaigns.
54. But see, for example, I. van Biezen, 'On the Internal Balance of Party Power: Party Organisations in New Democracies', *Party Politics*, 6(4) 2000, pp. 395-417; R. Harmel and R. Gibson, 'Party Families and Democratic Performance: Extraparliamentary versus Parliamentary Group Power', *Political Studies*, 46(3) 1998, pp. 633-50; K. Heidar and R. Koole (eds), *Parliamentary Party Groups in European Democracies* (London: Routledge, 2000).
55. van Biezen, 'On the Internal Balance'.
56. Cf. Katz and Mair, 'Changing Models'; Heidar and Koole, 'Parliamentary Party Groups'.
57. See van Biezen and Nassmacher, 'Political Finance'; other figures contradict this

observation and suggest that some parties (PS and PSD) spend about the same amount on a single election campaign as on their entire extra-parliamentary organisation in one year. See van Biezen, 'Party Financing'.

[58] Partly because parties (at least in Spain) seem to have established a quite extensive and costly extra-parliamentary structure, maintaining local headquarters throughout the country staffed by paid officials. See Heywood, 'Continuity and Change'.

[59] van Biezen, 'Party Financing'; van Biezen, 'On the Internal Balance'.

[60] van Biezen, 'Party Financing'.

[61] Parties are entitled to this money if they succeed in obtaining the number of seats or votes required for establishing a parliamentary group. The minimum number of seats for a parliamentary group in Spain is 15 for the lower and 10 for the upper chamber. In the lower chamber, parties that have obtained at least five seats and at least 15 per cent of the vote in the constituencies where they have presented candidates, or at least five per cent of the vote on the national level, can also establish a separate parliamentary group. Parties that do not meet these requirements are incorporated in the so-called mixed group (grupo mixto).

[62] R. Gillespie, 'Party Funding in a New Democracy: Spain', in P. Burnell and A. Ware (eds), *Funding Democratization* (Manchester: Manchester University Press, 1998), pp. 73-93.

[63] For more details see Kopecký, 'Parliaments in the'; and P. Kopecký, 'Building Party Government: Political Parties in the Czech and Slovak Republics', in P. Webb, S. White and D. Stansfield (eds), *Political Parties in Transitory Democracies* (Oxford: Oxford University Press), forthcoming.

[64] See Heywood, 'Continuity and Change'.

Aleks Szczerbiak
Cartelisation in Post-Communist Politics: State Party Funding in Post-1989 Poland

ABSTRACT

This paper considers the degree to which the new parties in post-communist Poland orientate towards, and are dependent upon, the state for their funding. All the main Polish parties and groupings surveyed believe that the state should play a continuing or greater role in providing them with financial support, and both the level and scope of state funding has been increased and extended since 1989. There is also some evidence pointing to the emergence of a party cartel with state funding provisions that discriminate heavily in favour of those that achieve the greatest electoral success. However, the Polish party system is still too fluid, undeveloped and lacking a stable enough pattern of interactions for a party cartel to have fully emerged. Moreover, the distinction between 'successor' parties with their roots in the communist period and completely 'new' parties is not necessarily as helpful in identifying the varying levels of state-orientation as hypothesised.

Although it has tended to be either undervalued or completely ignored in most assessments of party organisational change, the evolving relationship between parties and the state corresponds to each successive theoretical model of party organisation.[1] The nature of this change has been particularly evident in the ways that parties have sought to procure financial and material resources. Operating under a limited franchise, Duverger's cadre party was financed primarily through personal contacts. The later, post-universal suffrage mass party's main sources of finance was numerous small membership subscriptions and contributions together with the activities of collateral organisations such as party co-operatives and trade unions. Duverger regarded the changing system of party finances (which he characterised as replacing the "capitalist financing of electioneering by democratic financing") as fundamental to the differences between cadre and mass parties and interpreted it as part of the broader process of democratisation and political change.[2] In the catch-all/electoral professional model, political parties increasingly sought funding from a broader range of interest groups (and, to some extent, the state) rather than their own internally-generated resources. The emergence of this model, therefore, implied an erosion of the party-civil society linkage and foresaw the greater emphasis by parties on the state, with the latter offering the potential to compensate for the former.

More recently, Katz and Mair have carried forward this conception of contemporary parties increasingly seeking to anchor themselves in the state and hypothesised the emergence of a new cartel party model. They noted a series of social, cultural and political trends over the last two decades that have led to a general decline in the levels of party involvement and participation. Membership levels and commitment have failed to keep pace with the rapidly escalating costs of party activity in the modern state. Consequently, parties have been obliged to look elsewhere for their resources and, in this case, their actual or potential access to public office made it easy for them to turn to the state for the organisational resources required in order to maintain themselves. This ever closer symbiosis between parties and the state could be particularly observed in the latter's increasingly important role in helping parties to secure, and oversee the regulation of, financial subventions and material resources. While the pattern obviously varied from country to country, Katz and Mair found that state subventions often constituted an increasingly important source of party income and that this growth had "come to represent one of the most significant changes to the environment within which parties act".[3]

Katz and Mair's cartel party is, therefore, characterised principally by an increasing orientation towards, and dependence upon, the state as an institutional support structure. Consequently, the links between parties and their electorates become even looser and more remote as the hypothesised cartel party both colonises and becomes an integral part of the state:

No longer simple brokers between civil society and the state, the parties now become absorbed by the state. From having first assumed the role of trustees, and then later of delegates, and then later again, in the hey-day of the catch-all party, of entrepreneurs, parties have now become semi-state agencies.[4]

It should be emphasised that the role of 'the state' in these various developments should not simply be characterised as an exogenous factor influencing party life. On the contrary, it is the parties themselves in their role as governors and legislators who are ultimately responsible for influencing the rules that determine access to these resources and determined the framework within which they were allocated. Moreover, because, for example, state subventions are often tied to prior party performance or position (whether defined in terms of electoral success or parliamentary representation) they generally helped to sustain existing parties and privilege insiders. At the same time, they help existing parties to resist challenges from those on the margins and limit the scope for the emergence of 'new entrants'. Indeed, hypothetically, parties may have become so dependent on continuous access to these resources that winning or losing an election could, by determining a party's membership of this privileged circle, affect its very political survival. Thus, as Katz and Mair put it, "the conditions become ideal for the formation of a cartel".[5] In other words, this pattern of increasing dependence on the state is accompanied by inter-party collusion in the division of state resources in such a way that parties can be seen to be laying the basis for their own mutual survival.

This paper considers the degree to which the new parties in post-communist Poland orientate towards, and are dependent upon, the state for their funding. It begins by considering, hypothetically, what kind of party-state relationship we might expect to see developing among the new parties in post-communist Poland. In order to test these hypotheses it then moves on to consider what kind of state financial and material support parties *actually received* and what they *believe* should be the role of the state in this area. Finally, the paper examines the broader issue of whether or not there is evidence of a pattern of inter-party collusion to create a 'cartel' of privileged insiders.[6]

The paper focuses on the six main parties and groupings that emerged in the run up to the most recent September 1997 parliamentary elections. The two largest political groupings, Solidarity Electoral Action (Akcja Wyborcza Solidarność: AWS) and the Democratic Left Alliance (Sojusz Lewicy Demokratycznej: SLD), were both formed as conglomerates comprising a number of parties and other political groupings. AWS was established in June 1996 as an electoral alliance bringing together more than thirty centre-right political parties and other organisations although the hegemonic role was played by the Solidarity trade union. AWS emerged as the largest parliamentary grouping and main government coalition partner after the September 1997 election (33.83% and 201 seats in the Sejm, the more powerful lower house of the Polish parliament). The SLD also comprised around thirty trade unions, women's, youth and other social organisations that had enjoyed patronage during the communist era. However, it was dominated by the Social Democracy of the Republic of Poland party (Socjaldemokracja Rzeczpospolitej Polskiej: SdRP) which was formed in January 1990 at the final Congress of the communist Polish United Workers' Party (Polska Zjednoczona Partia Robotnicza: PZPR). The SLD was the largest grouping and senior government coalition partner during the 1993-97 parliament and its leader Aleksander Kwaśniewski was elected President of the Polish Republic in November 1995. However, in spite of increasing its share of the vote to 27.13% in September 1997 it was reduced to second place and saw its Sejm representation cut from 171 to 164 seats. The SLD was transformed into a single, unitary party in 1999 and SdRP was absorbed within it. AWS, on the other hand, remained a coalition but one whose viability was increasingly threatened following the defeat of its candidate in the October 2000 presidential election. For most of the 1997-2001 parliament, however, it was partially consolidated internally around four main parties but with the Solidarity union retaining a key role.[7]

The Freedom Union (Unia Wolności: UW) was formed in April 1994 following a merger of two liberal centrist parties that also emerged from within the Solidarity movement: the Democratic Union (Unia Demokratyczna: UD) and the Liberal Democratic Congress (Kongres Liberalno-Demokratyczne: KLD). The UW was the third largest grouping and main opposition party in the 1993-97 parliament but emerged as the new parliamentary 'kingmaker' in September 1997 with 13.37% of the vote and 60 seats. It went on to become AWS's junior coalition partner until it withdrew from the government in June 2000. The Polish Peasant Party (Polskie Stronnictwo Ludowe: PSL), on the other hand, was formed in May 1990 largely as the organisational successor to the communist's former satellite United Peasant Party (Zjednoczone Stronnictwo Ludowe: ZSL). The PSL won the second largest number of seats and was the SLD's junior coalition partner in the 1993-97 parliament, although in September 1997 it saw its share of the vote halved to 7.31% and its parliamentary representation slashed to 27.

The Movement for Poland's Reconstruction (Ruch Odbudowy Polski: ROP) was a right-wing party formed in November 1995 by the supporters of former Solidarity premier Jan Olszewski in an attempt to capitalise on his relatively good showing in the Presidential elections. The ROP won just enough support in September 1997 to secure parliamentary representation (5.56%) although this translated into only 6 seats in the Sejm. Finally, the Labour Union (Unia Pracy: UP) was formed in 1992 by a number of smaller groupings led by individuals from the Solidarity's social democratic wing and reformed ex-communists who chose not to join SdRP. Although it was the fourth largest grouping in the 1993-97 parliament, the UP narrowly failed to cross the threshold for parliamentary representation in September 1997 with 4.74% of the votes.

Post-communist party-state linkages

So what kind of party-state relationship might we expect to see in the light of west European experience developing among the new parties in post-communist Poland? A number of commentators who have attempted to make structured projections about the way party organisation is likely to develop in post-communist states. They have generally hypothesised that the growing emphasis on links with the state that is increasingly evident in Western democracies is likely to be replicated in the Polish (and, more generally, East European) experience.[8] Indeed, there are a number of reasons to assume that the newly emerging parties of Eastern Europe are, if anything, likely to be even more orientated towards the state than their counterparts in Western democracies when they were at a similar stage of development.

The new parties are operating within a political culture where the state was a highly prominent feature of the political landscape and in which it may prove difficult to engender a sense of it being separate from the party system. Moreover, despite the substantial progress made in terms of privatisation, the state has continued to play a prominent economic role throughout the region during the post-communist period. Civil society certainly appeared to assume a particularly important role in the ideology of the East European opposition movements that flourished at the end of the communist period. However, it went on to have much less political relevance as the new parties' focus shifted to the tasks of economic transformation and political reconstruction in which the state assumed much greater prominence and many of its potential leaders moved into the realms of party politics. Moreover, given the new parties' structural characteristics (the lack of a mass membership or any degree of social implantation together with the general weakness of their party organisation on the ground) it was natural that they should focus much of their attention on the state.[9] Similarly, the fact that party leaders played (and, in some cases, continue to play) a central role in party development also seemed likely to incline them towards developing a closer relationship with the state. Finally, the principle of state support for new political parties in terms of financial subsidies was quickly established in almost all the recent cases of democratisation[10] was, therefore, likely to be an means of party development in the post-communist states as well.[11]

However, as a caveat to this overall hypothesis we might (as a number of commentators have) draw a distinction between the organisational 'successors' to the ruling communist parties and their allies (the SdRP/SLD and PSL in the case of our sample) and those newly established parties which have had to develop without the benefit of an organisational legacy from the communist period (AWS, the UW, ROP and UP). Hypothetically, the 'successor' parties are more likely to retain, at least in relative terms and in a post-communist context, some of the former strengths of the traditional mass party model such as relatively high levels of membership, well-developed local organisational networks and a fairly robust financial and material base. Consequently, we might expect these two 'successor' parties to be correspondingly less orientated towards the state than the 'new' parties that did not enjoy this organisational legacy. This is particularly likely to be the case with the PSL which (at first sight) appears to display more of the characteristics of the mass party, and a broadly greater orientation towards civil society, than any of the other parties or groupings surveyed.[12]

Moreover, however striking the immediate similarities between the cartel party model and the new Polish parties may appear, we should also be cautious about taking these comparisons too far. In the first place, the accuracy of the model itself has been questioned.[13] Katz and Mair have themselves both cautioned against its general applicability and acknowledged that a party cartel is most likely to develop in those political cultures marked by a tradition of inter-party consensus and co-operation.[14] It is, therefore, much less likely to emerge in post-communist polities such as Poland were the emotional temperature and levels of polarisation along the cleavage of attitudes towards the past are likely to be very high for some time to come and parties themselves remain internally fissiparous. More generally, it is questionable whether the party system in Poland (or other parts of Eastern Europe for that matter) is developed or stable enough either for the key players to be clearly identified or for the likely members of a party cartel to agree on the shared political perspectives and mutual interests that are emphasised in that model. As Lewis points out, the essence of the cartel party model from the point of view of the voters lies in their ability to choose "from a fixed menu of parties" and it is precisely this fixed menu that is lacking in Poland and Eastern Europe more generally.[15]

State party funding in post-communist Poland

Until the passage of the 1997 Party Law, direct and ongoing state party funding did not formally exist in Poland and the reimbursement of election campaign expenses was the one possibility for financing political parties and groupings *directly* from the state budget. The 1993 Electoral Law introduced this major innovation into the Polish system of party funding as a result of which certain election committees (and, therefore, parties or coalitions of parties) received a one-off donation from the state budget to refund costs incurred during a parliamentary election campaign. These refunds were only paid to those election committees able to secure parliamentary representation. Refunds were paid in proportion to the total number of Sejm deputies and Senators (members of the less powerful upper house of parliament) elected, provided that the election committee published a financial report of their campaign accounts within three months of the election. The amount available for campaign refunds was set at 20% of the total expenditure assigned in the state budget to cover the costs of organising, preparing and conducting the election.

The financial role of the state in Poland certainly became evident after the September 1993 elections when every eligible party or political grouping received 14,500 new złoties (the equivalent of $7,650) for every seat won in either of the two chambers.[16] Although the refund only went to those parties that won parliamentary seats, it was paid directly to party central offices via the electoral committees submitting the candidates' lists from which the Sejm deputies or Senators were elected. These were either single parties or groupings (as in the case of the PSL, UW and UP) or electoral coalitions comprising a number of organisations (such as the SdRP-led SLD) which then divided the refund between their members. As **Table 1** shows, there were considerable variations in the amount paid to each of the groupings with the victorious parties receiving significant sums of money. By providing them with the possibility of earning funds to cover day-to-day political activities, these refunds, of course, further strengthened the position of the two victorious 'successor' formations, the SLD and PSL, and augmented the relatively extensive organisational resources already at their command. Those parties with only a few parliamentarians barely covered the repayment of the loans they had taken out to finance their campaigns.[17]

The other significant source of state financial support for Polish parties before 1997 was the provision of various forms of support for parliamentary groupings, together with salaries, expenses and other material resources for individual parliamentarians. A large part of the Polish parliamentary budget was used to help Sejm deputies and Senators perform their parliamentary duties, both at national and constituency level. Parliamentary clubs received standard monthly payments per deputy to finance their activities that was reduced as the size of the fraction increased. In 2000 this sum was 933 złoties per deputy for fractions with more than 100 members, 996 złoties for those with 50-100 deputies and 1062 złoties for those with less than 50.[18] Moreover, Sejm deputies and Senators also received: substantial allowances to run offices in their local electoral districts (7,500 złoties per month in 2000), essential office equipment supplied free by the Sejm and Senate Chancelleries, together with a general deputies' expense allowance. Full-time 'professional' deputies were paid wages on top of this in the form of a so-called *ryczałt*.[19]

It is, of course, questionable whether or not all of these sums can be included within the broad definition of 'state party funding'. Some of the salaries and expenses, for example, were intended as Sejm deputies and Senators' personal income. Similarly, parliamentary directives insisted that the office expense allowance should, in theory, "not be used to finance the activity of political parties, social organisations, foundations or charitable activity nor the activity of the parliamentary club".[20] Ultimately, of course, it was up to the individual parliamentarian, and not the parliamentary party leaderships, to decide how this particular allowance should be allocated. In practice, however parliamentary salaries and allowances were very closely linked with, and inevitably shaded into, the general question of parliamentary club and party funding in general. Many deputies and Senators regularly passed on part of their salaries and expense allowances for the needs of the parliamentary club as a whole, or even the party central office, as an established procedure. Similarly, given that many parliamentarian's constituency surgeries often doubled up as local party offices and performed a crucial role in their local organisational infrastructure,[21] it was often difficult to distinguish between the funds spent on constituency work and those used to promote local party activity. They should, therefore, properly be regarded as a *de facto* form of backdoor state financing for parties as a whole rather than for the individual parliamentarian. Indeed, as **Table 2** shows, the total amount allocated to support the activities of (mostly party-based) parliamentary clubs, together with individual parliamentarians' allowances and expenses, should not be regarded as a form of marginal funding.[22]

The 1997 Law on Political Parties introduced three significant changes to the Polish state party funding regime. Firstly, it established a new system of regular donations (known as 'objective' donations: *dotacje celowe*) to be paid to those election committees that specifically registered themselves as political parties (and not electoral coalitions). This was in addition to the one-off election refunds (henceforth known as 'subjective' donations: *dotacje podmiotowe*) which continued to be paid to all eligible electoral committees on the basis of the number of seats won. Secondly, although the level of election refunds and donations paid to each party was still determined by its electoral performance, the regular donations were paid in proportion to the number of votes obtained rather than seats won. Thirdly, the regular donations were paid to all parties that won more than 3% of the votes "cast for all political parties' candidates' lists across the whole country" and not just those whose electoral committees crossed the 5% threshold for parliamentary representation. The overall budget for state subventions remained unchanged with the new regular donations accounting for 60% of the total, paid in four annual instalments: 40% in the first year and 20% in the three subsequent years (uprated in line with inflation).

This new system of regular donations was (in theory, at least) accompanied by much greater financial transparency, with parties obliged to submit annual financial reports on "expenditure undertaken on their statutory objectives" or face the risk of losing their entitlement to receive further donations. Moreover, all parties (even those that didn't receive any election refunds or state donations) also had to submit details of any donations to their Election Funds which were ten times greater than the forecast average public sector salary for that year, together with a more general set of financial accounts. Failure to do so could result in the party's Election Fund being frozen or its deletion from the official register of political parties, respectively.

Following the 1997 parliamentary elections, the total amount allocated to all the election committees that qualified for refunds and regular donations was more than 14 million new złoties. As Table 3 shows, as electoral coalitions AWS and the SLD were not entitled to regular donations and only received one-off election refunds worth approximately 25,000 złoties for each parliamentarian elected - with AWS earning 6.3 million and the SLD 4.8 million. Meanwhile, those election committees that registered as political parties shared a total of 2.725 million złoties: 25,000 złoties per parliamentary seat multiplied by the 109 seats won by the three political parties which crossed the 5% threshold for parliamentary representation (the UW, PSL and ROP). These three parties also received one-off donations but only worth 10,000 złoties per seat, having to share the remainder set aside for the regular, 'subjective' donations with those parties that had not won any seats but still obtained more than 3% of the vote. Originally it was assumed (and was probably the intention of those who framed the legislation) that these regular donations were only payable to those parties which won more than 3% of the total number of votes cast for *all election committees*. In 1997, therefore, only the UP (which won 4.74% of the votes) would have been eligible among those parties that failed to cross the 5% threshold. However, it subsequently emerged that the 3% figure related only to the number of votes cast for *election committees that were specifically registered as political parties* without taking into account the votes cast for electoral coalitions such as AWS or the SLD. This made the *de facto* threshold for regular donations just over 1% and meant that the two pensioners' parties (KPEiR and KPEiR RP) that contested the 1997 elections (and won 2.18% and 1.63% of the votes respectively) were also eligible.

Election refunds, therefore, provided to parliamentary parties and the new system of regular state subventions played a critical role in helping parties to survive the single most expensive activity they were likely to be engaged in. Together with the new system of regular state subventions and the various forms of material and financial support provided to parliamentary parties state party funding also provided certain parties with some sort of secure financial base for their ongoing party activities. Clearly, without access to properly audited sets of party accounts over a number of years, it is impossible to make any definitive judgements as to how much importance each party attached to the various forms of state support compared with other, internally-generated sources of revenue. Unfortunately, in spite of the fact that the principle of transparency of funding was built into original 1990 Law on Political Parties, detailed information on Polish party funding has always been extremely patchy and difficult to obtain.

However, the more rigorous requirements placed on parties by the 1997 Party Law to publish annual financial accounts mean that a somewhat clearer picture of the relative importance of state party funding is slowly beginning to emerge. As Table 4 shows, the first set of published party accounts for 1997, 1998 and 1999 revealed that state subsidies and refunds only played a significant role in the finances of the ROP and UP, the two smaller parties that were the beneficiaries of state party funding. On the other hand, state funding appeared to play only a marginal role in the UW's and PSL's income stream. Table 4 also us with provides a graphic illustration of just how significant organisational inheritance was for securing the PSL's financial base. Income from business activities contributed between 77.48%-94.30% of the party's 10-12 million złoties annual income in the years 1997-99. The great bulk of this came from income obtained from renting out parts of its headquarters building that the party inherited from the ZSL and, thereby, made the PSL easily the best funded party in post-communist Poland.[23]

However, these figures are somewhat misleading and tend to underestimate the importance of state funding for the main political parties in post-communist Poland. Firstly, the two most significant beneficiaries from state party funding arising from the September 1997 parliamentary elections were, of course, the AWS and SLD electoral coalitions. Donations and bank loans taken out with the prospect that they would then receive refunds to pay them off funded their election campaigns. These refunds were channelled through AWS and the SLD and only a very small proportion of this found its way back to the parties that comprised them (none in the case of AWS) with the balance retained by the election committees. In other words, virtually none of this (more significant) flow of income from state funding is reflected in party financial statements. Secondly, and perhaps even more significantly, these figures do not show funds channelled to parties through various parliamentary allowances which are a much more significant means of providing parties with both ongoing funding and of local organisational infrastructure. As **Tables 1** and **2** show, the four largest parliamentary parties in the 1993-97 parliament actually received more than three times as much funding in this form in 1995 as their respective party central offices received in their entire one-off refund for the September 1993 election.

Attitudes to state party funding

The widespread practice of state financial support, particularly that channelled through the parliamentary party, appeared to be of prime importance to all parties and both its level and scope have been progressively increased and extended. Indeed, the growing significance of state party funding is reflected in the fact that most Polish politicians have consistently supported both its introduction and expansion.

The issue was first raised in the context of the debate on the 1993 electoral law when virtually every parliamentary fraction supported the introduction of the election refund.[24] All the six parties and groupings surveyed have subsequently argued strongly in favour of the state providing parties with greater financial support. The most enthusiastic supporters were traditionally the PSL and UP, both of whom sponsored legislation to introduce regular subsidies in addition to the one-off election refunds that culminated in the passage of the 1997 Party Law. Given its general organisational weakness, together with the fact that (at the time that the new Law was being debated) the party faced the direct threat of exclusion from parliament, the UP's support for broadening the scope of state party funding was fairly predictable. With its relatively well developed organisational base (by Polish standards at least) and alternative sources of internally generated income, the PSL's enthusiasm for increasing the role of the state was perhaps rather more surprising. However, state party funding has played a crucial role in the PSL's organisational strategy at various stages. For example, the party used most of its 1993 parliamentary election refund to assist local party organisations with the purchase of the buildings in which their headquarters were located.[25]

Indeed, of all the parties and groupings surveyed it was PSL spokesman who set out the case for direct state party funding most clearly and comprehensively during the debates on the 1997 Law. Firstly, they argued that parties were one of the main foundations of a democratic system and incurred certain unavoidable costs as a result of having to fulfil a number of essential functions. As PSL Vice-President Janusz Dobrosz put it speaking in the Sejm debate on the 1997 Party Law, "political parties are currently one of the basic elements of public life, an essential cell in the process of representing state interests as well as performing the government of the state. Political parties have their specific functions and tasks, which they are not in a position to realise effectively without subventions."[26] Secondly, without a basic state-guaranteed minimum level of finances, parties inevitably began to operate like "businessmen chasing profits" and became pre-occupied with the identifying new sources of income. In other words, turning one of the traditional arguments against state funding of parties on its head, the PSL argued that, by relieving them of the burden of fundraising, state funding actually gave parties greater opportunities to concentrate on their other functions and involve themselves in broader civic activities. Thirdly, the provision of state subsidies "significantly limits the dependence of parties and politicians on the vested interests of various potential sponsors" and "limits corruption and the influence of business, together with that of overseas funds, on the politics of the state." UP National Spokesman Tomasz Nałęcz also argued that it was, "more cost-effective for the state budget, the ordinary Pole, the average taxpayer, to put aside certain modest amounts openly and clearly for financing political parties than leaving this sphere of obligation in the current actual grey zone."

Both the SdRP/SLD and UW also supported the 1997 Law that continued and extended the scope of state party funding. SLD Parliamentary Club spokesman and SdRP Presidium member Zbigniew Zaborowski argued that, "extending the right of political parties to obtain subsidies for their statutory activities will increase the state budget deficit but I think that this deficit is in accord with the interests of society, enables the formation of a transparent, open system of financing political parties." UW Parliamentary Club spokesman Jerzy Ciemnewski also supported extending the scope of state support and argued that "from the point of view of the current requirements of constructing a democratic system" and specifically backed the proposal to finance parties that failed to enter parliament.

Of the six parties and groupings surveyed the ROP and AWS devoted the least attention to the implications of the 1997 Party Law. This was largely for the fairly obvious reason that, as relatively new organisations, they were pre-occupied with developing a basic organisational structure and broader programmatic questions in the run up to the September 1997 parliamentary elections when the new Law was being debated. However, both groupings appeared to be generally supportive of state party funding in principle and their spokesmen echoed a number of the arguments used by other groupings on the contribution that it could make to reducing corruption and helping parties to concentrate on their basic political functions. For example, ROP Supreme Council Vice-Chairman and Senator Zbigniew Romaszewski argued that state subventions were justified on the grounds that, "parties that carry out business activities . . . are a much greater threat to society than party finances from the budget in an open manner." Romaszewski was also one of the main parliamentary sponsors of the campaign to introduce a one złoty annual levy of taxpayers to fund parties[27] Similarly, AWS National Spokesman Tomasz Tywonek argued that "it is the state that is responsible for political cadres . . . in reality it is politicians who then form governments, it is politicians who draft laws and it is politicians who are responsible for improving the lot of the people" and "the state ought to be concerned that these politicians are as well prepared as possible to fulfil their mission." Consequently, "straightforward state financing is, quite simply, the thing that is easiest to control" with "the state treasury undoubtedly . . . (playing) . . . a key role."[28]

Since 1997, support for state party funding has, if anything, increased and hardened among all parties and there is now a strong consensus in favour of broadening its scope even among those parties that were not previously particularly enthusiastic. For example, re-iterating his party's support for state party funding SLD spokesman Lech Nikolski argued that, "eventually parties should be completely financed by the state".[29] The leader of AWS affiliate SKL Jan Maria Rokita also argued that either private firms that donate to political should be given tax breaks to encourage them to be more open about their donations or that parties should be funded directly from the state budget.[30] Other party spokesman such as UW General Secretary Mirosław Czech and the AWS Parliamentary Club Vice-Chairman Jacek Rybicki have also re-iterated their parties' support for increased state party funding, although mainly stressing its benefits as an anti-corruption measure.[31]

An emerging party cartel?

All the new Polish parties, therefore, displayed a keen interest in exploiting the potential resources provided by the state in terms of party funding. The pattern in post-communist Poland appeared to reflect (and, in terms of a comparable stage of party system development, go beyond) Western developments in terms of the provisions for and parties' expectations of state party funding. However, the message was much more mixed as far as the emergence of a cartel of privileged insiders that colluded to exclude new entrants was concerned.

There was clearly some evidence to support the notion that such a party cartel might be developing in post-communist Poland. Polish legislation certainly provided greater access to certain financial and material resources to those parties that achieved the greatest electoral success and parliamentary representation. As Tables 1 and 3 illustrate, the most successful parties in the 1993 and 1997 elections received a handsome financial premium for their electoral victories. This financial premium was exaggerated by an electoral system that, although proportional in theory, distinctly favoured the most successful parties through: the application of a relatively high (in the context of the highly fragmented Polish party system) 5% threshold for representation in the Sejm (8% in the case of electoral coalitions); the use of the d'Hondt system to determine the final division of seats within the local electoral districts; allocation of additional seats from a national list only to those parties and groupings winning over 7% of the vote; and the creation (in 1993) of a larger number of smaller multi-member constituencies compared to the 1991 Electoral Law. This is precisely what happened in September 1993 when the SLD and PSL won 20.4% and 15.4% of the votes but secured 37.7% and 29% of the seats respectively. As a result they obtained much larger election refunds than they would have done purely on the basis of the number of votes won, while several parties and groupings that fell just short of the 5% and 8% barriers did not benefit at all from re-imbursements. This was further exacerbated by the electoral system to the Senate, based on plurality voting in two or three member constituencies, that led to even greater distortions with the SLD and PSL winning 37% and 33% of the seats respectively. The 1997 Senate election saw similar disproportions emerge, most notably the fact that AWS won 51% of the seats on the basis of a 33.83% share of the national vote.

Moreover, the consequences of an electoral system that so clearly privileged the strongest parties were not confined solely to the question of election refunds. The various, extremely generous additional forms of funding for parliamentary clubs and individual parliamentarians provided those parties represented in parliament with a further obvious advantage over those that were excluded and, thereby, gave election winners a further premium for victory. To some extent, then, the existing rules for state access to parliamentary resources also limited the scope for new entrants by discriminating against parties that emerged in between elections unless they were formed on the basis of existing parties with parliamentary representation. Together with the system of electoral refunds, they represented a clear move towards the creation of a party cartel in Poland.

However, there was other evidence to suggest that Polish politics was still relatively fluid. Even the stringent post-1993 funding regime did not prevent the emergence of new entrants and 'freeze' the party system within the existing parliamentary configuration. This was exemplified by the subsequent formation and entry in parliament of both the ROP and AWS (the latter, admittedly, under the aegis of the Solidarity trade union). Indeed, although Polish parties were generally in favour of broadening the scope of state support, they did not yet support completely restricting access only to a narrow cartel of parties. This was based on a general nervousness about declaring unambiguously who was and who was not a member of the party cartel at this stage of the development of the Polish party system. This was felt particularly keenly among those parties, such as the UP, that operated on the margins of the 5% parliamentary threshold and were uncertain as to whether or not they cold sustain their 'insider' status. Moreover, by actually lowering the threshold for access to state party funding to 3% (and, thereby, providing the lifeline of continued state funding to some parties that failed to secure parliamentary representation) in some respects the 1997 Party Law actually represented a step away from the formation of a party cartel.

Indeed, some of the new Law's sponsors explicitly justified its provisions for broadening access to state funding to include non-parliamentary parties on the grounds that it gave them a 'second in what was still evidently a crystallising party system. There was, for example, undoubtedly an element of self-preservation that motivated the UP, one of the 1997 Law's main sponsors, which was concerned (correctly, as it turned out) that it would not be able to guarantee its own status as a member of the putative party cartel.[32] UP National Spokesman Tomasz Nałęcz, for example, argued that it, "is difficult to demand that parties should only have the right to exist when they reach a mature age. I think that the law-maker's intention should also be to enable them to have a fair childhood and a period of maturation." Similarly UW Parliamentary Club spokesman Jerzy Ciemniewski argued in favour of the 1997 Law on the grounds that, "financing parties which have not found themselves in parliament, but enjoy certain social support does not close off the party system in its current shape and allows other parties the opportunity for development and participation in electoral battles." In other words, as hypothesised, the shared political perspectives and notions of how parties could collectively further mutual interests (which underpin the pattern of inter-party collusion emphasised in that model) had simply not been firmly enough established for a relatively stable party cartel to properly emerge.

Conclusion

The overall pattern of party activity and attitudes, therefore, fitted broadly with our hypothesised projection that the new Polish parties would replicate the experience of contemporary parties in Western democracies in terms of their interest in exploiting the financial resources provided by the state. The various kinds of state financial support (election refunds, subventions to parliamentary parties, parliamentary allowances and, since 1997, direct, regular party funding) appeared to be of prime and growing importance. All the main Polish parties and groupings surveyed believed that the state should play a continuing or greater role in providing them with financial support and both the level and scope of state funding has, indeed, been progressively increased and extended since 1989.

Interestingly, however, the distinction between 'successor' parties with their roots in the communist period and completely 'new' parties was not necessarily as striking or as helpful an analytical tool in identifying the varying levels of state-orientation as hypothesised. It was fairly predictable that the relatively small and organisationally weak UP was one of the most enthusiastic supporters of a very pro-active state role in providing parties with funding and media access. It was more surprising that the PSL, arguably the party that bore the clearest resemblance to the mass party model in many other respects, was actually one of the most enthusiastic supporters of state party funding. In this respect at least it actually appeared to bear a closer resemblance to the cartel party model than most of the 'new' parties operating on the Polish political scene.

There was also some evidence pointing to the emergence of a party cartel in post-communist Poland with party funding provisions discriminating heavily in favour of those parties that achieved the greatest electoral success together with an electoral system that exaggerated the success of larger parties. However, while there may have been a number of important similarities with contemporary Western development, there were also significant differences and the comparisons should not be overdrawn. The provisions of the 1997 Party Law, which actually lowered the threshold for state party funding to include non-parliamentary parties, illustrate the consensus against declaring unambiguously who was and who was not a member of the cartel at this stage of party system development in Poland. The Polish party system is still too fluid and undeveloped, with the parties themselves of an unstable and often transient character. It is simply too soon for a stable enough pattern of inter-actions to develop which could form the basis for a party cartel to fully emerge.

Table 1: 1993 State Election Refunds
(Figures in new złoties)

Party/grouping	Expenditure	Income[33]	Parliamentarians	Refund
SdRP/SLD	1,870,000	1,787,000	208	3,016,000
PSL	1,488,700	1,491,300	168	2,436,000
UD (UW)	2,047,900	1,954,200	78	1,131,000
UP	362,200	336,300	43	623,500
KPN	841,300	504,800	22	319,000
BBWR	1,504,000	1,442,300	18	261,000

Source: Rzeczpospolita, 21 November 1996.

Table 2: 1995 Total State Funding of Parliamentary Clubs/Circles

Club/circle	Parliamentarians	Amount in new złoties
SdRP/SLD	204	9,792,000
PSL	165	7,920,000
UW	78	3,744,000
UP	39	1,872,000
KPN	16	768,000
BBWR	15	720,000
Solidarity trade union	10	480,000

Source: S. Gebethner, 'Problem Finansowania Partii Politycznych a System Wyborczy w Polsce w Latach 90', in F. Ryszka et al. (eds), Historia-Idee-Polityka (Warsaw: Wydawnictwo Naukowe Scholar, 1995), pp. 425-434, p. 431.

Table 3: 1997 Election Refunds and Donations
(Figures in new złoties)

Party/grouping	Expenditure	Income	Seats	Refunds	Donations
AWS	11,100,000	9,300,000	252	6,300,000	
SdRP/SLD	9,300,000	9,300,000	172	4,800,000	
UW	7,600,000	6,700,000	68	680,000	630,000
PSL	3,500,000	3,300,000	30	300,000	340,000
ROP	1,900,000	1,750,000	11	110,000	260,000
UP	973,000	993,000			220,000
KPEiR	513,000	475,000			100,000
KPEiR RP	123,000	105,000			80,000

Sources: Gazeta Wyborcza, 10 December 1997; and Rzeczpospolita, 23 December 1997.

Table 4: Sources of Party Income for 1997-1999

PSL:

Source of income	1997	1998	1999
Business activity, bank interest and loans	77.48%	87.96%	94.30%
Donations and public collections	22.21%	7.19%	4.20%
State funding	0.00%	4.43%	0.69%
Membership subscriptions	0.29%	0.37%	0.81%
Total (new złoties)	**12,109,775**	**10,472,809**	**11,146,614**

ROP:

Source of income	1997	1998	1999
Business activity, bank interest and loans	Not available	3.24%	6.63%
Donations and public collections	Not available	16.38%	15.13%
State funding	Not available	66.99%	63.98%
Membership subscriptions	Not available	13.38%	14.25%
Total (new złoties)	**Not available**	**345,936**	**90,846**

UP:

Source of income	1997	1998	1999
Business activity, bank interest and loans	8.18%	0.00%	0.04%
Donations and public collections	11.39%	0.00%	0.00%
State funding	78.33%[34]	100.00%	33.78%
Membership subscriptions	2.09%	0.00%	59.68%
Other	0.00%	0.00%	6.50%
Total (new złoties)	**390,306**	**101,513**	**146,885**

UW:

Source of income	1997	1998	1999
Business activity, bank interest and loans	9.58%	2.39%	6.90%
Donations and public collections	87.02%	70.23%[35]	23.16%
State funding	0.00%	11.63%	4.52%
Membership subscriptions	3.39%	15.75%	62.80%
Total (new złoties)	**7,109,878**	**8,454,648**	**3,091,906**

Source: Party accounts submitted to the Warsaw Regional Court.

Notes

1. See: M. Duverger, *Political Parties: Their Organisation and Activity in the Modern State* (London: Macmillan, 1954); O. Kirchheimer, 'The Transformation of Western European Party Systems' in J. LaPalombara and M. Weiner (eds), *Political Parties and Political Development* (Princeton, NJ: Princeton University Press, 1966), pp. 177-200; A. Panebianco, *Political Parties: Organisation and Power* (Cambridge: Cambridge University Press, 1988); and R.S. Katz and P. Mair, 'Changing Models of Party Organization and Party Democracy: The Emergence of the Cartel Party', *Party Politics* 1(1) 1995, pp. 5-28.
2. See: Duverger, *Political Parties*, p. 63.
3. See: Katz and Mair, 'Changing Models of Party Organisation and Party Democracy', p. 15.
4. Katz and Mair, 'Changing Models'.
5. Katz and Mair, 'Changing Models', p. 17.
6. There are, of course, other aspects of the party-state relationship worthy of consideration when attempting to identify a pattern of state dependence and cartelisation, particularly the extent to which parties are dependent on the state media. However, this paper focuses exclusively on state party funding which is both a recurring theme in all the contemporary party models and can be isolated and examined relatively easily.
7. These four parties are: the union based Solidarity Electoral Action Social Movement (Ruch Społeczny Akcji Wyborczej Solidarność: RS AWS), the Christian National Union (Zjednoczenie Chrześcijańsko-Narodowe: ZChN), the Conservative People's Party (Stronnictwo Konserwatywno-Ludowe: SKL) and the Polish Agreement of Christian Democrats (Polskie Porozumienie Chrześcijańskich Demokratów: PPChD).
8. See: P. Kopecky, 'Developing Party Organizations in East-Central Europe: What Type of Party is Likely to Emerge?', *Party Politics*, 1(4) 1995, pp. 515-534; P.G. Lewis and R. Gortat, 'Models of Party Democracy and Questions of State Dependence in Poland, *Party Politics*, 1(4) 1995, pp. 599-608, p. 603; P.G. Lewis (ed.), *Party Structure and Organization in East-Central Europe* (Aldershot: Edward Elgar, 1996), p. 15; and P. Mair, *What Is Different About Post-communist Party Systems?* (Glasgow: University of Strathclyde, 1996), p. 15.
9. See: A. Szczerbiak, 'Testing Party Models in East-Central Europe: Local Party Organization in Postcommunist Poland', *Party Politics*, 5(4) 1999, pp. 525-537.
10. See: P. Burnell and A. Ware, *Funding Democratization* (Manchester: Manchester University Press, 1998).
11. On the other hand, there are counter arguments to suggest that the new parties may be particularly anxious to distance themselves from a communist legacy where the party and state were inseparable. The ruling communist parties were,

of course, enmeshed in the state apparatus and enjoyed extensive (indeed, virtually unlimited) control over its resources, while the communist state was perceived to be the major agent of political repression and obstacle to democracy in Eastern Europe. Indeed, as Lewis points out, "particular care was often taken in drafting legislation to separate new parties from the sources of administrative and economic power that have been a central part of the political establishment under the former regime." See: P.G. Lewis, 'Party Funding in post-communist east-central Europe', in Burnell and Ware, *Funding Democratization*, pp. 139-40.

[12] For more on the apparent similarities and differences between the PSL and the traditional mass party model see: A. Szczerbiak, 'The Polish Peasant Party: A Mass Party in Post-communist Eastern Europe?', *East European Politics and Societies*, forthcoming.

[13] See: R. Koole, 'Cadre, Catch-all or Cartel? A Comment on the Notion of the Cartel Party', *Party Politics*, 2(4) 1996, pp. 507-523; and H. Kitschelt, 'Citizens, politicians and party cartelization: Political representation and state failure in post-industrial democracies', *European Journal of Political Research*, 37, (2000), pp. 149-179.

[14] See: Katz and Mair, 'Changing Models of Party Organization and Party Democracy', p. 17.

[15] See: Lewis, *Party Structure and Organization in East-Central Europe*, p. 12.

[16] All figures cited in this chapter are expressed in 'new' złoties that came into circulation on January 1st 1995 and were equivalent to 10,000 'old' złoties.

[17] Although any surplus from the refund was supposed to be assigned for "publicly beneficial purposes" parties discovered various ways to circumvent this provision. The party could also, of course, also earn bank interest on any excess sums that could then, quite legally, be spent on stricte party activities.

[18] Parliamentary parties' specialist and expert reports were largely paid for from these funds - although Sejm deputies and Senators who chaired parliamentary committees could also obtain additional sums which could also, of course, be utilised indirectly for party purposes.

[19] See: J. Paradowska, 'Lewa Kasa, Prawa Kasa', *Polityka*, 22 January 2000. Although this term is (somewhat confusingly) also used sometimes simply to describe parliamentarians' office expense allowances.

[20] See: A. van der Meer-Krok-Paszkowska and M. van der Muyzenberg, 'The Positions of Parties in the Polish and Hungarian Parliaments', Paper prepared for the Fourth Workshop on 'Transformation Processes in Eastern Europe', The Hague, February 1-2 1996, p. 8.

[21] See: Szczerbiak, 'Testing Party Models in East-Central Europe'.

[22] Gebethner's calculation included: the financial resources passed on directly to the parliamentary clubs and circles themselves, Sejm deputies and Senators' personal

expense allowances and the total amount allocated to parliamentary deputies to maintain their offices. Only the ryczałts (the lump-sums paid to 'professional' parliamentarians who had given up all paid employment to devote themselves to full-time parliamentary work) was excluded, since this was supposed to substitute for income foregone. Even these calculations did not include the various services-in-kind enjoyed by Polish deputies and Senators (such as free public transport by land or air and the free use of hotel accommodation in Warsaw) which it was impossible to calculate the exact value of.

[23] The income from this kind of organisational inheritance was not, however, available to SdRP that was forced to divest itself of nearly of the assets that it inherited from the PZPR.

[24] See: E. Czaczkowska, 'Partie oczekują na gest', *Rzeczpospolita*, 6 April 1992; and E. Szemplińska, 'Jałmużnicy: Z czego żyją partie', Wprost, 22 March 1992.

[25] See: *Rzeczpospolita*, 21 November 1996.

[26] Unless otherwise stated all citations are from the stenographic record of parliamentary debates on the 1997 Law.

[27] See: *Gazeta Wyborcza*, 24 February 1998.

[28] Author interview, 4 June 1997.

[29] See: *Gazeta Wyborcza*, 8 December 1999.

[30] See: *Gazeta Wyborcza*, 14 June 2000.

[31] See: *Gazeta Wyborcza*, 11 May 2000.

[32] The original proposal from the PSL (which was more confident about its ability to retain parliamentary representation) was that both regular donations and election refunds should be confined only to parliamentary parties in proportion to the number of seats won. This would, of course, have had the opposite, cartelising effect of re-inforcing the position of the strongest parties and groupings.

[33] The PSL, UD and BBWR's income included bank credits and other loans or credits of 657,300, 1,153,300 and 270,000 which obviously needed to be taken into account when considering the net profit or loss which each of these grouping's made on the election campaign after receipt of the election refund. See: Lewis and Gortat (1995: 606).

[34] Remainder of the party's 1993 election refund.

[35] 30.06% of this represents contributions from election candidates.

Seán Hanley

Are the Exceptions Really the Rule? Questioning the Application of 'Electoral-Professional' Type Models of Party Organisation in East Central Europe

ABSTRACT

Much writing on party organisational development in post-communist East Central Europe has argued that, with the partial exception of successor parties to former regime parties, political parties in the region will be state-centred, low-membership organisations dominated by political elites, which loosely approximate to the 'cartel' and 'electoral-professional' models of party identified by some scholars in Western Europe. This pattern of development in East Central Europe is seen as reflecting the specific opportunity structures of post-communist societies, which both shape politicians' organisational strategies and determine available resources for party building. Using a detailed re-examination of the Czech case, this paper questions the applicability of such models. It argues that their use is problematic not simply because of inherent difficulties of model-fitting, but because they underestimate the path-dependent character of party organisational development in the region, especially the extent to which viable parties appear to have drawn on organisational resources accumulated under the old regime and during transition. The combination of path-dependency and post-communist opportunity structures, it is argued, tends to create hybrid party organisations, which are removed from 'electoral-professional' type parties in a number of ways. The paper concludes by suggesting possible avenues for rethinking party organisational development in the region.

Introduction

While considerable scholarly attention has been devoted to emerging patterns of cleavage and inter-party competition in East Central Europe, research on parties in the region as *organisations* linking state and society has remained relatively underdeveloped. Moreover, much of the work that has been done on party organisational development in the region has focused heavily on attempts to apply models of party organisation developed in a West European context to East Central Europe. These have often proved problematic, however, especially when confronted with detailed empirical findings from the region. In this chapter I would like to address this broader debate by critically reassessing one aspect of current thinking on party formation and party organisation in post-communist East Central Europe: the expectation that the optimum, most efficient, and therefore most likely, model of party organisation will be (and is) a rough approximation to the elite-based 'electoral-professional' or 'cartel' type party said to be emerging in Western Europe. Using a detailed case study of party organisation and party development in the Czech Republic after 1989, I will argue that the difficulties in applying this model arise not only because of the inherent complexity of empirical data and the difficulty of exporting models developed for Western Europe, but also because, despite the caveats introduced by analysts, they tend to obscure the path-dependent *process* of party organisational development in the region and the resulting complexity of the organisations produced by this process.

On the basis of the Czech case, I will then suggest that the pattern of party organisation we might expect to find in East Central Europe is less a dichotomous split between small 'new' parties, roughly following the 'electoral-professional' model and a number of residual 'old', former regime parties, preserving elements of traditional 'mass' party organisation, than a series of path-dependently formed hybrids *all* of which are based on the transformation of pre-existing political organisation. By pre-existing political organisation, I suggest, we should understand not only the 'mass' legacy of former ruling and 'satellite' parties, but also the 'organisational capital' embodied in short-lived transitional mass movements and resources passed to 'historic parties' by political exiles and international actors. Such 'path-dependent' development implies that few, if any, viable real-life parties in East Central Europe will closely resemble the rational-efficient 'electoral professional' or 'cartel' type parties anticipated. I will conclude by briefly reflecting on the implications of these findings for the use of party models in the region and the ways in which post-communist party organisational development is theorised.

Towards the 'Electoral-Professional' Party in East Central Europe?

Most specialists agree that there are a number of historical, structural and conjunctural factors, which make the context of party organisational emergence in post-communist East Central Europe quite different from that in Western Europe in the late 19th and early 20th centuries. These factors include: an inherited 'anti-party' culture and a suspicion of politics and political organisation; the lack of clear (or clearly understood) social identities and socio-economic interests; the weakness of civil society and organised interest groups and, correspondingly, the relative importance of the state as a resource-base for parties; the fluid nature of post-communist electorates and tendency for electoral markets to be 'open'; the trend for parties to be founded 'internally' from above by transition-era elites, rather than 'externally 'on the basis of social movements; the growth in the reach and importance of the electronic media; and the greater need of parties to control and occupy the state, given the politically-led nature of post-communist transformation.[1]

There has also been broad consensus among scholars in deducing the *type* of party organisation that such a set of 'opportunity structures' should logically imply: small, low-membership organisations dominated by office-holders, political professionals and party elites, which neither have (nor seek) any real presence in civil society, but instead rely on the state, the media and the electoral nexus to link with voters. Kitschelt, for example, in an early and influential article, anticipated 'loose associations of professionals with little local entrenchment and no transmission belts into target constituencies'.[2] Mair, writing in the mid-1990s, spoke of 'the maintenance of' elitist party organisations, even in the medium to long term'.[3] Kopecký's more detailed study hypothesised 'formations with loose electoral constituencies, in which a relatively unimportant role is played by party membership, and the dominant role by party leaders'.[4] Similarly, Szczerbiak in his recent research on Poland postulates '[parties] characterised by a weak grounding in civil society arising from a low membership base and the low priority assigned to building up local structures and a high level of dependence on the state for financial and material resources . . . a centralised pattern of decision-making alongside a high level of autonomy given to basic and intermediary structures on local decisions'.[5]

Such expectations concerning East Central Europe have been conceptualised almost exclusively using theoretical models first developed in the literature on party organisational development in Western Europe. Indeed, many writers have structured their analyses of party development in the region largely in terms of investigating or testing the fit of such models. The literature on West European parties traces their development through a variety of organisational forms from the loose 'caucuses' of notables based on the parliamentary factions and elite social networks of a pre-democratic age; to the 'branch-mass' party or 'party of mass integration' of the late 19th and early 20th centuries; through an intermediate stage of the more loosely organised, less class-based post-1945 'catch-all party';[6] to the more streamlined 'electoral-professional party', 'cartel party' or 'business-firm'[7] models of party characterised by fluid and fragmented electorates, low memberships, elite domination, and a reliance on state resources, the electronic media and externally purchased professional expertise. It is to this final, most contemporary set of models that the type of party organisation implied by East Central European political and social conditions has usually been related. Indeed, it has even been suggested that, unencumbered by the historical, organisational and ideological baggage of long-established parties in Western democracies, East Central European parties are 'leapfrogging' West European parties in developing 'purer', more advanced 'electoral-professional' and 'cartel' party forms of organisation.[8]

At a high level of generalisation, such expectations are broadly confirmed. Leaving aside the exceptional cases of the Czech Communist Party of Bohemia and Moravia (KSĖM) and the Hungarian Christian Democrats, no truly 'mass' parties exist either in terms of size or encapsulation of distinct social constituencies.[9] Moreover, it is clear that levels of party membership, organisational density, voter-party identification and social implantation in East Central Europe are, in almost all cases, significantly inferior to those in both Western and Southern Europe.[10] Viewed in terms of internal power relationships too, in many cases, there is significant concentration and overlapping of party and state/parliamentary elites, who seem to enjoy significant autonomy.[11] Thus as in Poland, so in the region generally, it seems that parties 'exhibit more of the characteristics evident in contemporary models of party organisation - catch-all, electoral-professional and cartel - than those of the traditional mass party'.[12]

However, when empirical data on party membership and organisation in East Central European states are examined in detail a more complex picture emerges. While most 'new' parties descended from pre-1989 opposition groupings or formed after 1989 seem to conform to the 'electoral-professional' or 'cartel' model in terms of membership size and structure, former regime parties seem to retain significant aspects of traditional mass party organisation. Lewis, for example, notes 'the relative strength, organizational resilience and relatively high membership levels of former communist parties and allied organizations' as well as their good financial and material resource base.[13] Similar conclusions are reached by Kopecký in his detailed survey of party organisation in the Czech Republic, where both the Communist Party and the Christian Democratic Union-Czechoslovak People's Party, a former satellite party, stand out because of the size and density of their organisational networks and the loyalty and stability of their electorates.[14] Szczerbiak's regionally-based analysis of Polish party organisation in 1997 too reveals 'a sharp contrast between the two 'successor' parties and the three 'new' parties', with the former enjoying 'a relatively robust level of membership, organisation and material resources compared with those completely 'new' parties that have emerged since 1989'.[15]

Although analysts disagree over the scope and importance of organisational dissimilarities between 'successor' and 'new' parties,[16] on first examination the anomaly seems a relatively simple one, explicable in terms of the 'organisational inheritance' and cultural continuity from the communist regime and, in some cases, the pre-communist period.[17] Such organisational legacies, analysts suggest, might in a limited number of cases 'mask or simply work against' the general, underlying tendency for East Central European parties to evolve towards the 'electoral professional' model,[18] making successor parties 'partial exceptions' to this general tendency.[19]

However, close analysis of other aspects of party organisation, such as patterns of elite domination or professionalisation, reveals a number of further inconsistencies. Van Biezen's recent work on the internal power dynamics of parties in Hungary and the Czech Republic, for example, while highlighting the overlapping of parliamentary and party elites, suggests that party head offices, *not* parliamentary elites, are the more powerful actors.[20] Moreover, as Szczerbiak demonstrates, while Polish parties typically lack both significant mass memberships and large paid central apparatuses, there are only limited signs of the capital-intensive 'electoral-professionalisation' of party organisation and party campaigning through, for example, the buying in of media and policy expertise.[21]

Analysts engaged in such fine-grain research, have, therefore, tended to shy away from even qualified generalisations about the usefulness of models such 'electoral-professional' and 'cartel' party types in East Central Europe.[22] This uneasy relationship between detailed empirical research and existing models of party suggests that some degree of re-thinking may need to take place. In the following sections, I consider some possible lines along which such a rethinking might take place through a detailed re-examination and reinterpretation of the Czech case.

The Czech Case Revisited

As in many Central European democracies, Czech party politics has moved from a state of flux and instability following the collapse of communist rule to a semi-consolidated, programmatically-structured party system with 5-6 key actors.[23] In terms of party organisation and party-society links, the Czech case exhibits the same loosely 'electoral-professional' tendencies seen throughout the region,[24] but is unusual in that the Communist Party of Bohemia and Moravia (KSÈM) has retained a communist identity and mass organisation rather than becoming a post-communist social democratic party. In the following analysis, I therefore focus on the development of three mainstream parties, which by the late 1990s had emerged as the most powerful actors in the Czech party system, accounting for 69 percent of votes cast and 76 percent of deputies at the most recent (1998) legislative elections. These three parties are: the Czechoslovak People's Party (ÈSL),[25] a centre-right Catholic party with roots going back to the 19th century, which existed as a 'satellite' party under communist rule; the Social Democrats (ÈSSD), a 'historic' party banned under communist rule; and the powerful centre-right, Civic Democratic Party (ODS) led by Václav Klaus, a 'new' party formed in 1991. The analysis will trace the process of party formation and organisational development from 1989, paying particular attention to the 'genesis' period of the three parties in 1989-91.[26]

Detailed analysis of this period immediately raises a number of questions about accepted accounts of post-communist party development. The first point to emphasize is that the notion of 'organisational inheritances' needs extending to embrace not only 'frozen' organisational resources built up under communism and historical party traditions, but also the 'live' organisational legacies of political and social mobilisation in and around the 'transition' period in 1989-90. This can be illustrated by examining the impressive growth in 1989-90 in the memberships and organisational networks of the Czechoslovak People's Party (ÈSL), the former satellite party, and the revived 'historic' Czech Social Democratic Party (see tables 1 and 2). In the course of 1990, the Czechoslovak People's Party (ÈSL) more than doubled both its membership and the number of local branches, creating by late 1990 what can reasonably be termed a mass organisation of almost 100,000 members from a 'satellite' party membership of approximately 20,000 (see table 1).

Table 1: Organisational data on the Czechoslovak People's Party (ÈSL)
(later Christian Democratic Union - Czechoslovak People's Party
(KDU-ÈSL)) 1990-1999

Date	Direct members	No. of party basic units
1990 (1 Jan)	48,037*	1448
1990 (1 Apr)	87,237	2324
1990 (1 Sept)	96,372	no data
1990 (Dec)	95,435	2387
1991 (Feb)	95,056	2403
1991 (Aug)	94,377	2401
1992	88,737	2437
1993	100,000 (est)	no data
1995 (Nov)	80,000	no data
1999 (Feb)	60,396	no data

Note: * Later estimates imply a membership of 50,958 on 1 January 1990
Source: Internal party bulletins and Czech press

Table 2: Organisational Data on Czechoslovak Social Democracy
(later Czech Social Democratic Party) (ÈSSD) 1990-1999

Year	Direct members	No. of party basic units
1990 (Apr)	8,640 (est. 9-10,000)	est. 76
1990 (Sept)	11,823 (est. 13,000)	501 (est. 550-580)
1991 (Mar)	12,734 (est. 13,000+)	no data
1993	17,000	no data
1995 [Nov]	est. 12,500	no data
1997 [Dec]	est. 14,000	no data
1999 [Jan]	18,762	no data

Source: Internal party bulletins and Czech press (estimates from party sources)

The case of Czechoslovak Social Democracy reveals a similar pattern. ÈSSD was officially merged with the Communist Party in June 1948, but continued to exist in the West throughout communist rule as a network of political exiles. Although it had no real organisational resources in place in Czechoslovakia when the communist regime fell in November 1989, its status as a 'historic' party did give it a 'legacy' of resources to draw on. Its leaders were, for example, successful in reclaiming the party's valuable pre-1948 Prague headquarters building from the Communist Party in January 1990. They were also able to translate the exiled ÈSSD's associate membership of the Socialist International, which it had enjoyed since the 1950s, into significant donations from otherwise cautious SI parties. More significantly, however, in the first half of 1990, although it failed to create anything approaching a mass organisation, ÈSSD succeeded in creating a nationwide political organisation of 10,000-11,000 members and a professional national apparatus, numbering almost 200 staff by mid-1991. While, as with the People's Party, geographical patterns of support and breakdowns of party membership by age group and region, suggest ÈSSD was drawing on historic reservoirs of support and identification, once again these were unleashed and, to some extent augmented, by the wider political mobilisation of the transition period.[27]

A second key point that emerges in re-examining Czechoslovakia's transitional politics is that 'organisational inheritance' should be seen as a *general* phenomenon affecting most if not all viable parties that have developed in East Central Europe. While imperfectly understood, the operation of such inheritances for 'historic' and 'successor' parties like ÈSSD and ÈSL has been widely noted. However, it also seems to be the case that successful and organisationally viable 'new' parties draw on substantial organisational inheritances.

This can be seen through an analysis of origins of the most powerful and, in the long-term, only sustained 'new' Czech party: Václav Klaus's Civic Democratic Party (ODS) and its emergence from Civic Forum (OF), the broad-based social and political movement formed in November 1989, which headed both the interim administration after 1989 and the Czech and Czechoslovak governments elected in June 1990. Despite the looseness and instability of its structures, Civic Forum was a mass political organisation with hundreds of thousands of participants, which, in addition to state funding and the powers of patronage that incumbency implied, had by the end of 1990 (and probably earlier) created a nationwide network of local groups, a well-resourced headquarters and professionalised regional structures, which rivalled those of the Communist Party (KSÈM).[28] Much academic writing (and much of ODS's own rhetoric) has stressed that the party's formation represented a radical break with OF. However, while the break-up of Civic Forum may have represented an important change of *political* direction, in organisational terms ODS received a substantial organisational inheritance from the movement. This inheritance took the form of material resources, personnel, activists and organisational networks and structures[29] and was to be crucial for the viability of the newly-founded party, which did not receive state funding in its own right until after the June 1992 elections.

Table 3: Organisational Data on the Civic Democratic Party (ODS) 1991-1996

Year	Direct members	No. of party basic units
1991 (April)	est. 20,000	803
1992 (Mar)	'up to 30,000'	1000+
1993	22,000	no data
1994 (Dec)	23,489	1405
1995 (Aug)	21,365	1395
1995 (Nov)	21,803	1391
1996 (Nov)	23,434	1385

Source: Data in ODS party bulletins and estimates in Czech press.

By early 1991, riven with disagreements over issues such as economic reform, decommunisation, Czech-Slovak relations, and the future of the movement itself, Civic Forum was on the point of break-up. When plans by the Forum's right wing, led by Václav Klaus, to transform the movement into a centre-right party brought these to a head, it agreed to divide the movement and its assets into two 'successor parties': a right-of-centre party and a looser centrist grouping, Civic Movement (OH). On 23 February 1991 a special Civic Forum Assembly agreed that Civic Forum's assets at national level would be split evenly between ODS and OH, but would exclude all other political groups within the Forum. Local and district Civic Fora were to agree their own arrangements for the division of their property. Given Klaus's considerable grassroots support, most agreed that most or all of their assets would be passed to ODS. Moreover, in almost every district a majority of Civic Forum's full time professional district 'managers' (officials) - nationally approximately three quarters of the total - joined ODS, many beginning the 'pre-registration' of ODS members even before Civic Forum had formally been dissolved.[30] It is also significant that ODS membership (see Table 3), which reached 20,000 shortly after the party's foundation and remained remarkably stable thereafter, corresponds closely to the 3% of Civic Forum voters polled in November 1990, who said they would 'definitely' join Klaus's new party.[31] Contrary to suggestions that it 'developed from a parliamentary club',[32] it is therefore clear that the emergent ODS had considerable impetus at both elite (parliamentary) *and* grassroots level,[33] and derived an organisational legacy from Civic Forum without which it is unlikely that the party would have come into existence as an organisationally viable force.

The third striking point that emerges from re-examining the 'genesis' period of the three parties is that the organisational legacies built up during the transition period were, at least in part, fostered by quite explicit, if ultimately unsustainable, strategies of creating viable *mass* organisations. It is therefore not strictly accurate to assume that 'little effort is being made *or has been made* to build strong popular organizations' (my emphasis) in East Central Europe.[34] The vision of leaders of both of the Social Democrats and the People's Party, for example, in the early 1990s was that of the traditional mass-branch party based on historic identity, mass organisation and the encapsulation of distinct historic social constituencies. Czechoslovak People's Party (ÈSL) Chairman, Josef Bartonèík, for example, stated in January 1990 that he aimed 'to build an influential and fairly large party surrounded by a widely developed spectrum of loosely affiliated structures and the widest possible circle of sympathisers . . .'[35] In his view, the party would represent a distinct constituency of Christian voters and defend the interests of the Catholic Church. Similarly, Social Democrat leaders envisaged their party as 'a traditional workers' party' representing 'popular strata'[36] and planned their party's organisation and apparatus accordingly 'with its own night schools, travel agency and publishing house' as well as women's and youth organisations and sections for work in trade unions, supposedly following the blueprint of the Austrian SPO.[37] Civic Forum too, despite its loose 'movement' style of organisation and eschewal of hierarchy, and other trappings of 'party', clearly had an 'external' organisational strategy intended to promote *mass* citizen participation. In this regard, the Forum's (in)famous 1990 slogan that 'parties are for party hacks, Civic Forum is for everyone' was not merely an artefact of dissident 'anti-political' thinking, but also an aspiration to create a mass grassroots movement. Indeed, what is striking in this period is that, although the concept of the electoral-professional framework party - usually referred to in Czech as the 'electoral party' (*volební strana*) - was widely discussed in Czechoslovakia from at least late 1990, it was, with one exception, *not* consciously adopted by any important party. Moreover, the leaders of the Civic Democratic Alliance (ODA), the one party which did consciously seek to be a small, low membership formation based on parliamentary elites, did so *not* from considerations of 'electoral-professional' organisational rationality, but because of Burkean notions of representation, reflecting a neo-conservative ideology developed by its intellectual founders before 1989.

The organisational strategies of all three Czech would-be mass organisations of the early 1990s quickly floundered. The two historic parties' early strategies, while partially successful in recreating elements of the mass party organisation, proved wholly unrealistic and unsuccessful as a means of capturing significant loyal electorates[38] and even less successful in gaining social implantation. The People's Party, for example, despite its mass membership and socially and geographically concentrated bases of support, failed to create affiliated organisations with memberships of more than a few thousand. Civic Forum, by contrast, while highly successful both electorally and as a vehicle for mass participation, saw its founders' 'mass' organisational strategy crumble in 1990 because of a lack of traditional party-mindedness on the part of its ex-dissident leaders and a failure to appreciate the need for party discipline, structures of internal democratic accountability and paid officials, sufficiently quickly or clearly.[39] All such failed 'mass organisations', however, handed on organisational legacies, which were to enable and constrain the subsequent development of the three parties discussed.

Party Organisational Development and Path-Dependency

The 'locking in' of aspects of initial organisation to a party's later organisational development is something which has been widely noted in relation to the historical formation of West European parties. It is implicit, for example, in Lipset and Rokkan's thesis about the 'freezing' of West European party systems or in Panebianco's account of party institutionalisation.[40] More recently a number of US scholars, drawing on the burgeoning 'new institutionalist' literature, have attempted to theorise party organisational development in terms of 'path dependency'.[41] The literature on post-communist East and Central Europe has seen widespread discussion of 'legacies', usually seen in terms of socio-cultural factors or regime types.[42] Such structural notions of legacies have also been applied to party system formation in the region.[43] However, despite a number of attempts to trace stages of party system evolution in post-communist Europe, analysis of the path-dependent development of party organisation across these 'stages' has remained largely descriptive and *ad hoc*.[44] Moreover, as analysis of the Czech case suggests, the nature and influence of the legacies left by early transitional organisational strategies has been overlooked, even among authors who attempt to relate the concept of 'path-dependency' to East European party organisation.[45] Such analyses, however, overlook the fact that path-dependent development is determined not only by external constraints, such as institutions, social structures or communications technologies but also by the pre-existing distribution of organisational resources. As Stark famously observed, this implies that political actors in East Central Europe are:

> rebuilding organizations and institutions not *on the ruins* but *with the ruins* as they redeploy available resources in response to their immediate practical dilemmas . . . it is through adjusting to new uncertainties that new organizational forms emerge.[46]

The existence of significant 'inheritances' in the organisational 'ruins' of the transition period, however, is of more than purely historical importance. It has important implications for type of party organisation we should anticipate in contemporary East Central Europe. The key implication is, perhaps, that *most viable parties develop on the basis of previously existing organisations, which have already choked off genuinely new parties, by effectively monopolising most organisational 'start-up capital'*. Pure 'electoral professional' parties of the type frequently inferred and anticipated for the region were, therefore, always unlikely to develop. What we should, in fact, anticipate, in East Central Europe is the emergence of parties which are *organisational hybrids*, combining substantial elements of the organisations they evolved from and substantial elements of the 'electoral-professional' model, which post-communist social and political conditions taken in isolation imply as the optimal rational-efficient form for inter-party competition. 'Partial exceptions' to the 'electoral-professional' type party may therefore be the rule. I will now consider, how such hybrid organizational forms emerged in the Czech Republic in the 1990s.

Party Evolution in Czech Republic: The Transformation of Failed 'Mass' Organisation

All three Czech parties under consideration became stable and successful actors in the mid-late 1990s after partial and limited development along broadly 'electoral-professional' lines. In all cases the party organisations that emerged were characterised by tensions between an 'electoral-professional' rationality introduced by post-transitional leaderships and the legacies left by the would-be mass party organisations which were (re)founded immediately after the collapse of communism.

In November 1990, the Czechoslovak People's Party (ÈSL) elected Josef Lux as its new leader in place of Josef Bartonèík marking an important change in the party's organisational and political strategy. Rather than be an advocate for a Christian constituency, Lux wanted ÈSL to be 'a conservative, popular. . . . genuinely right-wing party close to the centre' which would 'defend and embody the interests and needs of ordinary people'.[47] While Bartonèík had assumed that the party could attract a large bloc of Christian-oriented voters relatively easily, Lux was aware that, beyond its limited traditional support bases, the party had little obvious appeal in a largely secular society, historically lukewarm towards Catholicism. This implied that to attract a sizeable electorate the party had to appeal to voters in programmatic terms, rather than relying on the automatic and organised support of a loyal traditional constituency. This shift was visible in the greater weight the party gave to centralised policy formation, as well as its adoption of a more explicit ideology (right-wing and conservative after 1990, centrist and social market after 1994). As part of broader policy objectives such as the creation of a civil society and the maintenance of 'social peace', however, the party also sought to advocate the interests of certain groups - families with children, pensioners and disabled people[48] and, Lux later suggested, like the German CDU, the embryonic, Czech middle classes.[49] Under Lux, ÈSL also abandoned the idea of building up mass auxiliary organisations, a change in priorities visible in the party's decline in membership from the heights of the 90-100,00 recruited in 1990. By contrast, from 1996 the party moved towards centrally-run media-based campaigning centring around the personality of its leader, projecting the party as a 'tranquil force' in Czech politics. Despite enjoying much more limited electoral success compared to the Social Democrats and ODS, KDU-ÈSL did nevertheless succeed in moving beyond its largely elderly rural Catholic 'historic' constituency[50] and establishing itself as the organisational and political core of the centre-right Four Party Coalition grouping that emerged in the late 1990s after Lux's death.[51]

In 1993 Czech Social Democrats also elected a new leader, former Civic Forum MP Miloš Zeman. Zeman sought to accelerate the transformation of ÈSSD's from a political sect with significant organisational assets but little electoral support into '... a model of a broad pluralistic party, a party which is left-wing, but which reaches into the political centre...'[52] capable of capturing around 30 per cent of the vote. This was to be achieved by offering an alternative vision of social transformation with broad appeal, rather than projecting a historic party identity, which excluded many potential supporters (such as, for example, former communists). In November 1996 Zeman even stated that this implied that 'because of our, to a certain extent, centrist position *(støedovou pozicí)*, we are what is termed in English a 'catch all party',... a party that very broad strata of people can vote for'.[53] As in the case of the People's Party, ÈSSD began to re-conceive its constituency less in terms of an established, pre-existing working class with a natural loyalty to Social Democracy and more in terms of the *prospective* or emerging interests of likely 'losers' in transformation as carried out by the Right. From the mid-1990s ÈSSD programmes therefore increasingly stressed the idea of defending the life chances of working people and vulnerable groups *as individuals* rather than as distinct social groups. Rather than justifying its advocacy of particular interests on the grounds of history or tradition, these programmes related them to policies seen as beneficial to society as a whole or necessary to transformation.[54] As far as party-society links were concerned, while ÈSSD did seek to establish contacts with pensioners', tenants' and consumers' groups, under Zeman these were seen more as a source of potential new party members, than a means of establishing mass social presence or a base in civil society.[55] In organisational terms, Zeman abandoned the 'Austrian' model, calling merely for the extension of ÈSSD organisation at local level and an increase of the party's membership from 10,000-15,000 to 40,000.[56] However, the organisational and political model adopted under Zeman stabilised the party and brought previously unattainable electoral success, with ÈSSD emerging as the main opposition party in 1996 with 26% of the vote (compared with 4% in 1990 and 7% in 1992) and becoming the largest Czech party in 1998 with 32%.

If the transformation of the two 'historic' parties along more 'electoral-professional' lines, implied *broadening* their electoral appeal beyond limited constituencies and assigning a lower priority to 'party building', in the case of ODS, emergence from Civic Forum implied a transformation to create *narrower* but clearer organisational and ideological boundaries. ODS leaders sought to create a smaller, more disciplined formation with a greater degree of centralised control and a distinct (anti-communist, neo-liberal) ideology, which would contrast markedly with the all-embracing mass movement-party that Civic Forum had (briefly) been. ODS leaders' vision was of programmatically-oriented, office-seeking party with an electorally mediated relationship to individuals and groups in society, rather than Civic Forum's 'corporatist' vision of substituting for an absent civil society. They therefore hoped to create a party whose estimated membership would be in the range of 20-60,000, not a 'mass Leninist party' or a 'boundless' mass movement.[57] In contrast to ÈSSD and ÈSL, for whom a paid party apparatus was self-evident, political professionalism in the form of a powerful Head Office and network of regional 'managers' was also central to ODS's internal structure and ethos.[58]

In the 1990s, therefore, all three parties began to approximate to a greater degree 'electoral-professional' and 'cartel' type models as a result of internal transformations and reforms. Indeed, the tendency has been towards a scaling back of even the modest organisational goals initially set by the new wave of party transformers. Thus, although ÈSSD membership, for example, increased slightly in the late 1990s, when the party first gained government office, memberships have remained low - below even limited goals set by party leaderships - and seem to have been largely static and, in the case of ODS stagnant, since the early 1990s with significant local activism confined to small groups within these memberships.[59] Despite ritual appeals to increase party membership, it is also clear that, once incumbent, Czech party leaders gave a low priority to building or maintaining the party organisation. Indeed, Václav Klaus's lack of interest in his party work and party fund-raising after 1992 led some to remark that he would happily have dissolved ODS and re-founded it three months before the next election.[60] Such membership levels have, in conformity with the 'cartel' and 'electoral professional' typologies, left all three parties heavily dependent on the state for resources.[61] Indeed, as early as 1991 even ÈSL's relatively large membership was insufficient to finance even the party's district apparatuses. Moreover, as internal party critics in both ODS and ÈSSD have noted, on entering government in 1992 and 1998 policy formation in both parties was effectively transferred from the party to government, depriving both party members and party managers of any real influence.[62] In both parties the overlapping of party, parliamentary and government elites has bolstered the autonomy of such elites,[63] reflecting a 'stratarchic relationship'[64] between elite and grassroots, with ordinary members largely absorbed in local parish pump politics and ignorant of, or uninterested in, national politics.[65] Moreover, since the mid-1990s, tacit agreements between ODS and ÈSSD to tolerate each other's minority administrations have increasingly led the two to act in a cartel-like fashion in 'colonising' public bodies and corporations, dividing senior posts between supporters of the two parties.

However, despite such 'electoral professional' tendencies, *the three party organisations that have developed nevertheless embody significant legacies from the unsuccessful organisational strategies of the post-transition period that give them a 'hybrid' quality*. This can be seen in a number of ways. Firstly, however insubstantial they may appear by West European standards, the structures and organisational networks of the three parties extend considerably beyond what they require for national electoral competition or elite recruitment. Indeed, the effective redundancy of local and regional structures is arguably at the root of the 'stratarchic' tendencies and elite-grassroots tensions visible in all three parties. In the case of ODS, in particular, 'stratarchic' tendencies appear less a facet of the 'electoral professional' model *per se*, than a direct legacy from Civic Forum, whose regional and intermediary structures were notoriously weak.

Secondly, however removed from the day-to-day or month-to-month exercise of power, such path-dependently inherited structures and/or grassroots memberships are far from merely passive appendages to powerful central leaderships. In 1997 Václav Klaus was moved to complain of '... insufficient understanding of internal loyalty in ODS, clearly motivated by fear of some kind of *diktat* from the political leadership', criticising local and regional ODS organisations which 'oscillate between passivity and a tendency towards oversimplified and somewhat radical views'. In October 1997, Miloš Zeman too complained that the Social Democratic Party's fractious regional organisations were constantly challenging the party leadership rather than recruiting new members.[66] In ODS, as in Civic Forum, district managers are paid employees of party headquarters who rival and overlap elected district and regional leadership bodies, making the party's regional organisations a complex and powerful cockpit of contending interests.

Moreover, particularly at moments of party crisis, such regional and grassroots structures can exert a decisive influence on parties' internal dynamics. In ODS on several occasions in the 1990s, grassroots delegates have used Congresses to veto Klaus's proposals (over, for example, his choice of candidate Deputy Chairs). However, in 1997-8, in the wake of an explosive party financing scandal, when he found himself politically isolated within the ODS leadership, Klaus was able to mobilise grassroots majority support to defeat his political opponents using the party's limited, but functional, democratic mechanisms at a special party Congress. ÈSSD regional organisations are also a key resource for those seeking to build or challenge the 'dominant coalition' within the party. The party's Central Bohemian organisation, for example, has proved an important base for a faction challenging the leadership of Miloš Zeman, whose leaders would otherwise be dependent on his prime ministerial *largesse*.

Moreover, the dynamics of candidate-selection in the Czech Republic, often taken as an approximate gauge of power relations within parties, are also highly revealing. As detailed analysis of Czech parties' nomination procedures for parliamentary candidates for the 1996 and 1998 legislative elections shows, in all three parties regional and district party organisations played the key role in candidate-selection.[67] Although the dominant actors were usually regional and district executives, in some cases, as in some regions in the Social Democratic Party in 1996, there was direct balloting of grassroots members. Correspondingly, there was only a *limited* degree of intervention in the process by national leaderships, even where, as in the case of ODS, they had wide formal powers to do so.[68] Although the regional constituencies and list-based PR used in Czech legislative elections may partly explain the relative strength of regional organisations in candidate-selection, it is clear that the internal dynamics of the parties surveyed contrast markedly with those of a purer 'electoral professional' or 'business firm' party such as Italy's *Forza Italia*, where the 'grassroots' can be effectively and continually bypassed by party elites.[69]

Overall, therefore, it can be seen that from the early 1990s onwards there has been a tendency for major Czech parties to *converge* around a number of features, which amount to an organisational form at one step removed from the electoral-professional type patterns usually deduced from the political opportunity structures of post-communist East Central Europe or accepted, with certain qualifications, by default, as the result of a model-fitting exercise. These features can be summarised as: (1) a medium-large national organisation with a limited but effective local presence run by a professional bureaucracy at central and regional level, originating in failed 'mass' transitional strategies and elements of mass organisation existing under the communist regime; (2) internal dynamics characterised by elite domination, to some extent countered by 'redundant' regional and local structures; (3) a political appeal based on a detailed programme relating to post-communist socio-economic transformation; and (4) a broad (but limited) electoral base of support defined in terms of social groups created by transformation amounting to no more than 30% of the electorate.

Conclusions

This chapter has argued, on the basis of the Czech case, that the expectation that parties in East Central Europe can best be understood essentially as rough approximations to models such as the 'electoral-professional' or 'cartel' party needs to be reassessed and reconceptualised. It has suggested, in the light of evidence about the *processes* of party formation and the detailed organisational characteristics of the resultant parties, that organisationally and electorally viable formations, which draw on and adapt previous organisational forms to create 'hybrid' organisations may be less the exception than the rule in post-communist East Central Europe. A renewed focus on the path-dependent evolution of party organisation in the region may, therefore, yield fresh insights.

The research presented here also contains a number of implications for the comparative study of party organisation in the region. Firstly, it should be noted that the nature and tempo of transitional mobilisation and its significance for subsequent party organisational development will vary between states. Thus, for example, in contrast to the Czech case where transitional mobilisation took the form of an intense burst of mass civic activism in and around the final collapse of the regime in 1989-90, in a country like Poland social mobilisation was characteristic of the *whole* of the late communist period and was historically waning at the time of Polish transition in mid-late 1989.[70]

Secondly, the analysis presented here can be seen as feeding into a broader stream of criticism of 'cartel' type models which sees them as misstating and oversimplifying the relationship between state and civil society, and as overstating the insulation of party elites from societal, grassroots and competitive pressures.[71] In this connection, the Czech case suggests that, even in Eastern Europe, the formation of party organisation is less easily accomplished through purely elite action than is often assumed, and that, as in Western Europe, the autonomy of party elites from grassroots pressures, however inconsistently exerted, should not be overestimated. However, the conclusion of this chapter in this regard is less that 'cartel', 'electoral professional' and 'business firm' models of party lack value as heuristic devices or ideal types in conceptualising recent *trends* in East Central European party organisational development than that their centrality to the debate about the type of party emerging in the region has muddied the waters by obscuring the *overall* process of party formation in the region since 1989 and diverting scholarly attention from systematic consideration of the complex organisational forms repeatedly highlighted by empirical findings.

Future research should perhaps therefore be directed away from snapshot studies which adopt a model-fitting approach towards more longitudinal analysis of ongoing *processes* of party formation and development taking place through the path-dependent interaction of a varied succession of 'models' and organisational strategies. This might be attempted either through theorising from first principles, in the manner of for example 'new institutionalist' writers such as Aldrich,[72] or through the creative reinterpretation and reapplication of existing literatures. Otto Kirchheimer's seminal essay on the 'catch-all' party, for example, might merit re-reading less for its anticipation of 'electoral-professional' and 'cartel' trends than for intuitively capturing the path-dependent character of parties' organisational development and the hybrid forms this tends to produce. There seem to be clear parallels between the post-war transformation of traditional Western mass parties into 'catch-all' formations and the way parties in post-communist East Central Europe have been built up path-dependently 'with the ruins' of defunct organisations and subsequently adapted imperfectly and partially to the imperatives of open electorates, technological change and the absence of a well-defined class structure.[73] The broader implication is perhaps that the formation or re-formation of viable party organisation during *any* period of regime change will occur path-dependently, producing organisations that are from the very outset elegant hybrids rather than organisational types that can be esentially summed up using a single, logically consistent ideal type.[74]

The third main implication of this chapter is that the assumptions concerning electoral and organisational rationality embodied in 'cartel' and 'electoral-professional' type party models as applied to East Central Europe may be in need of more sophisticated analysis. In contradiction to the implicit assumptions of much writing on the subject, for example, it appears that parties' and party leaders' organisational strategies in East Central Europe have, very often, *not* been guided by a rational calculus realistically matching organisational costs, benefits and resources to electoral ends within a relatively fixed and known set of opportunity structures. As the Czech case suggests, the early transition period at the very least was characterised by misperceptions stemming both from the uncertainty of the situation and normative desires to (re)institutionalise historic parties' or civic oppositions' organisational principles.[75] Moreover, subsequent organisational strategies were *strategies of transformation* re-combining and reshaping pre-existing organisational resources, which required a complex political crafting not reducible to a single formula. The effectiveness of such crafting will clearly therefore vary unpredictably from case to case. Polish political elites, for example, in contrast to the political acumen of Václav Klaus, appear to have allowed the grassroots organisational potential of the Solidarity Citizens' Committees movement, Civic Forum's Polish equivalent, to dissipate when it started to fragment in the early post-transition period in 1990-1.[76]

The apparently hybrid nature of successful parties also raises questions concerning the time-horizons over which the rationality of party organisation should be judged. Hopkin and Paolucci have recently suggested that strongly 'electoral-professional' and 'business firm' type parties achieve only *short-term* electoral and organisational efficiency and that they do so at the expense of the *longer-term* organisational stability that elements of more traditional party organisation bring.[77] This may imply that such path-dependent 'hybrid' creations of the type identified by reanalysis of the Czech case might be less a 'sub-optimal' deviation from a rational-efficient ideal than an organisational form efficiently reconciling a variety of demands well adapted to survival over the medium-long term.

Notes

1. H. Kitschelt, 'The Formation of Party Systems in East-Central Europe', *Politics and Society,* 20(1), (1992), pp. 7-50; P. Kopecký, 'Developing Party Organizations in East-Central Europe: What Type of Party is Likely to Emerge', *Party Politics,* 1(4) 1995, pp. 515-34; P.G. Lewis, 'Political Institutionalisation and Party Development in Post-Communist Poland', *Europe-Asia Studies,* 46(5) 1994, pp. 779-800; P.G. Lewis and R. Gortat, 'Models of party development and questions of state dependence in Poland', *Party Politics,* 1(4) 1995, pp. 599-608; D. Perkins, 'Structure and Choice: The Role of Organizations, Patronage and the Media in Party Formation', *Party Politics,* 2 1996, pp. 355-375; P. Mair, *What is Different about Post-Communist Party Systems?,* (Glasgow: University of Strathclyde, 1996); A. Szczerbiak, 'Party Structure and Organisation in Post-Communist Poland', paper presented at the PSA 50th Annual Conference 10-13 April 2000, LSE, London; I. van Biezen, 'On the Internal Balance of Party Power: Party Organizations in New Democracies', *Party Politics,* 6(4) 2000, pp. 395-417.
2. Kitschelt, 'The Formation of Party Systems', p. 42.
3. Mair, *What is different*, pp. 12 and 13.
4. Kopecký, 'Developing Party Organizations', p. 517.
5. A. Szczerbiak, 'Testing Party Models in East-Central Europe: Local Party Organization in Postcommunist Poland', *Party Politics,* 5(4) 1999, pp. 525-37, citation p. 526.
6. For an overview see Mair (ed.), *The West European Party System* (Oxford University Press: Oxford: 1990).
7. A. Panebianco, *Political Parties: Organisation and Power*, (Cambridge: CUP, 1988). R. Katz and P. Mair, 'Changing Models of Party Organization and Party Democracy: The Emergence of the Cartel Party', *Party Politics,* 1(1) 1995, pp. 5-28. J. Hopkin and C. Paolucci, 'The business firm model of party organisation: Cases from Spain and Italy', *European Journal of Political Research,* 35 1999, pp. 307-39.
8. Perkins, 'Structure and Choice'; D. Olson, 'Party Formation and Party System Consolidation in New Democracies in Central Europe', *Political Studies,* 46(3) 1998, pp. 432-65.
9. See Z. Enyedi, 'Organizing A Subcultural Party in Eastern Europe: The Case of the Hungarian Christian Democrats', *Party Politics,* 2(3) 1996, pp. 397-96 and S. Hanley, 'Towards Breakthrough or Breakdown? The Consolidation of KSÈM as a Neo-Communist Successor Party in the Czech Republic', *Journal of Communist Studies and Transition Politics,* 17(3) 2001, pp. 96-116.
10. Kopecký, 'Developing Party Organizations', p. 524; Mair, *What is different*, p. 14.
11. Kopecký, 'Developing Party Organizations'; Szczerbiak, 'Party Structure and Organisation'; van Biezen, 'On the Internal Balance'.
12. Szczerbiak, 'Testing Party Models', p. 535.

[13] P.G. Lewis, 'Introduction and Theoretical Framework' in P.G. Lewis (ed.), *Party Structure and Organization in East-Central Europe* (Aldershot: Edward Elgar, 1996), pp. 1-17, citation p. 16.
[14] Kopecký, 'Developing Party Organizations'.
[15] Szczerbiak, 'Testing Party Models', p. 527 and p. 526 respectively.
[16] Kopecký's analysis of the Czech case identifies them as significant, while Szczerbiak (2000: 31; see also 12-13) sees differences in resources and membership as overridden by factors such as parties' participation in electoral or parliamentary blocs. 'Developing Party Organizations', p. 528 and 'Party Structure and Organisation', pp. 12-13 respectively.
[17] M. Waller, 'Party Inheritances and Party Identities' in G. Pridham and P.G. Lewis (eds), *Stabilising Fragile Democracies: Comparing New Party Systems in Southern and Eastern Europe*, (London/New York: Routledge, 1996), pp. 23-43.
[18] Kopecký, 'Developing Party Organizations', p. 532.
[19] Szczerbiak, 'Testing Party Models', p. 535.
[20] Van Biezen, 'On the Internal Balance'.
[21] A. Szczerbiak, 'The Professionalisation of Party Campaigns in Post-Communist Poland' in P.G. Lewis (ed.), *Party Development and Democratic Change in Eastern Europe*, (Frank Cass: London and Portland, OR, 2001), pp. 78-92.
[22] Kopecký concludes that the six Czech parties he examines 'do not display characteristics which would point to a distinctive model of party organisation'. 'Developing Party Organizations', p. 529. Szczerbiak introduces 'caveats and qualifications' relating to, for example, absence of cartel type behaviour among political elites and weakly established notions of 'party'. 'Party Structure and Organisation', pp. 31-4. Van Biezen notes the 'limited values of established models of party formation and organization'. 'On the Internal Balance', p. 410.
[23] H. Kitschelt et al., *Post-Communist Party Systems: Competition, Representation and Inter-Party Collaboration*, (Cambridge: CUP, 1999).
[24] Kopecký, 'Developing Party Organizations'; A. Kroupa and T. Kostelecký, 'Party Structure and Organization in the Czech Republic' in P.G. Lewis (ed.), *Party Structure and Organization in East-Central Europe*, (Aldershot: Edward Elgar, 1996), pp. 89-115.
[25] Later re-named the Christian Democratic Union-Czechoslovak People's Party (KDU-ÈSL).
[26] This concept is developed by Panebianco in, *Political Parties: Organisation and Power*.
[27] S. Hanley, 'Normative Concepts of Party in Post-Communist Party System Formation: the Czech Case 1990-1998', (unpublished PhD thesis, University of Birmingham, 2000), pp. 308-10.
[28] M. Hadjiisky, *La fin du Forum civique et la naissance du Parti democratique civique*

(janvier 1990-avril 1991), (Prague: Documents du travail du CEFRES no. 6, 1996); Kroupa and Kostelecký, 'Party Structure'; Hanley, 'Normative Concepts'.

The exact extent of organisation is unclear, as the movement had no formal membership or centralised records. In a poll in May 1990 8.86% of Czech respondents claimed to be 'members' of Civic Forum, implying a 'membership' of 650,000. See M. Boguszak, I. Gabal and V. Rak, *CSFR 90: Pre-Election Study*, (Berlin: Wissenschaftszentrum Berlin fur Sozialforschung, Maschninenlesbares Codebuch Nr. 2560, 1996).

[29] Another important political 'inheritance' was arguably political prominence its leader Klaus had acquired as Finance Minister in the Civic Forum-led government.

[30] Hanley, 'Normative Concepts', pp. 188-214 and 347-8.

[31] 'Of politickou stranou?', *Svobodné slovo*, 27 November 1990.

[32] Kopecký, 'Developing Party Organizations', p. 529.

[33] See Hadjiisky, *La fin du Forum civique*; Hanley, 'Normative Concepts'.

[34] Mair, *What is different*, p. 13.

[35] 'Nástup ÈSL do volební kampaní', *Lidová demokracie*, 19 January 1990, p. 2.

[36] ÈSSD, Program Èeskoslovenské sociální demokracie, (Prague: ČSSD, 1990).

[37] U. Lindstrom, 'East European Social Democracy: Born to be Rejected' in L. Karvonen and J. Sundberg (eds), *Social Democracy in Transition: Northern, Southern and Eastern Europe* (Aldershot: Edward Elgar, 1991), p. 248.

[38] In the June 1990 elections the Social Democrats polled 4% and failed to enter the Czechoslovak or Czech parliaments. The People's Party gained only 8%.

[39] Hadjiisky, *La fin du Forum civique*; Hanley, 'Normative Concepts'.

[40] S.M. Lipset and S. Rokkan, 'Cleavage Structure, Party Systems And Voter Alignments: An Introduction' in *Party Systems And Voter Alignments: Cross National Perspectives* (New York: Free Press, 1967), pp. 1-64; Panebianco, *Political Parties: Organisation and Power*.

[41] J. Aldrich, *Why Parties? The Origin and Transformation of Political Parties in America* (Chicago: University of Chicago Press, 1995); S. Kalyvas, *The Rise of Christian Democracy*, (Cornell University Press, Ithaca and London, 1996); Perkins, 'Structure and Choice'.

[42] See, for example, S. Hanson, 'The Leninist legacy and institutional change', *Comparative Political Studies*, 28(2) 1995, pp. 306-14 or G. Schopflin, 'An Analysis of Post-Communism' in *Nations, Identity, Power* (London: Hurst, 2000), pp. 170-88.

[43] See M. Cotta, 'Building party systems after the dictatorship: the East European cases in comparative perspective' in G. Pridham and T. Vanhanen (eds), *Democratisation in Eastern Europe: Domestic and International Perspectives*, (London and New York: Routledge, 1994), pp. 99-128 and Kitschelt et al., *Party Systems*.

[44] M. Marody, 'Three Stages of Party System Emergence in Poland', *Communist and Post-Communist Studies*, 28(2) 1995, pp. 263-70; J. Bielasiak, 'Substance and Process in the Development of Party Systems in East Central Europe', *Communist and Post-Communist Studies*, 30(1) 1997, pp. 23-44.

[45] Perkins, for example, merely concludes that parties in the region are 'essentially leapfrogging their Western counterparts' in becoming media-based cadre parties. 'Structure and Choice', p. 369.

[46] D. Stark, 'Path Dependence and Privatization in East Central Europe', *East European Politics and Societies*, 6(1) 1992, pp. 17-54, citation pp. 20-1.

[47] J. Lux, 'Kvalitnì, konstruktivnì a kvalifikovanì', *Lidová demokracie*, 15 October 1990, p. 1.

[48] KDU-ÈSL, Volební program 1996, (Prague: KDU-ÈSL, 1996) and Prùvodce politikou KDU-ÈSL - Podrobný volební program 1998, (Prague: KDU-ČSL, 1998).

[49] J. Lux, 'Volièi se vidí správnì', *Lidové noviny*, 10 May 1995.

[50] By the end of 1997 45 per cent of its voters were under 45. See remarks by head of the STEM polling organisation Jan Hartl in 'Je to tøetí síla?', *Týden*, no. 49, 1998.

[51] Lux resigned as party leader and left politics in 1998 after being diagnosed with leukaemia. He died in 1999.

[52] Press conference of 29 June 1993. 'Parlamentní informaèní servis', *Zpravodaj*, no. 7, 1993 [ÈSSD Archive, Fond 44 sl 42].

[53] M. Zeman, 'Zeman chce vyhrát v boji o Senát a pak ho možná zrušit', *Mladá fronta Dnes*, 12 November 1996, p. 4.

[54] ÈSSD, Východiska volebního programu Èeské strany sociálnì demokratické, (Prague: ÈSSD, 1995); Lidkost proti sobectví, (Prague: ÈSSD, 1996) and Alternativa pro naši zemi, (www.cssd.cz.: ČSSD, 1997).

[55] 'Zeman potøebuje desetitisíce nových straníkù', *Mladá fronta Dnes*, 11 October 1997, p. 2.

[56] See the appeal by Jana Volfová, 'Výzva k zakládaní místních organiací', *Zpravodaj*, 1, 1993, p. 3 [ÈSSD Archive, Fond 44 sl 38.].

[57] V. Klaus, 'Projev na pracovním setkání Obèanských fór v Olomouci dne 8.12.90' [Speech to Working Meeting of Civic Fora in Olomouc on 8.12.90] in V. Klaus, O tváø zítøka (rok devádesátý), (Prague: Pražská imaginace, 1991).

[58] Hadjiisky, *La fin du Forum civique*; Hanley, 'Normative Concepts'.

[59] Indeed, in 1996 ODS officials have publicly noted that most party members do no more than pay dues and that most local party work was carried out by a handful of activists, holding multiple offices. See L. Novák, 'Odcházím s pocitem, že jsem se vždy o slušné øešení alespoò pokusil', *Bulletin ODS*, 18/1996, p. 9.

[60] B. Peèinka, 'Klausova strana a frakce', *Lidové noviny*, 19 May 1997, p. 8.

[61] Van Biezen, 'On the Internal Balance'.

[62] On ODS see J. Zieleniec, 'Projev místopøedsedy Josefa Zieleniece na Kongresu ODS v Brnì 7.12.1996', *Bulletin ODS*, 18/1996, pp. 23-4; on ÈSSD see S. Kotrba, 'As They Sow, So Have They Reaped - The Czech Social Democrats in Power', Electronically published by *Central Europe Review* (www.ce-review.org), 2001.

[63] Until 1996, many party leaders and government office-holders were not deputies in the Czech parliament or deputies in the Czechoslovak Federal Assembly which ceased to exist in 1992 after the division of Czechoslovakia.

[64] Kopecký, 'Developing Party Organizations', p. 526.

[65] 'Klaus vytýká ODS stejné problémy jaké vidí Zeman v sociální demokracii', *Mladá fronta Dnes*, 3 November 1997, p. 2.

[66] 'Klaus vytýká ODS . . .', *Mladá fronta Dnes*, 3 November 1997.

[67] S. Saxonberg, 'Gender and Parliamentary Representation in the Czech Republic', chapter in S. Saxonberg, *Czech Politics in a New Millenium: Politics, Parties and Gender*, (Boulder, CO: East European Monographs, forthcoming).

[68] In only one case, that of KDU-ÈSL in 1996, did the national leadership play a dominant role in candidate-selection and, even here, a procedure based on regional ballots of members was introduced for 1998.

[69] See Hopkin and Paolucci, 'The business firm model'.

[70] Moreover, Polish popular mobilisation took predominantly 'industrial' and 'social' forms with purely civic movements playing a relatively secondary role. G. Ekiert and J. Kubik, *Rebellious Civil Society: Popular Protest and Democratic Consolidation in Post-Communist Poland 1989-1993*, (University of Michigan Press: Ann Arbor, 1999).

[71] See R. Koole, 'Cadre, Catch-All or Cadre? A Comment on the Notion of the Cartel Party', *Party Politics*, 2(4) 1996, pp. 525-534 and H. Kitschelt, 'Citizens, Politicians and Party Cartellization: Political Representation and State Failure in Post-Industrial Democracies', *European Journal of Political Research*, 37, 2000, pp. 149-179.

[72] Aldrich, *Why Parties?*

[73] Given the weaker institutionalisation of earlier organisational forms in East Central Europe, however, it may be that the erosion of organisational legacies by pressures towards 'electoral professionalisation' will be more pronounced and rapid than in post-war Western Europe.

[74] This is, for example, suggested by the conclusions reached by Kalyvas in relation to the emergence of Christian Social parties in the late 19th century. Kalyvas, *The Rise of Christian Democracy*.

[75] Such normative and cultural factors seem in need of more explicit and more general incorporation into discussions of party organisational development. While parties increasingly organised according to 'electoral-professional', 'cartel' or 'business firm' logics of organisation might be more rational-efficient engines for electoral competition, party-voter linkage, and even governance, this case study suggests

that even in a region with strong anti-party traditions, such streamlined elite creations may lack the deeper cultural and historical legitimacy still accruing to mass organisational forms.

[76] T. Grabowski, 'The Party That Never Was: The Rise and Fall of the Solidarity Citizens' Committees in Poland, *East European Politics and Societies*, 10(2) Spring, 1996, pp. 214-245. In this light, the organisational weaknesses of the numerous ex-Solidarity parties in Poland may appear less a rational-efficient response to poorly defined social interests and a weak civil society, than a negative confirmation of the importance of both path-dependently supplied organisational resources and effective political crafting in recuperating them for party building.

[77] Hopkin and Paolucci, 'The business firm model'.

Nick Sitter
Cleavages, Party Strategy and Party System Change in Europe, East and West

ABSTRACT

This chapter analyses the development of competitive party politics in post-communist East Central Europe from a comparative perspective. The central concerns are party system stabilisation and change in Hungary, Poland, the Czech Republic and Slovakia, and implications for comparative theory. Starting from Lipset and Rokkan's 'cleavage model', the chapter assesses the relevance of their key variables for party politics in the 1990s. Although there are considerable similarities (particularly in terms of choice of electoral systems), the cleavages, relationships between voters and parties, and the very nature of parties all differ considerably from the early Twentieth Century West European cases. Party strategy emerges as the key variable in explaining patterns of party system stability and change. Variations result from: (i) the prevalence of catch-all type strategies; (ii) interest representation strategies; and (iii) the presence of parties that have staked out positions on the flanks of the system. The conclusions concerning the central role of party strategy are not confined to East Central Europe, but are also pertinent to the study of party system change in Western Europe.

Introduction

More than a decade after the collapse of communism in East Central Europe the question of party system consolidation and stability remains somewhat contentious. It is sometimes argued that these systems are more unstable than their western counterparts, because of the nature of the transitions, the instability of the parties or the volatility of the electorates in East Central Europe. However, analysed from a comparative perspective the party systems of Hungary, Poland, the Czech Republic and even Slovakia reveal underlying patterns of stability. Developments since the 1997-98 round of elections in the region are perhaps better analysed in terms of party system change than as indications of continued instability. In what follows, the development of competitive politics in the region is analysed from a comparative perspective, building on the West European politics literature in general and Lipset and Rokkan's 'cleavage model' of party system development in particular.[1] This warrants reconsidering some of the assumptions in the West European literature in the light of the post-communist context, which in turn permits some tentative conclusions about party system stability and change in general. The political parties, and particularly party strategy, emerge as the central variable in this analysis.

The following analysis takes Lipset and Rokkan's model of party system formation as a starting point, albeit more as a heuristic device than as a construct to be applied directly to post-communist East Central Europe. The first section therefore constitutes an effort to adapt the model for application beyond its core cases, reconsidering some of the explicit and implicit assumptions about institutional design, cleavages, voters, and parties in the light of the conditions of post-communism. The second section turns to party strategy, suggesting that post-communist parties have been free to adopt a range of party strategies, some more successful than others. The third section briefly addresses the development of systematic party competition in a selection of East Central European cases (namely Hungary, Poland, the Czech Republic and Slovakia), suggesting that a degree of party system stabilisation was evident by the late 1990s in terms of patterns of party competition and government formation. The concluding section considers the implications for party system stability and change in Europe more generally, both East and West.

Cleavages, Parties and Party System Development: Extending the Lipset-Rokkan Analysis beyond its Core Cases

The emergence of competitive multi-party politics after the collapse of communism in East Central Europe soon prompted questions about the applicability of West European comparative theories. Despite some obvious differences in the nature of political parties and dimensions of conflict and competition, the processes of establishing new institutions and patterns of competition were comparable to those that had taken place earlier in Western Europe. Perhaps the most obvious points of comparative reference were the Mediterranean transitions to democracy in the 1970s, or the processes of post-war democratisation in Germany and Italy.[2] However, given the very rapid completion of transition and consolidation in the minimalist sense of all main actors accepting the new rules of the game, the operation and stabilisation of competitive politics became the central questions.[3] Here the political parties play a key role, hence the focus on the development and stabilisation (or otherwise) of multi-party systems. Hence Lijphart's application of Rokkan's work on institutional design to analyse the newly negotiated electoral and parliamentary systems of Poland, Hungary and Czechoslovakia.[4] In similar vein, Smith drew on West European literature to analyse post-communist developments, but raised questions about whether the new parties could 'leap over' the stages of development from mass party to catch-all party and about the implications of relatively un-aligned electorates.[5] Lewis added questions about the implications of low party institutionalisation.[6] Kitschelt argued that economic and political competition produced patterns of voter and party alignments that differed from Western Europe, because political and economic liberalisation would be aligned under post-communism in contrast to the western combination of political conservatism and free markets.[7] Mair took this a step further by focussing on differences in patterns of party competition and government formation.[8] In short, while theories of West European politics proved pertinent to analysis of developments in post-communist politics, they raise questions about differences and exceptions.

These questions in turn raise the issue of the implications for party system theory. Referring to the debate on party system freezing and change, Mair suggests that 'it is only by comparing established party systems with those which are still in their infancy that we can really begin to understand the freezing process.'⁹ Much of the literature on the development, freezing and changing of West European party systems builds on assumptions that do not necessarily hold for post-communist party systems, or even beyond the core West European cases. Though the Lipset-Rokkan model of party system formation was developed with reference to Western Europe as a whole, is has an in-built bias towards the northern monarchies bordering on the Atlantic, Norway in particular. Application of the model to the Mediterranean states and peripheral states like Finland or Ireland is more problematic, particularly in the light of territorial change and civil war.[10] Sinnott argues that the model can only be applied to Ireland if the state is considered part of a wider political system including the UK (taking 1918 as the starting point).[11] The relevance of territorial change, revolution and civil war to the Finnish party system is less contentious, but still generates challenges for the Lipset-Rokkan approach.[12] Analyses of the new Greek, Portuguese and Spanish party systems that emerged in the 1970s, a decade after the Lipset-Rokkan model was elaborated, invited questions about the extent to which it applied in a late Twentieth Century context: the changing Italian party system of the 1990s carried similar implications.[13] Application of the model to East Central Europe merely multiplies these problems and, like some of these Western cases, provides opportunities to revisit and develop party system theory.

The Lipset and Rokkan Model and the Development of Competitive Party Systems in East Central Europe: Reconsidering the Parameters

Although Lipset and Rokkan's analysis is sometimes interpreted as a sociological model that focuses on structures, the actors - the political parties - are allocated a central role. Their 'freezing hypothesis' - that 'the party systems of the 1960s reflect, with few but significant exceptions, the cleavage structures of the 1920s' - probably generated more controversy and debate than their analysis of party system development.[14] Approaching 'freezing' as a party-driven process, Sartori commended Lipset and Rokkan's focus on the role of political parties in translating cleavages into party competition.

> The 1920 freezing of party systems and alignments is intriguing only as long as we persist in understanding party systems as dependent variables. It is not intriguing, however, if we realise that a frozen party system is simply a party system that intervenes in the political process as an inde-

pendent *system of channelment,* propelled and maintained by its own laws and inertia.[15]

In other words the party system, once developed, contributes to its own perpetuation. It is not merely the result of other forces, but an independent factor contributing to its own stability. The party system is by and large the product of the *interaction* between parties.[16] Their strategies for building alliances (combining cleavages) and mobilising voters explain the differences among West European party systems. Hence the argument that the development of party systems is driven by *party strategy*, within parameters set by *cleavage structures, institutions, voting patterns* and *party organisation,* and that the conditions of post-communism place far fewer constraints on party leaderships than was the case in early Twentieth Century Western Europe. These are considered briefly in turn below.

First, the central point in Lipset and Rokkan's analysis is how and in what sequence *four sets of cleavages* were translated into political competition. But this list is hardly exhaustive, even as far as Western Europe is concerned. Two emerged from the 'national revolutions': centre - periphery cleavages between the core nation-builders and political, ethnic or cultural peripheries, and state - church cleavages pitting secular against religious forces. Two more were caused by the industrial revolution: rural interests (primary industry, including agriculture) against urban industry, and owners and employers versus workers. Different patterns in the central nation-building elites' commitments on the religious and economic fronts, i.e., respectively to a secular state or a church on the first front, and to urban or landed interests on the second, explain the main differences among West European party systems (Table 1). On the other hand the politicisation of the fourth cleavage, workers versus owners, made for increasing similarities between the party systems because socialist parties emerged across Western Europe, and usually succeeded in redefining the left side of the political spectrum. To reiterate, however, this list of cleavages is hardly exhaustive.

To be sure, Parsons' schema, from which Lipset and Rokkan derived these cleavages, purports to be a *general theory*, but it has been criticised for being excessively static and equilibrium-oriented.[17] Bartolini and Mair's definition of cleavages as featuring three elements, *empirical, normative* and *organisational,* where 'a cleavage has to be considered primarily as a *form of closure of*

Table 1: Lipset & Rokkan's eight-fold typology

	Central core of nation-builders' alliance on the religious front	Nation-builders' economic alliance	Examples of nation-builders	Periphery or opposition's response	Examples of opposition
1	National church dominant (i.e. allied with the state)	Rural: landed interests	Britain: Conservative	Dissident religious, urban	Liberal
2	National church dominant	Urban: commercial and industrial	Scandinavia: Conservative	Dissident religious, rural	Liberal or 'old' left
3	National church dominant, Catholic strong minority	Rural	Prussia/Reich: Conservative	Secular, urban vs. Catholic	Liberals vs. Catholic
4	National church dominant, Catholic strong minority	Urban	Netherlands: Liberal	Dissident rel., vs. Catholic vs. rural	Religious parties
5	Secular state against Catholic Church	Rural	Spain: Liberal	Urban vs. Catholic	Catalans vs. Carlists
6	Secular state against Catholic Church	Urban	France, Italy: Radicals, Liberals	Catholic, rural	Conservative Catholics
7	State allied with Catholic Church	Rural	Austria: Catholics	Secular, urban	Liberals, Pan-Germans
8	State allied with Catholic Church	Urban	Belgium: Catholics vs. Liberals	Rural	Flemish separatists

social relationships', opens the possibility that other events may generate cleavages.[18] Analysis of Italian, Finnish and Irish politics suggest (albeit not without some controversy) that regime change could cause cleavages, and a similar argument has been put forward regarding European integration.[19] In any case there is no *a priori* reason why such 'non-structural' cleavages (that lack the objective element) should not be as divisive or decisive as structural cleavages.[20] Applied to post-communist politics, this suggests that non-structural cleavages that centre on regime change or approaches to nationalism may be as significant as the socio-economic cleavages generated by the process of economic transition.[21] An example analogous to Lipset and Rokkan's eight-fold typology is set out in Table 2, although this holds only for the first and second parliaments, and even then is a considerable over-simplification.

Moreover, the *institutions*, or *rules of the game*, are less problematic in the post-communist context. As far as the development of party systems is concerned, the initial period is characterised by institutional flux rather than stability. The new rules of the game enjoy legitimacy precisely because they are the result of negotiations between the main protagonists on the political scene. Hence the introduction of PR electoral systems in early Twentieth Century Western Europe, as the conservative and liberal parties sought to limit any

Table 2: A possible post-communist eight-fold typology

	First Governments, ca. 1990-1993 period	Government's economic strategy	Examples of first governments	Periphery or opposition's response	Examples of opposition
1	Former opposition, commitment to secular state (civic nationalism)	Fast pace of reform	Poland: Liberal wing of Solidarity	Nationalist vs. Reform communists	Populists, Reform communists
2	Former opposition, commitment to secular state (civic nationalism)	Moderate pace of reform		Nationalist vs. Reform communists	
3	Former opposition, nationalist posture (ethnic nationalism)	Fast	Czech lands: Klaus's Civic Forum technocrats	Civic vs. Reform communists	Social liberals, social democrats, communists
4	Former opposition, nationalist posture (ethnic nationalism)	Moderate	Hungary: Christian national gov't Slovakia: Meciar	Civic vs. Reform communists	Liberals vs. Reform communists
5	Former Communist (civic nationalism)	Fast	Bulgaria	Nationalist	
6	Former Communist (civic nationalism)	Moderate	Yugoslavia	Civic vs. nationalist	
7	Former Communist (ethnic nationalism)	Fast	Romania	Civic	
8	Former Communist (ethnic nationalism)	Moderate	Serbia	Civic	

potential manufactured majority the socialist parties might be accorded under a plurality electoral system, while the social democrat parties sought to guarantee their parliamentary presence.[22] Lijphart has demonstrated that the same logic explains institutional choice in post-communist East Central Europe.[23] Institutions such as electoral systems are therefore dependent rather than independent variables during the early phases of party system development, except when they are imposed from the outside or reflect earlier systems. Hence the adoption of proportional electoral systems in Poland and Czechoslovakia, although a combination of historical factors and negotiating positions contributed to a semi-majoritarian solution in Hungary. These institutions help shape party system 'freezing' inasmuch as they establish the levels at which barriers to new entrants are set. Moreover, all four states have modified their electoral systems since 1990 by raising these barriers. The relationship between voters and parties, reflected in voting patterns, has proven the most controversial aspect of application of West European theories to post-communist East Central because the very existence of pluralist civil society has been retarded.[24] Although Lipset and Rokkan did not make this explicit, their analysis was predicated on strong links between parties and voters. On the socialist left, trade unions played a major role in tying voters to parties, while churches played a similar role for part of the old centre-right.[25] To be sure, several analyses point to or demonstrate the effect of social structures on post-communist voting patterns.[26] However, the combination of disaggregated interests and weak extra-parliamentary organisational support for parties, notably in the form of the Church and trade unions playing a small role in politics, weakens the basis for voters' party identification.[27] Moreover, the costs of economic transition alone suggest that voters might turn against incumbents come election time.

> Given the large number of economic and social problems each rebuilding democracy usually faces, and given the propensity of the winning party to place all of the problems on their initial agenda, it is unlikely that any governing party could achieve complete success before the second election.[28]

The less than surprising result has been a propensity for East Central European voters to reject the incumbents come election time. Yet far from causing party system instability, this tendency to propel opposition parties into government after elections has forced almost all parties to engage in coalition building, thereby accelerating the process of party system development. By the end of the 1990s, all major parties in Hungary, Poland, Slovakia and the Czech Republic had taken part in coalitions, and therefore developed more systematic and stable patterns of interaction. In some cases these patterns have proven more stable than the party organisations. Although new parties emerged in Poland and Slovakia before the 2001 and 2002 elections, taking advantage of the anti-incumbency effect, the most significant effect in post-communist voting patterns appears to be that anti-incumbency voting accelerated the stabilisation of party systems by prompting bloc-building and the government - opposition competition.

Finally, it should be said that the *nature of political parties*, or more specifically their organisation, remains an implicit factor in Lipset and Rokkan's model but emerges as a key variable for analysis of party system development outside their core cases. Their analysis is based on the Nineteenth Century elite parties being challenged by emerging mass parties on the socialist left, and the assumption that the latter articulated a relatively clear set of interests linked to the 'workers' side in the owner - worker cleavage.[29] Yet party organisation had changed considerably by the late 1960s, as Kirchheimer and others have shown - relaxing ideological stances, relying more on party professionals and the media than on the mass membership in campaigns, and seeking to extend their appeal across cleavages to most of the electorate.[30] Katz and Mair have found evidence of further professionalisation of West European parties, to the extent that they come closer to a 'cartel party' ideal-type that represents the state to society rather than vice versa, and focuses more on public relations techniques and issues or general competence in campaigns.[31] To be sure, several parties have chosen not to compete along the main left - right dimension, and to maintain a focus on the interests of a more clearly delineated constituency, or to adopt more leadership-dominated 'new populist' strategies.[32] It should therefore come as no surprise that extension of Lipset and Rokkan's analysis to cases that feature very different forms of party organisation has proven more problematic, as the Irish and Greek cases have illustrated.[33]

Unsurprisingly, party organisations in post-communist East Central Europe hardly conform to the mass party ideal type, being leadership dominated and more precarious because of limited or weak institutionalisation.[34] At least four types of party emerged on the scene after the fall of communism: (i) the reformed communist parties, which is as close as the region comes to the catch-all ideal type in terms of organisation and evolution; (ii) new parties born out of the opposition movements, which have attempted Smith's 'evolutionary leap' straight to catch-all or cartel type; (iii) interest-oriented parties, often reviving predecessors from the inter-war or immediate post-war era; and (iv) new populist parties that have much in common with their new West European counterparts. Electoral alliances of varying longevity make up a possible fifth category, but they usually fall into one of the four ideal-types or represent a hybrid. This means that the mass party organisation, a key factor in the stabilisation of the older West European party systems, hardly features under post-communism.

The parameters within which post-communist parties operate therefore differ considerably from those of early Twentieth Century Western Europe, in terms of cleavages, voters and the very nature of political parties, if less in terms of institutional contexts. In Lipset and Rokkan's analysis relatively strongly institutionalised parties translated a clearly defined set of cleavages into party politics. This was a step-by-step process, which brought about stable alliances and prompted gradual revision of the rules of the game to accommodate new challenges. Parties built close links with voters through extra-parliamentary organisations. Most of these assumptions do not hold for post-communism. The result has been parties that operate under less constraining parameters, and are freer to experiment with different types of strategies. Somewhat paradoxically, this happened at the same time as actual *policy choices* were constrained by the overwhelming consensus in favour of West European type liberal democracy and free markets, which meant operating within IMF guidelines and designing public policy compatible with the EU's *Acquis Communautaire*. Party strategy therefore became the key factor shaping the development and stabilisation of party systems (Figure 1).

Party Strategy and the Emergence of Competitive Multi-Party Politics in East Central Europe: Three Dimensions of Opposition

The transition from communism is probably the wave of democratisation in which the parties have been most 'free to choose'. Whereas some invoked West European ideologies, mainly social democracy and liberalism, and a

Figure 1: The development of competitive politics

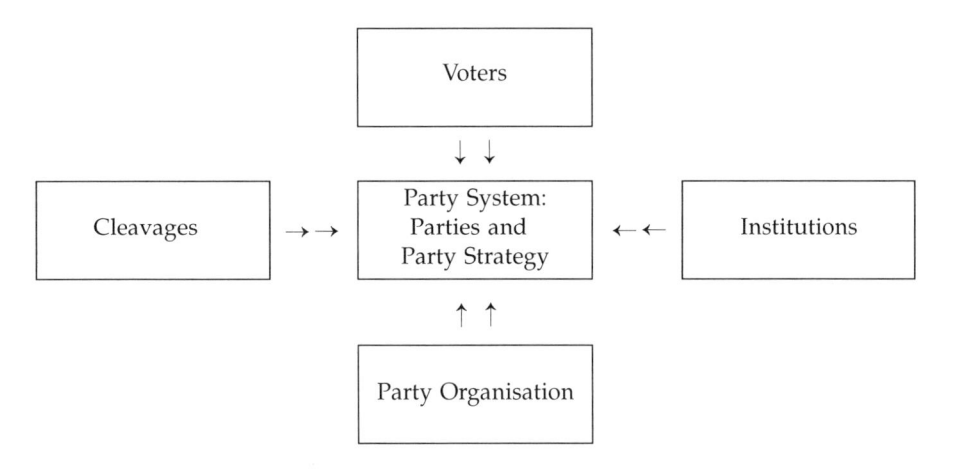

```
                    ┌─────────┐
                    │ Voters  │
                    └─────────┘
                        ↓ ↓
┌──────────┐       ┌──────────────┐       ┌──────────────┐
│ Cleavages│ →→    │ Party System:│  ←←   │ Institutions │
│          │       │  Parties and │       │              │
│          │       │Party Strategy│       │              │
└──────────┘       └──────────────┘       └──────────────┘
                        ↑ ↑
                  ┌──────────────────┐
                  │Party Organisation│
                  └──────────────────┘
```

'return to Europe', others sought to invoke inter-war or immediate post-war ideology, the struggle against communism or even to focus on the problems of post-communist state-building. Within this diversity, three broad patterns of opposition emerged. These amount to three broad strategies of party competition. To the extent that the communist parties sought to abandon communism and stake out a centre-left position, the most attractive option was simply invoking the West European social democratic tradition. The opposition tended to divide into a more individualistic and market oriented liberal right, which invoked West European or US liberalism, and a more traditional Christian national right that looked to national identity and faced the somewhat difficult task of defining conservatism after four decades of communism.[35] First, as the opposition movements' successor parties engaged in a struggle to define the 'right' in East Central Europe, the social democrats (including reformed communists) defined the 'left'. Second, several parties sought to revive pre-communist organisations or dimensions of competition, establishing so-called 'historical parties' based on ethnic or regional identity and/or economic interest. Inasmuch as these parties failed to shape left - right competition, or chose to cross-cut it, their strategy developed into a second dimension of opposition. The third dimension of opposition is made up of the parties that established themselves on the flanks of the party system, be they unreformed communists or workers parties on the left or nationalist parties on the radical 'right'.

The First Strategy of Opposition: Shaping Left - Right Competition

The first strategy of government - opposition competition, characteristic of most of the catch-all and cartel parties of Western Europe, entails competition along the main left - right dimension of the party system. This has usually been linked to issues related to market regulation, the welfare state and redistribution of resources, though as the Irish case illustrates, this is not always the case. In fact, definition of the main dimension of competition has usually been contentious in Western Europe, and in some cases the liberal - conservative contest as to which party would represent the main opposition to the social democratic left produced a three-bloc party system. This question was of central concern in Kitschelt's 1992 analysis, where he suggested that party alignments in East Central Europe would reflect different combinations of positions on the economic policy dimension (political or market redistribution) and a non-economic dimension running from cosmopolitan libertarian to authoritarian particularist politics.[36] In Western Europe the bulk of voters, and therefore the most successful parties, lie in the upper-left and lower-right quadrants in figure 2 (underlined text). However, the fact that post-communist voters interested in fast economic change would also be oriented toward rapid opening of society, while some would resist, meant that most of them would be found in the upper-right and lower-left quadrants. The more successful parties would therefore be located in these quadrants (bold text in Figure 2). In these terms, the left - right dimension in East Central Europe was at ninety degrees to that familiar from West European politics. Although post-communist parties emerged in all four quadrants, the most successful were expected to lie at the upper-right and lower-left. However, as Kitschelt has since noted, the inter-party contest to define and shape the left - right dimension would prove more complex, and involve some parties' invoking cleavages related to national identity.[37] The bulk of this contest took place during the first two or three parliaments.

The parties that defined the 'left' include the ex-communist Hungarian Socialist Party (MSzP), the Alliance of the Democratic Left (SLD) in Poland, and Party of the Democratic Left (SDL) in Slovakia, as well as the Czech Social Democratic Party (CSSD), a revival of the party that was merged with the communists in 1948. All four invoked West European social democratic ideas, advocating relatively rapid economic transition, and took relatively secular approaches

Figure 2: Competitive space in European party systems

Libertarian-Cosmopolitan Politics

West European Social Democrat Left	**Post-Communist Liberals**
Political	*Market*
Redistribution	*Allocation*
Post-Communist Christian Nationals and Communists	West European Conservative Right

Authoritarian Particularist Politics

Note: Adapted from Kitschelt, 'The Formation of Party Systems in East Central Europe'.

to nationalist issues. The Polish and Hungarian parties won executive office as early as 1993 and 1994 respectively, and the Hungarian party proceeded to accelerate its predecessors' economic reforms. Although the CSSD did not gain executive office until 1998, it represented the main alternative to the Klaus government in the 1996 elections. Only the SDL has seen less success in its efforts to stake out a strong position on the left, despite its erstwhile co-operation with the Slovak Social Democrats (SDSS). In Poland, the old regime - opposition divisions contributed to the independent survival of the ex-Solidarity social democrat Union of Labour (UP).

On the centre-right, two broad sets of parties have struggled to shape the right wing of the spectrum, with clearer outcomes in the Czech and Hungarian cases than in Poland and Slovakia. In the Czech case, the technocratic free-market wing of the Civic Forum in form of Klaus's Civic Democratic Party (ODS) initially won this contest, and it soon absorbed the Christian Democrat Party (KDS). It was flanked on its immediate left and right by the smaller Christian Democratic Union-Czechoslovak People's Party (KDU-CSL) and the Civic Democratic Alliance (ODA), but would find its dominance of the right reduced after a large faction opposed to Klaus split off to form the Freedom Union (US) in late 1997. By contrast, both Christian national and liberal parties prospered well into the late 1990s in Hungary, Poland and Slovakia. In the Hungarian case, the liberal Alliance of Young Democrats' (Fidesz) change in strategy after losing the 1994 election allowed it to encroach on the Christian national right's territory and eventually become the main right-wing party. With the other liberal party, the Alliance of Free Democrats (SzDSz), having joined the MSzP in coalition government for the duration of the 1994-98 parliament, Hungary was well on the way to a two-bloc system by 1998.

The Polish right remains more divided, and the Slovak right is somewhat problematic to define given Meciar's interventionist economy policy. The Polish Christian national parties, most of which combined in Solidarity Electoral Action (AWS) before the 1997 election, and regrouped as the smaller Solidarity Electoral Action of the Right (AWSP) in 2001, are usually considered as the 'right' in that country. The more economic reform-oriented liberals, initially the Liberal Democratic Congress (KLD), Democratic Union (UD) and the free market wing of the Polish Beer Lovers' Party (PPPP), which eventually united in the Freedom union (UW) in 1994, made up the liberal free market 'centre-right'. It was squeezed out in the 2001 elections by the newly formed Civic Platform (PO), whose founding members came from the UW and AWS and positioned their new party between the two. Meciar's Movement for a Democratic Slovakia (HzDS), which combined emphasis on Slovak national interests and moderately paced economic reform, came closest to defining a post-communist 'right' that belongs in Kitschelt's lower-right quadrant. Apart from the SDL, Meciar's main opposition between 1992 and 1998 consisted principally of the small liberal Democratic Party (DS, comparable to the Czech ODA), the Christian Democratic Movement (KDH), and the Democratic Union (DU, formed and reinforced by HzDS dissidents and expellees). In the run-up to the 1998 election these parties formed the Slovak Democratic Coalition (SDK), with the Greens (SZS) and Social Democratic Party of Slovakia (SDSS), with the explicit aim of defeating Meciar's government. Efforts to turn the SDK into a party were only partly successful, yielding the Slovak Democratic and Christian Union (SDKU), but not integrating the KDH. In addition, the Slovak scene has seen a number of populist parities attempting to establish themselves as the main alternatives to Meciar, with considerable but short-lived success in the case of the Party for Civic Understanding (SOP), and potentially, Direction (Smer). Both have aligned themselves on the centre-left.

The Second Strategy of Opposition: Cross-Cutting Competition and Territorial Opposition

A number of parties opted for strategies that involved efforts to appeal to a more clearly identified electorate. This strategy is comparable to that developed by regional, agrarian and dissident religious parties in Western Europe that have eschewed the trend toward catch-all strategies. This has involved drawing on the economic, political or cultural (including ethnic) interests of peripheries against the administrative centre.[38] In East Central Europe the most successful examples include parties targeting agrarian and regional interests, primarily the Polish Peasant Party (PSL), the Independent Smallholders' Party (FKgP) in Hungary, the Czech and Slovak Christian democrat parties, and the parties representing the Hungarian minority in Slovakia. The KDU-CSL and KDH come close to the West European Christian democrat model, whereas the Christian National Union (ZChN) in Poland and the KDNP have adopted a Christian national appeal that increasingly diverged from the Polish and Hungarian mainstream right. Lepper's Farmers' Self-Defence (Samobroona) represent a hybrid of this strategy and the third strategy, an interest group turned populist political party, operating on the left flank. Like most East Central European parties, these tend to be hierarchically organised and weakly institutionalised, which exacerbates the consequences of internal divisions regarding strategy. This proved the undoing of the KDNP in 1997, when the party split over relations with Fidesz and lost several of its members to that party. The FKgP suffered similarly in the run-up to the 2002 election.

The Third Strategy of Opposition: Competition at the Flanks of the Party System

Finally, a number of parties have chosen a third strategy of opposition, on the flanks of the party system. In West European politics this strategy was first defined by anti-system parties on the communist left and fascist right, particularly during the inter-war years, although these parties have yielded ground to the 'new left' and new populist parties over the last few decades. In East Central Europe the unreformed communists have been relegated to this kind of opposition, and a number of hard-line nationalists have taken up positions on the right flank of the party systems (but are hardly enthusiastic about liberalised markets). The Communist Party of Bohemia and Moravia (KSCM, successor to the Communist Party of Czechoslovakia, KSC) and The Hungarian Truth and Justice Party (MIEP) epitomise these two variants. A host of other parties have adopted more or less populist and anti-system positions, such as the Czech Republicans (SPR-RCS) and the Movement for the Reconstruction of Poland (ROP). Something similar applies to the two parties that were formed from AWS's populist right wing in 2001, the League of Polish families (LPR) and the Law and Justice party (PiS). Apart from the KSCM, left wing success has been confined to the Association of Slovak Workers (ZRS), while the Polish and Hungarian far left have fared much worse or chosen to remain within the reformed parties. Other manifestations of 'new politics' on the left, such as feminist and green movements, have been far less successful. Perhaps the most interesting case is the hybrid HzDS, which to some extent constituted an anti-system party within the Czechoslovak context, but came to define the 'right' in Slovakia after independence. Although the extreme right is comparatively weak in East Central Europe in 2002, it played a considerable role in right-wing politics in three of the four cases during the 1990s. The Czech Republic is the exception, where the Republicans never played a significant role in either coalition games or party politics on the centre-right.

In short, the East Central European Parties have been relatively free to choose strategies, and have tested the full range, some far more successfully than others. The first dimension of government - opposition competition features parties that come close to the evolution from (communist) mass to catch-all party, as well as parties that 'leapt' straight to the 'cartel' type or mixed this with the East Central European brand of Christian nationalism and new populism. While the liberal successor-parties tended to focus on economic transition, their Christian national rivals have more often than not invoked anti-communism and ethnic approaches to nationalism. In this sense they can be said to have translated different cleavages into politics. However, a number of parties have opted for competition along a second dimension of opposition, mobilising voters along divisions that are very much like Lipset and Rokkan's state - church, centre - periphery and urban - rural divisions. Finally some parties have positioned themselves at the flanks of the party systems, rejecting or circumventing the left - right dimensions and therefore constituting a third dimension of opposition. Unlike the parties competing along the first and second dimensions, these parties have mostly been excluded from government. Therefore, although the parties may differ considerably from their West European counterparts, broadly similar patterns or dynamics of competition can be found. The next section turns to how this has played out in the development, stabilisation and change of party systems in Hungary, Poland, the Czech Republic and Slovakia.

The Development of the East Central European Party Systems: Changing Patterns of Competition and Bloc-Building

The first decade of competitive politics in East Central Europe constituted a testing ground for a wide range of party strategies (see Table 3). In the Hungarian and Czech cases the process of testing and adjusting strategies produced relatively stable party systems, and in Poland it produced clear patterns of bloc-building and competition, if not stable party organisations. The Slovak scene is more fluid, particularly in terms of the actual parties, and new parties retain the potential to change patterns of competition and coalition politics. The former opposition came to power in all four cases, albeit in different forms. Whereas the liberal wing of the opposition came to dominate the executive during the first four years in the Czech lands and Poland, the Christian national or populist elements won power in Hungary and Slovakia. This first phase therefore saw the beginning of an answer to the question of who made up the 'right', while the reformed communist parties and the CSSD established dominance on the left. The SLD and MSzP's positions were consolidated during the second phase, after their election victories in 1993 and 1994, which prompted the right to regroup in both countries. The same process came four years later in the Czech Republic. All three cases therefore saw considerable party system stabilisation through the development of stable patterns of competition and coalition building, even though their party systems have since seen further change. By contrast, the decade since Slovak independence has produced repeated efforts to build a stable alternative to Meciar's HzDS, without yielding the same degree of stabilisation.

Only in Hungary did the first elections produce a clear winner in the contest between the liberal and Christian national opposition. Invoking national identity and anti-communism, the MDF-KDNP-FKgP coalition defeated the

Table 3: Patterns of party competition in East Central Europe since 1989

Poland	1989 Election	1991 Election	1991-1993	1993 Election	1997 Election
Left flank social democrat	SLD **Solidarity:** UP	SLD Solidarity UP	SLD <u>Solidarity</u> UP	**SLD** UP	SLD
Liberal right	**Solidarity: ROAD**	UD KLD PPPP	**UD KLD PPPP**	UD(+KLD + PPPP), becomes UW	**UW**
Christian national right	**Solidarity:** PC ZChN KPN	**PC** ZChN	PC **ZChN**	BBWR	**AWS**
Others (agrarian)	PSL (ex-communist) **Solidarity:** PSL-PL	<u>PSL</u> PSL-PL	<u>PSL</u> **PL**	**PSL**	PSL
Right flank		KPN	KPN	KPN	ROP

Hungary	1989/1990	1990 Election	1994 Election	1998 Election
Left flank Social democrat (formerly communist)	MSzP	MSzP	**MSzP**	MSzP
Liberal right (centre)	SzDSz Fidesz	SzDSz Fidesz	**SzDSz** Fidesz	SzDSz
Christian national right	MDF	**MDF**	MDF	**Fidesz** **MDF**
Others (Christian, agrarian)	KNDP FKgP	**KNDP** **FKgP**	KNDP FKgP	**FKgP**
Right flank		MIEP	MIEP	MIEP

liberal challengers and remained in power through the full parliamentary term. Fidesz and SzDSz's focus on economic transition, in effect mobilisation along a different cleavage, not simply the other side of a given set of cleavages, proved less effective. Elsewhere the elections were won by broad movements in the form of Solidarity, Civic Forum (OF) and the Public Against Violence (VPN), all of which would break up along lines similar to those that divided the liberal and Christian national camp in Hungary. Solidarity's split between ROAD (Citizens' Movement for Democratic Action) and the Centre Alliance (PC), later replaced by Walesa's anti-party Bloc for Reform (BBWR, borrowing its initials from Pilsudski's inter-war populist party), set the scene for the division of the right into two blocs emphasising respectively economic shock therapy and conservative values. Despite coming out stronger in the 1991 election, the Christian national right proved unable to build a stable coalition. Suckocka's liberal-led coalition survived longer than expected, falling after a year in 1993, and losing the subsequent election to the reformed communist PSL-SLD coalition. In Czechoslovakia the OF and VPN fragmented into two wholly separate party systems, a range of liberal and conservative parties coming to dominate the Czech scene, while a fragmented system centred on support for and opposition to Meciar emerged in Slovakia. Meciar's combination of advocacy of slow economic transition and emphasis on Slovak nationalism confounds description of the Slovak party system in terms of left and right, although his HzDS would dominate, if not define the 'right' in that country. All four cases thus institutionalised divisions on the 'right', and with the exception of the Czech lands, this entailed competition between liberal free market parties and a more Christian national right which fits Kitschelt's model well. In contrast, the split in OF reflected a division between the technocrats led by Klaus (ODS) and the former dissidents in the Civic Movement (OH) and the ODA on the economic right.

The second series of fully free elections, 1992 in Czechoslovakia, 1993 in Poland and 1994 in Hungary, set off a second phase of party system development, as success or failure at the polls and in the subsequent coalition games shaped the consolidation of patterns of competition. The somewhat unexpected election victories of the SLD and MSzP changed the dynamics of bloc-building on both the left and right in Poland and Hungary, whereas Klaus's and Meciar's victories in the Czech lands and Slovakia reinforced their emergent patterns of political competition. In Hungary, the SzDSz's pre-election drift to the left was reinforced by its governing coalition with MSzP, while Fidesz's tendency in the opposite direction was firmly established at its 1995 party conference by way of a decision to adopt a more nationalist profile. Come 1998 the party's effort to establish itself as the main party on the right had paid off, as it absorbed elements of the KDNP and MDF, and Hungary's two-bloc system was all but consolidated. Fidesz' election victory that year, and its four-year coalition with the rump-MDF and FKgP, followed by the MSzP-SzDSZ victory in 2002, completed the consolidation.

By contrast, the retrenchment of the Polish right, although successful inasmuch as UW and AWS defeated the SDL-PSL coalition in 1997, yielded much less institutionalised parties. Considerable divisions remained, particularly within the AWS, to the extent that it is difficult to talk about stabilisation of political parties on the Polish right. However, the pattern of left - right competition was stabilised, to the extent that both the 1997 and 2001 elections saw competition between relatively clearly defined blocs. Although the AWS-UW coalition lasted out the four-year term, the parties did not. The SLD-PSL coalition that took office after the 2001 elections faced a fragmented opposition, including a more West European style conservative party in the PO. The two party systems have thus moved closer to the West European pattern of competition identified by Kitschelt (figure 3), with the proviso that the right-liberals are not always the most enthusiastic proponents of international free markets economics.

The stabilisation and change of the Czech party system also fits a pattern of re-alignment towards the West European dynamic, whereas the Slovak system remains dominated by Meciar even after HzDS lost the 1998 election. The split in ODS after the Klaus government fell in November 1997 (over a party finance scandal) helped consolidate a Scandinavian-style three-bloc system, with the ODS in the lower right quadrant, the CSSD in the upper left, and centre parties between the two in the upper right quadrant. The 'Opposition Agreement', which secured ODS support for a minority CSSD government, removed the need for further coalition games before the 2002 election. With the 1998 election, the consolidation of the centre-right parties into the SDK coalition and an alliance of SDK with SDL to build an alternative to Meciar's

Figure 3: A possible realignment of party competition in East Central Europe

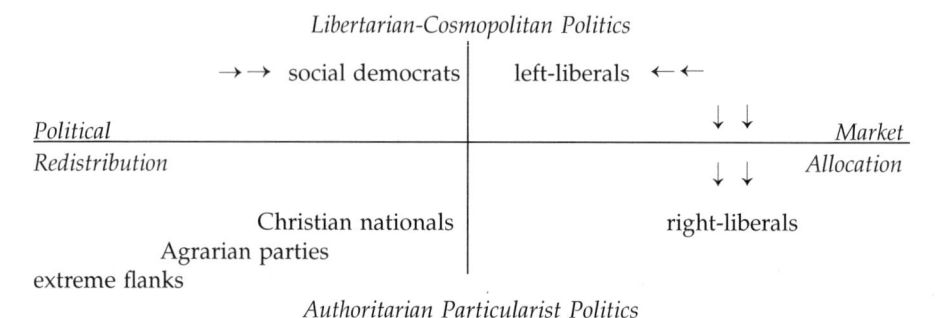

Libertarian-Cosmopolitan Politics

→ → social democrats | left-liberals ← ←

Political | ↓ ↓ *Market*
Redistribution | ↓ ↓ *Allocation*

Christian nationals | right-liberals
Agrarian parties |
extreme flanks |

Authoritarian Particularist Politics

198 • Nick Sitter

government appeared to herald a consolidation of Slovak politics into a more stable pattern. Meciar's efforts to build and maintain coalitions, his defeat in 1994, subsequent election victory and new coalition games produced a dynamic similar to the competition between Berlusconi and the centre-left in Italy. However, the success of SOP in the 1998 election, and strength of Smer and the newly formed New Citizens' Alliance (ANO, Slovak for 'yes') in pre-election polls in 2002, suggests that new parties retain a considerable potential to cause further change in the party system.

The fact that most parties that have developed cross-cutting or flanking strategies of competition are located in the lower-left quadrant of figure 3, and that these parties have been marginalised in Hungary and the Czech Republic, contributes further to the picture of stable party systems. In Hungary the KDNP divided over questions of strategy, and specifically over its relationship with Fidesz, which all but killed the KDNP. The FKgP, which had split over its relationship with the MDF-led government in the early 1990s, suffered similar problems in the Fidesz coalition. In 2002, unlike 1994, this cost the party its parliamentary representation. MIEP's failure to pass the threshold in the 2002 elections confirmed the shift to the two-bloc system, the party's position on the nationalist right having been squeezed considerably by Fidesz shift to the right. The Parties on the Czech flanks, the communist KSCM and the Republicans, have likewise been marginalised, if not eliminated from parliament, by the logic of coalition games among the three main blocs. The regionalist Movement for Moravia and Silesia (HSD-SMS) saw only temporary electoral success, as did the Liberal and Social Union (LSU), which included agrarians and greens. By contrast the Hungarian Coalition (MK, later SMK) in Slovakia and the agrarian PSL in Poland have successfully maintained stable support by appealing to a clearly delineated electorate. The agrarian elements of solidarity (PSL-PL, the Polish peasant Party-Peasant Alliance, later simply PL) joined AWS. Only in Slovakia has a party of the far right retained consistent support, the Slovak National Party (SNS) securing representation in every Slovak parliament so far. However, the effort to integrate the Polish right in AWS contributed to blurring the boundaries between the Christian national and far right, the Confederation for an Independent Poland (KPN) joining AWS, and the right-populist LPR subsequently leaving the alliance. With the transformation of Samobroona into a left-flank agrarian party, which like the LPR successfully campaigned on Euro-sceptic platforms, both Polish flanks remain populated and somewhat volatile.

Summing up, four broad trends can be discerned. First, among the parties that compete along the main left - right dimension a combination of personality politics and weakly institutionalised parties keeps the number of parties volatile. This appears to wreak greater havoc on the right than the left, and features mainly in Poland and Slovakia. While it has not changed the dynamic of party competition or government - opposition relations dramatically in Poland, the Slovak party system appears more vulnerable to full-blown party system change. Second, with the exception of the PSL and the Hungarian minority in Slovakia, the parties that opted for strategies involving cross-cutting competition along a second dimension of opposition have generally fared badly, dividing over how to align with the parties that position themselves on the main dimensions. Third, on the flanks, electoral support for the extreme right and left appears to be declining, suggesting that this type of opposition is not a particularly succesful strategy in the region. Fourth, however, the impending enlargement of the European Union has introduced a new potential 'touchstone of dissent' - Euroscepticism - which may be mobilised by the parties competing on the second or third dimension.[39] The different degrees of party system change thus produced are set out in figure 4, which combines change or stability in the set of parties and patterns of competition between them. Stabilisation of the party system in Hungary and the Czech Republic in the second half of the 1990s also involved changes in the patterns of bloc building and competition, whereas the Polish party system has remained remarkably stable in terms of patterns of competition compared to the number of parties. There is less evidence that Slovakia has stabilised either of the two.

Conclusion: The Changing East Central European Party Systems

Returning to the central questions about the applicability of West European comparative politics theory to post-communist East Central Europe and the implications for party system theory, three sets of conclusions and suggestions are warranted. First, application of theories developed for the comparative analysis of West European cases to the new party systems of East Central Europe is pertinent, but raises important questions about the theories' assump-

Figure 4: Party system change

	Stable Patterns of Competition	Changing Patterns of Competition
Stable set of parties	I **Party System Stability**	II - Hungary, Czech Rep. **Party System Adaptation** Patterns of competition and coalition-building evolve
Changing set of parties	III - Poland **Party System Modification** Parties change, patterns of competition remain	IV - Slovakia **Party System Change** New parties cause changes in competition, or vice versa

tions. In the present analysis, the role of actors - parties and their strategic choices - emerges as stronger than in most interpretations of Lipset and Rokkan's model. Cleavages, institutions, voting patterns, and to some extent even party organisations, are parameters within which parties' strategic decisions impact on the development and stabilisation of party systems. In East Central Europe, these factors have combined to produce a setting that enhances the importance of how parties choose to compete.

Second, the development of competitive multi-party systems in East Central Europe has been driven by the contest between parties to define the post-communist 'right'. The stabilisation of the party system reflects directly the extent to which this contest has been resolved, and this has meant that the competition between a liberal free market right and Christian national right has been accorded a prominent role. Defining the left proved easier, particularly in the Polish case where it reflects old regime - opposition divisions, but even in the Slovak case, where the left is comparatively weak. Most parties competing on cross-cutting or flanking dimensions have been marginalised, agrarian parties in particular experiencing limited success outside Poland.

Third, the development of more or less stable party systems has been largely a party-driven process. Party system stability depends on both the number of parties and their strategies (Figure 4). Adaptation, where existing parties modify their strategies to maintain or enhance their position in the party system, is common in West European politics, as are adjustments to coalition games. In this sense party system adaptation or modification is more common that radical change, in East Central as well as in Western Europe. Therefore, if theories of party system change and stability contribute to the analysis of party system development in East Central Europe, it is perhaps equally significant and more interesting that party system development in East Central Europe contributes to general theories of party system stability and change. The East Central European experience suggests that parties themselves, as in recent cases in Western Europe, are the main drivers behind party system change and stability. In short, the parties have stolen the show.

Notes

[1] S.M. Lipset and S. Rokkan, 'Cleavage Structures, Party Systems, and Voter Alignments: An Introduction', in S.M. Lipset and S. Rokkan (eds.), *Party Systems and Voter Alignments: Cross-National Perspectives*, (London: The Free Press, 1967).

[2] A. Agh, 'The "Comparative Revolution" and the Transition in Central and Southern Europe', *Journal of Theoretical Politics*, 5 (1993), pp. 231-252; G. Pridham and P.G. Lewis (eds.), *Stabilising Fragile Democracies: Comparing New Party Systems in Southern and Eastern Europe* (London: Routledge, 1996); J.J. Linz and A. Stepan, *Problems of Democratic Transition and Consolidation: Southern Europe, South America, and Post-Communist Europe* (Baltimore: John Hopkins University Press, 1996).

[3] G. Di Palma, 'Parliaments, Consolidation, Institutionalization: A Minimalist View', in U. Liebert and M. Cotta (eds.), *Parliaments and Democratic Consolidation in Southern Europe* (London: Pinter Publishers, 1990).

[4] A. Lijphart, 'Democratisation and Constitutional Choice in Czecho-Slovakia, Hungary and Poland 1989-91', *Journal of Theoretical Politics*, 4(2), 1992, pp. 207-223. This study is based on the model set out by S. Rokkan, *Citizens, Elections, Parties: Approaches to the Comparative Study of the Process of Development* (Oslo: Universitetsforlaget, 1970).

[5] G. Smith, 'Transitions to Liberal Democracy', in S. Whitefield (ed.), *The New Institutional Architecture of Eastern Europe* (Basingstoke: Macmillan, 1993).

[6] P.G. Lewis, 'Political Institutionalisation and Party Development in Post-Communist Poland', in *Europe-Asia Studies*, 46(5), 1994, pp. 779-799.

[7] H. Kitschelt, 'The Formation of Party Systems in East Central Europe', *Politics and Society*, 20(1), 1992, pp. 7-50.

[8] P. Mair, 'What is Different about Post-Communist Party Systems?', *Studies in Public Policy No. 259*, (University of Strathclyde, 1996), reprinted in P. Mair, *Party System Change: Approaches and Interpretations* (Oxford: Clarendon Press, 1997), chapter 8.

9. Mair, *Party System Change*, p. ix.
10. B. Kissane, 'The Not-So Amazing Case of Irish Democracy', *Irish Political Studies*, 10, 1995, 43-68.
11. R. Sinnott, 'Interpretations of the Irish Party System', *European Journal of Political Research*, 12(3), 1984, pp. 289-307.
12. E. Allardt and P. Pesonen, 'Cleavages in Finnish Politics', in Lipset and Rokkan (eds.), *Party Systems and Voter Alignments*; J. Mylly and R.M. Berry (eds.), *Political Parties in Finland: Essays in History and Politics* (Turku: Grafia Oy, 1984).
13. See e.g. G. Pridham, 'Political Actors, Linkages and Interactions: Democratic Consolidation in Southern Europe', *West European Politics*, 13, 1990, pp. 103-117; G. Pridham (ed.), *The New Mediterranean Democracies: Regime Transition in Spain, Greece and Portugal* (London: Frank Cass, 1984); S. Gundle and S. Parker (eds.), *The New Italian Republic: From the Fall of the Berlin Wall to Berlusconi* (London: Routledge, 1996).
14. Lipset and Rokkan, 'Cleavage Structures, Party Systems, and Voter Alignments', p. 50. On stability, see Bartolini and Mair, *Identity, Competition, and Electoral Availability: the Stabilization of European Electorates 1885-1985*, (Cambridge, Cambridge University Press, 1990); on change see R.J. Dalton, S.C. Flanagan and P.A. Beck (eds.), *Electoral Change in Advanced Industrial Democracies: Realignment or Dealignment?*, (Princeton, Princeton University Press, 1984); H. Daalder and P. Mair (eds.), *Western European Party Systems: Continuity and Change*, (Cambridge, Cambridge University Press, 1983); M. Pedersen, 'The Changing Dynamics of European Party Systems: Changing Patterns of Electoral Volatility', *European Journal of Political Research*, 7, 1979, pp. 1-26; S.B. Wolinetz, 'The Transformation of Western European Party Systems Revisited', *West European Politics*, 2(1), 1979.
15. G. Sartori, 'The Sociology of Parties: A Critical Review', in O. Stammer (ed.), *Party Systems, Party Organisations, and the Politics of New Masses*, (Berlin, Free University of Berlin, 1968), p. 21, emphasis in original.
16. G. Smith, 'What is a Party System?', *Parliamentary Affairs*, 19(3), 1966, pp. 351-362; G. Smith, 'Western European Party Systems: On the Trail of a Typology', *West European Politics*, 2(1), 1979, pp. 128-143.
17. M. Black, 'Some Questions about Parsons' Theories' in M. Black (ed.), *The Social Theories of Talcott Parsons*, (Englewood Cliffs, NJ, Prentice-Hall, 1961).
18. Bartolini and Mair, *Identity, Competition, and Electoral Availability*, p. 216.
19. G. Sartori, 'European Political Parties: The Case of Polarized Pluralism', in J. La Palombara and M. Weiner (eds.), *Political Parties and Political Development*, (Princeton, Princeton University Press, 1966), *Political Parties and Political Development*; Allardt and Pesonen, 'Cleavages in Finnish Politics'; R.K. Carty, *Parties and Parish Pump: Electoral Politics in Ireland*, (Waterloo, Ontario, Wilfrid Laurier University Press,

1981); S. Hix, 'The Study of the European Community: The Challenge to European Politics', *West European Politics*, 17(1), 1994, pp. 13-44.

[20] A. Zuckerman, 'Political Cleavage: A Conceptual and Theoretical Analysis', *British Journal of Political Science*, 5(2),1975, pp. 321-248; see also R. Dahl, 'The American Oppositions: Affirmation and Denial', in R. Dahl (ed.), *Political Oppositions in Western Democracies*, (New Haven, Yale University Press, 1966); H. Daalder, 'Parties, Elites, and Political Developments in Western Europe' in LaPalombara and Weiner (eds.); A. Lijphart, *Democracies: Patterns of Majoritarian and Consensus Government in Twenty-One Countries* (New Haven, Yale University Press, 1984).

[21] G. Schöpflin, *Politics in Eastern Europe: 1945-1992*, (Oxford, Blackwell, 1993).

[22] Rokkan, *Citizens, Elections, Parties*.

[23] Lijphart, 'Democratisation and Constitutional Choice in Czecho-Slovakia, Hungary and Poland 1989-91'.

[24] M. Waller, 'Groups, Interests and Political Aggregation in East Central Europe', *Journal of Communist Studies*, 8(1), 1992, pp. 128-147; J. Curry, 'Pluralism in East Central Europe: Not Will it Last, but What is it?', *Communist and Post-Communist Studies*, 26(4), 1993, pp. 446-461; I. Crewe, 'Voters, Parties and Leaders Thirty Years On: Western Electoral Studies and the New Democracies of Eastern Europe', in I. Budge and D. McKay (eds.), *Developing Democracy: Comparative Research in Honour of Jean Blondel*, (London, Sage, 1994).

[25] M. Duverger, *Political Parties: Their Organisation and Activity in the Modern State*, (London, Methuen and Co, 1954); D. Epstein, *Political Parties in Western Democracies*, (London, Pall Mall Press, 1967).

[26] Kitschelt, 'The Formation of Party Systems in East Central Europe'; G. Evans and S. Whitefield, 'Identifying the Bases of Party Competition in Eastern Europe', *British Journal of Political Studies*, 23, 1993, pp. 521-548; H. Kitschelt, Z. Mansfeldova, R. Markowski and G. Toka, *Post-Communist Party Systems: Competition, Representation and Inter-Party Cooperation*, (Cambridge, Cambridge University Press, 1999).

[27] C. Schnabel, 'Die Arbeitsbeziehungen im Osteuropäischen Transformationsprozess', in O. Vogel (ed.), *Osteuropa auf dem Weg in die Marktwirtschaft*, (Köln, Deutscher Instituts-Verlag GmbH, 1993); T. Cox and L. Vass, 'Civil Society and Interest Representation in Hungarian Political Development', in T. Cox and L. Vass (eds.), *Hungary: The Politics of Transition*, (London, Frank Cass, 1995); M. Kramer, 'Polish Workers and the Post-Communist transition', in *Communist and Post Communist Studies*, 28(1), 1995, pp. 74-114; S.L. Wolchik, 'Democratisation and Political Participation in Slovakia'; and D.M. Olson, 'The Experience of the Czech Republic', both in K. Dawisha and B. Parrott (eds.), *The Consolidation of Democracy in East-Central Europe*, (Cambridge, Cambridge University Press, 1997).

[28] A.W. Turner, 'Postauthoritarian Elections: Testing Expectations about 'First' Elections', *Comparative Political Studies*, 26(3), 1993, pp. 330-349, p. 345.

[29] A. Panebianco, *Political Parties: Organisation and Power* (Cambridge: Cambridge University Press, 1988).

[30] O. Kirchheimer, 'The Transformation of West European Party Systems', in J. La Palombara and M. Weiner (eds.), *Political Parties and Political Development* (Princeton: Princeton University Press, 1966; A. Panebianco, *Political Parties*.

[31] R. Katz and P. Mair (eds.), *How Parties Organize: Change and Adaptation in Party Organizations in Western Democracies* (London: Sage Books, 1994); A. Katz and P. Mair, 'Changing Models of Party Organisation and Party Democracy: The Emergence of the Cartel Party', *Party Politics*, 1(1), 1995, pp. 5-28.

[32] D. Arter (ed.), *From Farmyard to City Square? The Electoral Adaptation of the Nordic Agrarian Parties* (Aldershot: Ashgate, 2001); P. Taggart, 'New Populist Parties in Western Europe', *West European Politics*, 18(1), 1995, pp. 34-51.

[33] C. Lyrintzis, 'Political Parties in Post-Junta Greece: A Case of 'Bureaucratic Clientelism?'' *West European Politics*, 7(2), 1984; P. Mair, *The Changing Irish Party System: Organisation, Ideology and Electoral Competition* (London: Pinter, 1987).

[34] P.G. Lewis, 'Political Institutionalisation and Party Development in Post-Communist Poland', *Europe-Asia Studies*, 46(5), 1994, pp. 779-799; P.G. Lewis, 'Democratization and Party Development in Eastern Europe', *Party Politics* 1(3), 1995, pp. 391-405; P. Kopecky, 'Developing Party Organisations in East Central Europe', *Party Politics*, 1(4), 1995, pp. 515-534.

[35] R. Scruton, 'The New Right in Central Europe', *Political Studies*, 36, 1988, pp. 449-462 and pp. 638-652; G. Schöpflin, 'Postcommunism: The Problems of Democratic Construction', *Dædalus*, 123(3), 1994, pp. 127-141; J. Szacki, *Liberalism after Communism* (Budapest: Central European University Press, 1995).

[36] Kitschelt, 'The Formation of Party Systems in East Central Europe', p. 17.

[37] H. Kitschelt, 'Formation of Party Cleavage in Post-Communist Democracies: Theoretical Propositions', *Party Politics*, 1(4), 1995, pp. 447-472.

[38] S. Rokkan and D. Urwin, *Economy, Territory, Identity: Politics of West European Peripheries*. (London: Sage, 1983).

[39] P. Taggart, 'A Touchstone of Dissent: Euroscepticism in Contemporary West European Party Systems', *European Journal of Political Research*, 33, 1998, pp. 363-388.

Paul Taggart and Aleks Szczerbiak
Europeanisation, Euroscepticism and Party Systems: Party-based Euroscepticism in the Candidate States of Central and Eastern Europe

ABSTRACT

In this chapter, we assume that we can usefully examine the emergence of party-based Euroscepticism in the party systems of the candidate states and that we can account for (some of) the differences between the states by looking at their party systems. In order to do this we begin by offering a definition of Euroscepticism that differentiates between 'hard' and 'soft' variants. We map these types of Euroscepticism in parties in the candidate states of central and Eastern Europe. Looking at the nature of party systems we suggest that there is a need to rethink how we conceptualise and categorise them if we are to extend our Western models to central and Eastern Europe, and we offer some suggestions as to how this might be done. Using these models of party systems in relation to the candidate states of central and Eastern Europe we examine how this relates to the incidences of party-based Euroscepticism and reflect on the issues involved in applying West European models to East European cases.

Introduction

The issue of European integration is not confined to European Union (EU) member states. European integration is neither the exclusive historical preserve of the EU nor do the current EU member states constitute the only states affected by European integration and 'Europeanisation' in contemporary Europe.[1]

Obviously, the enlargement process incorporating ten states of central and Eastern Europe brings those states into the integration process. But the issue of 'Europe' is not confined to EU accession and is bundled up into other processes of democratisation and prospective trajectories in a range of European states that are not EU member states. For many in the candidate states EU accession is only one part of a larger process of 'returning to Europe'.[2] Looking at the candidate states of central and Eastern Europe allows us a fuller, and better, picture of the European issue.

European integration holds out the de facto possibility of a wider Europe unified under a substantial institutional structure and giving rise to broadly similar political and policy processes. In this sense, it provides us with a challenge to make our academic models conform to new European realities. In another sense, it provides us with an opportunity to test out the models of politics that have been developed in relation to Western Europe on a whole new set of cases. It provides us with comparative possibilities that increase the range of empirical data we can gather and, perhaps more importantly, it allows us to improve our conceptual range as we develop concepts that are pan-European in their application.

In looking at the specifics of what has been occurring in Europe recently, the term Europeanisation has come into use to describe the processes and impact of European integration.[3] The focus of those who use the term has primarily been on institutional and policy (process) change and there has been less spill-over of the term into the study of mass politics than we might expect. This is despite the recent growth of interest in the comparative politics approach to understanding the EU.[4] Europeanisation needs to be linked to polity, policy and *politics* if we can really talk about it as a process of profound change. The growth of interest in the role of parties in European integration and in the politics of the EU provides an excellent test bed for us to investigate the effects of Europeanisation on mass politics at the domestic level.[5] It is also notable that the concept of Europeanisation has largely been applied to existing member states and there has been little focus on the study of the candidate states to see how far they have been affected by European integration.[6]

Political parties are important gate-keepers in the process of European integration. The processes of integration and policy-making are often portrayed as technical, technocratic, elite-driven and complex. It is often forgotten that elites are selected by, beholden to, or are themselves active members of political parties. European Councils, as one visible manifestation of the EU, can be portrayed as aloof, opaque gatherings of Euro-elites. However, they are also gatherings of party politicians. The European Commission, as the embodiment of non-national identity, is made up of ex-party politicians proposed by governments that comprise 'not so ex'-party politicians. And the European Parliament is self-consciously constructed around party groupings and displays many of the features of party competition that we associate with national parliaments.[7]

Political parties as domestic political actors have also begun to incorporate Europe as an issue into their political agendas. This is partly because the decline of the permissive consensus about European integration means that we have seen the rise of political forces expressing scepticism or opposition to aspects of European integration. Moreover, to some extent, Europe is used as an issue in domestic party politics to reinforce domestic identities.[8] But we also need to be clear that EU politics are becoming increasingly incorporated into and inseparable from many political issues that would previously be regarded as purely 'domestic'.

There have been a number of studies that have charted the response of member state parties to the European issue. Leonard Ray's expert survey[9] of the position of political parties on Europe provided the basis for many other studies and for the replication and extension by Marks et al.[10] Gary Marks, Liesbet Hooghe and Carole Wilson have attempted to trace the left-right dimension and the role of the new politics dimension in determining party positions.[11] Hix and Lord have mapped party positions according to the stances taken by party activists.[12] What is notable is that there has been very little attention to the role of political parties in the integration process in the candidate states.

With the process of enlargement, the role of domestic politics in the candidate states becomes a central feature in the European integration process itself. Enlargement can only occur with the consent of the European Commission and the existing member states but it also depends on the support of the governing political parties in the candidate states and on their ability to win referendums ratifying accession. Accession has to be consistently sought by the candidate states. The competition between parties and the party system creates opportunities and incentives for parties to use the European issue for domestic electoral and strategic advantage. There is evidence that dissent about the process or the goal of accession has recently emerged at the peripheries and, in some cases, at the heart of the candidate states' party systems.

In this chapter, we assume that we can usefully examine the emergence of party-based Euroscepticism in the party systems of the candidate states and that we can account for (some of) the differences between the states by looking at their party systems. In order to do this we begin by offering a definition of Euroscepticism that differentiates between 'hard' and 'soft' variants. We then map these types of Euroscepticism in parties in the candidate states of central and Eastern Europe. In the next section we turn to the nature of party systems and suggest that we need to rethink how we conceptualise and categorise them if we are to extend our Western models to central and Eastern Europe. The reason for this, we argue, is not simply that there are new forms of party system in central and Eastern European states, but also because there are inherent limitations to the existing party system typologies in the Western European context. In the penultimate sections we apply our model of party systems to the candidate states of central and Eastern Europe and examine how this relates to the incidences of party-based Euroscepticism. In the conclusion we offer a summary and a discussion of the issues of extending the understanding of Euroscepticism and party systems from a West European to an East European context.

The chapter argues that Euroscepticism exists in virtually all of the party systems in the candidate states. While hard, rejectionist Eurosceptic parties are peripheral to the party systems, soft Eurosceptic parties that broadly support EU membership but use contestation of the EU as part of their rhetoric are much more prevalent and are even sometimes governing parties. Party system format and dynamics, however, provide only a partial explanation for the levels of party-based Euroscepticism in a party system and whether or not it manifests itself in governing parties.

Conceptualising Opposition to Europe

In exploring the meaning of Euroscepticism in the candidate states of central and Eastern Europe we are making the assumption that scepticism about

European integration has an equivalent meaning in those states to that which it has in the present West European member states. Clearly the context is different in that the states are both 'non-Western' and non-members. This does not mean that we abandon the usefulness of Euroscepticism in the central and Eastern European context but that we need to broaden out our conceptualisation of Euroscepticism so that it covers both realms.

Looking at only West European states we have defined Euroscepticism as 'the idea of contingent or qualified opposition, as well as incorporating outright and unqualified opposition to the process of European integration'.[13] However in bringing in the central and Eastern European states we see the need to differentiate types of Euroscepticism so that we can distinguish between those who are broadly opposed to Euroscepticism in principle and those who oppose European integration because of the form it takes. We find it useful to break down the Euroscepticism manifest in Eastern and central Europe into 'hard' and 'soft' Euroscepticism. Bearing in mind that all the cases under examination have a relatively high degree of consensus among political elites about the positive nature of European integration and specifically about their respective state's need to join, we can differentiate between those who are outside the consensus and do express hostility to the idea of European integration, and those that express specific limited objections to the nature of the accession process.

Hard Euroscepticism implies outright rejection of the entire project of European political and economic integration and opposition to one's country joining or remaining a member of the EU. Theoretically, hard Euroscepticism encompasses those with principled objection to the idea of any European economic or political integration. In reality such a position is too abstract to be applicable. In practice hard Euroscepticism can be identified by the principled objection to the *current form* of European integration in the EU. The principled objection comes from belief that the EU is counter to deeply held values or, more likely, is the embodiment of negative values. Examples of this would be the objection that the EU is too liberal/capitalist/socialist. In the case of the candidate countries we suggest that some parties might adopt Eurosceptic language in terms of micro and rhetorical positions while still maintaining a nominal commitment to accession. We are therefore assuming that, in such cases, nominal commitments to accession owe more to the existence of overwhelming elite consensus over Europe than to the 'heart' of the party's position. There may also be a sense that the EU has a form that is not desirable but that there is no alternative, or that the alternative is to return to communist rule and this is an even less desirable goal. Soft Euroscepticism, on the other hand, involves contingent or qualified opposition to European integration. Soft Euroscepticism is, therefore, contingent as it does not imply an opposition to integration on principled grounds but does imply that if there were alterations to either a policy area or a shift in national interest, European integration in its current form could be supported or even encouraged. Although we are using this distinction specifically to analyse party-based Euroscepticism in candidate states it works equally well for existing member states and elsewhere we have used it to analyse patterns of party-based Euroscepticism in a pan-European context.[14]

Mapping Euroscepticism in Central and Eastern Europe

Mapping party-based Euroscepticism in the candidate states of central and Eastern Europe gives us data that should help us in projecting the way in which accession will or will not occur in those states. It also provides us with a lens through which we can see how an issue refracts through the party system. This means that the European issue gives us the potential to understand something of both 'international' and domestic politics.

In reality the distinction between hard and soft Euroscepticism is not a hard and fast one and it is likely to be distributed along a spectrum. But in operationalising the terms we have sought to differentiate which end of the pole parties expressing some Euroscepticism are closer to and have therefore opted for a nominal differentiation. The purpose of this is to allow us to make comparisons across the range of party systems represented in the candidate states of central and Eastern Europe. The data is based on our own research and on the collation of the input of a range of experts of the particular party systems.

Table 1 lists the parties in each of the candidate countries that can be regarded as displaying either the hard or soft variants of Euroscepticism. We have also attempted to list (where we have information) factions within parties that display Euroscepticism that is at odds with the official position of their

Table 1: Contemporary Political Parties with Hard and Soft Euroscepticism in the Candidate Countries of Central and Eastern Europe

	Hard	Soft
Bulgaria	None	None
Czech Republic	Communist Party of Bohemia and Moravia (11.0-1998)	Civic Democratic Party (27.7-1998) Association for the Republic-Republican Party of Czechoslovakia (3.9-1998)
Estonia	Estonian Christian People's Party (2.43-1999) Estonian Future Party [16] Republican Party [17]	Centre Party (23.41-1999) Estonian Rural People's Party (7.27-1999)
Hungary	Hungarian Justice and Life Party (5.5-1998) Hungarian Workers' Party (4.1-1998)	FIDESZ/Hungarian Civic Party (28.2-1998) FKGP Independent Party of Smallholders (13.8-1998)
Latvia		Latvian Social Democratic Alliance (12.9-1998) Conservative Union for Fatherland & Freedom (14.2-1998)
Lithuania		The Centre Union of Lithuania (2.86-2000) Lithuanian Peasants Party (4.08-2000)
Poland	Self Defence (10.2-2001) League of Polish Families (7.87-2001)	Law and Justice Party (9.5-2001) Polish Peasant Party (8.98-2001) Christian National Union (faction in Solidarity Electoral Action)
Romania		Greater Romania Party (19.48-00)
Slovakia		Movement for a Democratic Slovakia (27.0-1998) Slovak National Party (9.1-1998) Christian Democratic Movement (faction in Slovak Democratic Coalition)
Slovenia	New Party (Drevensek & Reven) (0.59-2000)	Slovenian National Party (4.38-2000)

Note: Percentage share of vote won in parliamentary elections, and year of elections, are reported in brackets.

Sources: Bulgaria - Deyan Kiuranov, (the Centre for Liberal Strategies), Elena Iankova (Cornell University); Czech Republic - Sean Hanley (Brunel University), Kieran Williams (SSEES/UCL); Petr Kopecky (University of Sheffield); Estonia - Evald Mikkel (University of Tartu); Hungary - Agnes Batory, (University of Cambridge); Latvia - Gunta Misane (Latvia Bureau of European Information); Lithuania - Ruta Buienevita (Sussex European Institute); Poland - Aleks Szczerbiak (Sussex European Institute); Romania - Sorin Ionita (Georgetown University), Norma Nitescu (Sussex European Institute); Slovakia - Karen Henderson, (University of Leicester), Kieran Williams (SSEES/UCL); Slovenia - Alenka Krasovec (Ljubljana University).

Table 2: Cumulative Share of the Vote for Party-Based Euroscepticism in Parliamentary Elections for Lower Chamber by Country and Type of Euroscepticism

Country	Hard	Soft	Total
Bulgaria	0	0	0
Slovenia	0.59	4.38	4.97
Lithuania	0	6.94	6.94
Romania	0	19.48	19.48
Latvia	0	27.1	27.1
Estonia	2.43	30.68	33.11
Slovakia	0	36.1	36.1
Poland	18.07	18.48	36.55
Czech Republic	11.0	31.6	42.6
Hungary	9.6	42.0	51.6
Average	*4.17*	*21.68*	*25.85*

parties. We have also listed their share of the vote at the most recent parliamentary elections and aggregated this in Table 2. This gives some idea of the relative importance of the parties within their party systems. We should be clear that this figure does not amount to the size of a potential Eurosceptical electorate as many parties have Europe as a very minor issue and in some countries the issue has a very low salience in the party system as a whole.[15] The two concepts in fact measure somewhat different phenomena. The share of vote for hard Eurosceptic parties illustrates how opposition to EU membership *currently finds expression* in the party system. The level of support for soft Eurosceptic parties, and total share for all Eurosceptic parties, is more an indication of the potential for Euroscepticism to find expression in the party system because these are parties that, while they do not currently oppose EU membership outright, are clearly comfortable with using rhetoric that contests aspects of European integration as part of their political repertoire. Taken together these two totals provide us with a crude indicator of the total level of party-based Euroscepticism in the party system.

The picture that this presents allows us to make a number of observations. The first is that Euroscepticism, broadly understood, is a feature of all the party systems of the central and Eastern European candidate states with the one exception of Bulgaria. This is an important finding as it demonstrates the highly politicised process of accession and also demonstrates that, even where the stakes are high, the issue of European integration can become an issue of party competition. The permissive consensus that was seen to underlay early European integration is something that cannot be assumed among the candidate states of central and Eastern Europe.

The second observation is that while it is almost ubiquitous, Euroscepticism remains usually a minority concern and is often the preserve of parties that garner relatively low shares of their national vote. Indeed, that is precisely why in our research we did not confine ourselves to parliamentary parties as it is often the case that any Euroscepticism is found in parties at the margins of their party systems.

The third observation is that soft party-based Euroscepticism is more present than hard Euroscepticism. It is the case that there are more parties in the soft Eurosceptical category and that they are more significant in terms of vote shares than their hard Eurosceptic counterparts. Even if we aggregate the vote shares of all parties in each country expressing hard and soft Euroscepticism (see table 2 above) we can see that the average aggregate vote share for hard Eurosceptic parties is 4.17 per cent compared with 21.68 per cent for soft Eurosceptical parties.

The fourth observation is that the patterns of party-based Euroscepticism in the candidate states of central and Eastern Europe are remarkably similar to those in the member states. Data presented elsewhere[18] demonstrate that the three above observations apply equally to these states as they do to the fifteen existing member states. The pattern of small parties with a range of ideological positions taking Eurosceptical stances is one that is pan-European. This is evidence of the Europeanisation of the European issue in party systems.

The question then becomes what explains the variation in the numbers and types of parties advocating Euroscepticism? Drawing from our experience of party-based Euroscepticism there is a strong case to suggest that the nature of the party system has some bearing on that. Once again, looking at party systems across Europe necessitates some rethinking about our categorisations of party systems and it is towards this that we turn in the following section.

Categorising Party Systems

The literature on the categorisations of party systems is extensive but the most widely used and sophisticated comparative typology is that provided by Sartori.[19] Previous schemas relied heavily on the numbers of parties[20] but

Sartori suggests that the number of parties alone is insufficient to capture the real dynamics of a party system and the structure and direction of competition that they engender.[21] Sartori's framework seeks to sub-divide the large multi-party category by focusing on the different ways that the parties interact in different systems.

For our purposes we can focus primarily on the multi-party category as all of the candidate states fall broadly into this bracket. Indeed the overwhelming majority of European party systems fall into this category. This is why the sub-division between moderate and polarised pluralism provided by Sartori is so potentially useful. In this Sartori was essentially differentiating between those systems where the dynamic of competition was towards the centre and consensual (moderate pluralism) and those where competition drove the parties towards the poles of the party system and towards a more fractious type of politics (polarised pluralism).[22] The two types of multi-party system have different properties and generate different types of interaction, and this is potentially important in considering *how* central and Eastern European party systems manifest the European issue.

In trying to categorise the systems of central and Eastern Europe according to Sartori's types we come across a difficulty. The characteristics of the polarised pluralist party system are that they tend to have a dominant centre party, anti-system parties at the poles and have a centrifugal dynamic, whereas moderate pluralist systems have a centripetal logic and will not tend to have dominant centre parties. In the case of the candidate states, although there are parties which can be clearly categorised as anti-system, in spite of some commentators' expectations, they have not produced polarised party systems with a dominant centre party facing bi-polar opposition. The experience of one-party rule during the communist period as well as the problems of transition combine to militate against the presence of dominant centre parties. This means, in short, that all the states we are looking at broadly fit into the one category of moderate pluralism. (This is also increasingly true of most West European party systems following the collapse or social democratisation of communist parties.)[23] However, this finding is clearly at odds with the general observation of comparative scholars who note the variation in the forms of these party systems. Sartori's distinction does capture an important difference that is, to an extent, manifest in the candidate states of central and Eastern Europe. However, we need some way of capturing what is quite a real variation in the types of party system and which also fits with the spirit of Sartori's differentiation that captures the importance of the patterns of interaction between parties.

There are many problems in attempting to categorise central and Eastern European party systems that go beyond the particularities of Sartori's differentiation.[24] Not the least of these is the lack of 'system-ness' and the sense that these systems are in flux. This means that scholars of central and Eastern Europe have the sense that they are aiming at a moving target. Paul Lewis, in his wide-ranging survey of party systems across the whole of central and Eastern Europe, grapples with this issue and comes to the conclusion that he has little certainty that 'anything like a proper system of stable interactions has developed in any of the countries of the region'.[25] Certainly there is a high degree of change in these party systems and this causes some problems.

However, as Lewis also acknowledges, the difficulty can easily be exaggerated and we feel that there is utility in treating the party systems as systems.[26] West European party systems, often assumed to be the models of stable party systems, are less 'static' than sometimes they appear to be. We need only look at dramatic shifts in the British and Italian party systems in the past decade to witness two party systems that, according to Sartori's categories, could be said to have shifted location. Britain has gone from being a 'dominant' party system with the Conservatives winning a majority of parliamentary seats for three elections in a row, (back) to being a two-party system. Italy, the archetype of Sartori's polarised pluralism for most of the post-war period, underwent the equivalent of a revolution in the early 1990s to become a case of moderate pluralism. The assertion that central and Eastern European party systems are too much in flux to be categorised implies that they are qualitatively different from comparable party systems. We want to work here with the assumption that they might be *quantitatively* different in that they may have a higher level of variation, but they are not *qualitatively* different (i.e. that we can usefully compare them).[27] All systems are in flux, to different degrees admittedly, and therefore our categorisation needs to build in this possibility as part of the schema and not as something rendering the systems as less system-like.

There is a danger that the alleged specificity of the democratisation paradigm has become so embedded in approaches to central and Eastern Europe that an unease manifests itself in any attempt to treat these states as comparable to Western European states. The belief that the cases of central and Eastern European party systems have not yet established some sort of stability not only assumes that other (i.e. Western European) systems have stability, it also assumes that there is some sort of 'normality' that will eventually manifest itself in these systems when they 'settle down'. We suspect that there is no settling down for these party systems and that rather than trying to think *diachronically* and categorise single party systems across a period of time (e.g. the post-War British system has been two-party), it is more useful to think *synchronically*. This builds in *change* as a norm and also allows us to make time-specific comparisons. A dynamic conception of party systems, as we outline below, works on the assumption that any 'normality' is more likely to be manifest in change than in stability.

Party systems are best conceived of as categories *between* competing models so that at any one point in time we can 'plot the position' of a party system in relation to the two most apposite models. Taking us away from the strict criteria of Sartori's categories but keeping to the sense that there is something significantly different between systems with dualistic tendencies and those with more pluralistic, multi-polar tendencies, we propose to offer a new simple differentiation of party systems. For our purposes we can limit ourselves to two models that apply to multi-party systems.[28] Our differentiation is therefore between the models of party systems with *bi-polar* competition and those with *multi-polar competition*.

Party systems that are nearer to the bi-polar model are those where the structure of competition is between two sets of parties who tend to form coalitions in broadly the same configuration and where neither of these coalitional groups is electorally dominant. The most obvious form of bi-polarity is between right and left wing blocks or centre-left and centre-right blocks. Party systems nearer to the multi-polar model are those where coalitions vary radically in composition and where no single party dominates. Bi-polar systems will tend to manifest different types of debate and political discussion from multi-polar systems. To put this point more dryly, different types of party systems iterate issues in different types of ways. Bi-polar systems may be characterised most clearly when there is competition over one dominant issue, one dominant force (or individual) or between pro- and anti-system forces. Thus, in the case of Slovakia, the figure of Meciar serves as a lightning rod so that politicians can be characterised by their attitude towards him and his party, and the very existence of the governing coalition derives from the shared goal of keeping him out of the premiership. In categorising party systems we do not see systems neatly conforming to each ideal type but we can say that parties are nearer to one type than the other and we can accommodate the fact that systems may be in flux between different models at any one time.

We suggest that a more open, multi-polar system is liable to give more space and incentive for the expression of Euroscepticism than a closed dualistic system. We expect party systems that are bi-polar to have less 'space' for the expression of Euroscepticism whereas multi-polarity will not only provide more space for parties to carve out distinct party systems but will also provide increased incentives for them to do this. Why is this likely to be the case?

The dynamics of multi-polarity are such that peripheral parties can use a second-order issue such as European integration as one of multiple techniques for differentiating themselves from other more established parties. In short, our proposition is therefore the more multi-polar a party system the greater the aggregate level of party-based Euroscepticism in that system.

In other work we examined the proposition, derived from work on Western European systems, that Euroscepticism is the preserve of non-governmental parties in the candidate states of central and Eastern Europe but we found a different pattern.[29] As Table 1 shows, it is clear that, while peripheral parties do use Euroscepticism as means of differentiating themselves from the centre parties in central and Eastern Europe, Euroscepticism is also expressed by major parties of government. Indeed, this may also be becoming more possible in Western Europe. This means that there may be some mileage in developing a two-stage model for accounting for the emergence of party-based Euroscepticism in relation to types of party system, and so we suggest a second proposition relating to party systems that we can investigate.

This proposition centres around the idea that there is something about the nature of Euroscepticism that specifically relates to the oppositional dynamic in party systems such that we might expect multi-polar party systems to generate Euroscepticism in non-governmental parties but bi-polar systems to generate (soft) Euroscepticism among governing parties.

Party Systems and Euroscepticism

In seeing whether there is a relationship between the type of party system and the strength of party-based Euroscepticism we categorise each of the candidate states in terms of their party system, but this yields non-quantitative data, so we can only offer a simple visual comparison. Using our own assessments of the party systems, we classify Bulgaria, the Czech Republic, Estonia, Latvia, Lithuania, Poland, Romania and Slovenia as having multi-polar systems and Hungary and Slovakia as having bi-polar party systems. This is tabulated with levels of support for party-based Euroscepticism and laid out below in figure 1. This allows us to evaluate our first party system proposition that the more multi-polar a party system is, the greater the aggregate level of party-based Euroscepticism in that system.

Figure 1 shows that while there is no straightforward relationship between the level of party-based Euroscepticism and type of party system there does seem to be some sort of relationship. Four of the six countries with high party-based Euroscepticism - the Czech Republic, Latvia, Estonia and Poland - are multi-polar party systems. On the other hand, the two bi-polar systems Slovakia and Hungary are somewhat exceptions to this. The case of Slovakia

Figure 1: Levels of Party-Based Euroscepticism by Type of Party System

	Bi-Polar Party Systems	Multi-Polar Party Systems
Low Party-Based Euroscepticism		Bulgaria Slovenia* Romania Lithuania
High Party-Based Euroscepticism	Hungary* Slovakia	Czech Republic* Latvia Estonia* Poland*

* Has party in system expressing hard Euroscepticism

may be accounted for by the role of Meciar in his party system: the bi-polarity in the Slovakian case reflects the presence of pro- or anti-Meciar forces in the Slovakian party system. A recent fragmentation of the anti-Meciar party forces may indicate that the system is becoming more multi-polar. On the other side of the equation we can see that Bulgaria, Lithuania, Romania and Slovenia falls outside the expected relationship, being multi-polar systems with low levels of party-based Euroscepticism. However, until their most recent elections three of these party systems (Bulgaria, Lithuania and Romania) would have been categorised as bi-polar and therefore been located in the top left hand column as hypothesised. It may simply be that there is a time lag operating here and that the parties in these systems have not responded to the new opportunity structure that a multi-polar system creates.

Turning to our second proposition, that multi-polar party systems generate Euroscepticism in non-governmental parties but bi-polar systems generate (soft) Euroscepticism among governing parties, we found that governing parties in six states expressed soft Euroscepticism.[30] These states are the Czech Republic, Hungary, Poland, Slovakia and Slovenia. We have laid out in figure 2 the relationship between party systems with and without governing parties expressing Euroscepticism by type of party system. It is clear from the table that in six of the ten cases the hypothesised relationship does occur. Both party systems with governing parties expressing soft Euroscepticism are in the bi-polar category (Hungary and Slovakia). However, four of the eight multi-party systems also have a Eurosceptic governing party, while

Figure 2: Presence of Party-Based Euroscepticism Among Parties of Government by Type of Party System

	Bi-Polar Party Systems	Multi-Polar Party Systems
Euroscepticism in Governing Parties	Hungary* Slovakia	Slovenia* Czech Republic* Estonia* Poland*
Euroscepticism not in Governing Parties		Bulgaria Romania Latvia Lithuania

* Has party in system expressing hard Euroscepticism

the other four do not. We can however note that all multi-polar systems that contain governing parties expressing soft Euroscepticism also have parties expressing hard Euroscepticism in their party systems. This might mean that multi-polar systems offer greater opportunities for expressing Euroscepticism and that a particular incentive is offered to governmental parties expressing soft Euroscepticism, but that hard Euroscepticism is necessary as a means of differentiation for the parties taking advantage of the space to express Euroscepticism.

Looking at the type of party system offers us one piece of the puzzle in explaining how or whether Euroscepticism finds purchase within national party systems. It is clear that the national contexts and the different way the European issue is framed in domestic debate, as well as the variation in the status of the countries as candidates, will also play a role. But we can see that the nature of the system needs to be one component in any model of party-based Euroscepticism.

Conclusion

The proposed enlargement of the EU is part a conscious process of Europeanisation through institutionalisation and through convergence in policymaking. Our research demonstrates that, partly as a reaction to enlargement, the Europeanisation of mass politics has preceded those processes. At the level of domestic politics, European integration has become an issue of contestation and a part of the domestic political agenda.

This chapter shows that Euroscepticism broadly understood is a feature of all the party systems of the central and Eastern European candidate states with the one exception of Bulgaria. However, while it is almost ubiquitous, hard party-based Euroscepticism remains usually a minority concern and is often the preserve of parties that garner relatively low shares of their national vote. There are more parties in the soft Eurosceptical category and they are more significant in terms of vote shares than their hard Eurosceptic counterparts. In this respect, patterns of party-based Euroscepticism in the candidate states of central and Eastern Europe are remarkably similar to those in the member states.

In attempting to account for this, the format and dynamics of the party system offers a partial explanation for the varying levels of party-based Euroscepticism. Bi-polar party systems do not seem to discourage the emergence of party-based Euroscepticism while multi-polar party systems appear to be equally likely to produce systems with low levels of party-based Euroscepticism. On the other hand, when one bears in mind that three of the four multi-polar party systems with low levels of party based Euroscepticism were, until recently, bi-polar systems there is a clearer 'fit' in terms of the hypothesised relationship. Similarly, both bi-polar party systems have soft Eurosceptic parties. While only half of the multi-polar party systems have no soft Eurosceptic governing party, the four that do also have a hard Eurosceptic party in their system which may partly account for this. Clearly there are other variables that need to be considered to properly account for this relationship.

Notes

[1] H. Wallace 'Europeanisation and Globalisation: Complementary or Contradictory Trends?' *New Political Economy* 5(3), (2000), pp. 369-82, pp. 372-4.

[2] K. Henderson (ed.) *Back to Europe: Central and Eastern Europe and the European Union* (London: UCL Press, 1999).

[3] The literature is voluminous but key contributions are R. Ladrech 'Europeanisation of Domestic Politics and Institutions: The Case of France', *Journal of Common Market Studies* 32 (1994), pp. 69-88, C.M. Radaelli, 'Whither Europeanisation? Concept stretching and substantive', *European Integration online Papers* (EIoP) 4(8) 2000; http://eiop.or.at/eiop/texte/2000-008a.htm B. Kohler-Koch and R. Eising (eds.), *The Transformation of Governance in the European Union* (London: Routledge, 1999), C. Knill and D. Lehmkuhl, 'How Europe Matters: Different Mechanisms of European Integration', *European Integration on-line Papers* 3, 1999, http://eiopo.or.at.eiop/texte/1999_07a.htm. and, M.G. Cowles, J. Caporaso, and T. Risse (eds.) *Transforming Europe: Europeanisation and Domestic Change* (Ithaca, NY: Cornell University Press, 2001).

[4] S. Hix, *The Political System of the European Union* (Basingstoke: Palgrave, 1999), J. Richardson (ed.) *European Union: Power and Policy-Making* (London: Routledge, 2nd edn., 2001).

[5] See, for example J. Gaffney (ed.), *Political Parties and the European Union* (London: Routledge, 1996), S. Hix and C. Lord *Political Parties in the European Union* (London: Palgrave, 1997).

6. Notable exceptions to this tendency are K. Goetz 'European Integration and National Executives: A Cause in Search of an Effect', *West European Politics* 23(4), 2000, pp. 211-231, and H. Grabbe, 'Europeanising public policy in Central Europe: asymmetical relations and uncertainty', paper presented at the Seventh Biennial International Conference of the European Community Studies Association, 31 May-2 June, 2001, Madison, Wisconsin.
7. Hix and Lord, *Political Parties*, p. 1; T. Raunio, *The European Perspective: Transnational Party Groups in the 1989-1994 European Parliament* (Aldershot: Ashgate, 1997).
8. P. Taggart, 'A Touchstone of Dissent: Euroscepticism in Contemporary Western European Party Systems', *European Journal of Political Research*, 33, 1998, pp. 363-388.
9. L. Ray, 'Measuring Party Orientations Towards European Integration: Results from an Expert Survey', *European Journal of Political Research*, 36, 1999, pp. 283-306.
10. Survey conducted by Gary Marks, David Scott, Marco Steenbergen and Carole Wilson's replication (reported in L. Hooghe, G. Marks and C. Wilson 'Party Positions on European Integration: New Politics vs. Left/Right', paper presented at the Seventh Biennial International Conference of the European Community Studies Association, 31 May-2 June, 2001, Madison, Wisconsin).
11. Hooghe, Marks and Wilson, 'Party Positions'. G. Marks and L. Hooghe 'National Parties and the Contestation of Europe' in T. Banchoff and M.P. Smith (eds.), *Legitimacy and the European Union* (London: Routledge, 1999). G. Marks and C.J. Wilson 'The Past in the Present: A Cleavage Theory of Party Response to European Integration', *British Journal of Political Science*, 30, 2000, pp. 433-459. L. Hooghe and G. Marks, *Multi-Level Governance and European Integration* (Lanham: Rowman and Littlefield, 2001).
12. Hix and Lord, *Political Parties*, Ch. 2.
13. Taggart 'A Touchstone', p. 366.
14. P. Taggart and A. Szczerbiak, 'Crossing Europe: Patterns of Contemporary Party-Based Euroscepticism in EU Member States and the Candidate States of Central and Eastern Europe' paper presented at the annual meeting of the American Political Science Association, 29 August-2 September, 2001, San Francisco.
15. A. Batory, 'Hungarian Party Identities and the Question of Europea', Opposing Europe Research Network, Working Paper No. 4 (Brighton: Sussex European Institute, 2001) available at http://www.sussex.ac.uk/Units/SEI/pdfs/wp49.pdf.
16. This party failed to be registered for the 1999 elections and so no vote share is shown.
17. This party has been formed since the 1999 elections and so no vote share is shown.
18. Taggart and Szczerbiak 'Crossing Europe.'

[19] G. Sartori, *Parties and Party Systems* (Cambridge: Cambridge University Press, 1976).
[20] The classic example being M. Duverger, *Political Parties: Their Organisation and Activities in the Modern State* (London: Methuen, 1956).
[21] Sartori, *Parties*, p. 120.
[22] Ibid., 179, pp. 130-9.
[23] P. Webb, 'Party systems, Electoral Cleavages and Government Stability', in P. Heywood, E. Jones and M. Rhodes (eds) *Development in West European Politics 2* (Basingstoke: Palgrave, 2002), 115-34.
[24] See, for example H. Kitschelt, Z. Mansfeldova, R. Markowski and G. Tóka, *Post-Communist Party Systems: Competition, Representation and Inter-Party Competition* (Cambridge: Cambridge University Press. 1999), P.G. Lewis, *Political Parties in Post-Communist Eastern Europe* (London Routledge, 2001).
[25] Lewis, *Political Parties*, p. 124.
[26] Ibid., p. 149.
[27] For arguments stressing the specificity of the central and Eastern European experience see P. Mair, *Party System Change: Approaches and Interpretations* (Oxford: Clarendon Press, 1997), Ch. 8, and K. Henderson 'Euroscepticism or Europhobia: Opposition Attitudes to the EU in the Slovak Republic', Opposing Europe Research Network Working Paper No. 5 (Brighton: Sussex European Institute, 2001) available at http://www.sussex.ac.uk/Units/SEI/pdfs/wp50.pdf.
[28] In reality we expect that party systems will generate a range of models and that some of these models might be context-specific but that in building up a battery of different models generated in different contexts we may start to see comparative patterns and we can also improve on our specific understanding of particular party systems at particular points in time.
[29] P. Taggart and A. Szczerbiak, 'Parties, Positions and Europe: Euroscepticism in the EU Candidate States of Central and Eastern Europe', Opposing Europe Research Network Working Paper No. 2 (Brighton: Sussex European Institute, 2001) available at http://www.sussex.ac.uk/Units/SEI/pdfs/wp46.pdf) and Taggart 'A Touchstone'.
[30] Taggart and Szczerbiak, 'Parties'.

Paul G. Lewis
European Parties East and West: Comparative Perspectives

What general conclusions can be drawn from this survey of parties in contemporary central and eastern Europe (CEE) in the light of developments in established west European democracies and the analytical models this experience has engendered? The articles in this special issue provide extensive new material in this area and bring to bear a range of valuable insights into such questions. Most contributions point to broad and quite rapidly established similarities with, however, some significant differences and particular regional characteristics. In this they follow recent general studies of new parties in CEE and of post-communist party system development in broad terms.[1] The observations in this issue of PEPS cover a number of interrelated aspects of party development. They concern:

- the key institutional frameworks within which parties operate and which critically affect the parties' modes of behaviour;
- the nature of the parties themselves, the way in which they are organised and their manner of operation;
- the relation of CEE developments to theoretically embedded conceptions of modern parties and the general fit of these patterns to the models of party structure and activity commonly applied in the west.

In terms of the context of party activity and the central institutions that underpin the operation of parties, the *electoral systems* currently operating in the east are very similar to those in western Europe and the outcomes they produce are very much in line with the practice of established democracies (see article by Sarah Birch). Party systems are slightly larger in the east (in terms of the effective number of elective and parliamentary parties) and less likely to take the form of a two-party system. The ratio between the number of elective and parliamentary parties is nevertheless higher than at equivalent stages of west European development. This means that contemporary CEE electoral systems play a significant political role in their own right and have a much more restrictive effect on the size of party systems than their equivalents in western Europe. The main agency through which this is achieved is the high threshold of representation applied in CEE (and not alternative features of the electoral system like, for example, variable constituency size). The relatively swift consolidation of the new party systems has thus been achieved by conscious institutional decision and the use of 'artificial' devices like thresholds rather than the more natural but lengthy evolution of competitive party systems as seen in the west.

This, in turn, is likely to be the result of efforts consciously made by successful new parties to consolidate their strength by blocking access to the central political arena for potential competitors. Although not explicitly suggested in Birch's article, it is a view that carries strong overtones of the cartelisation extensively discussed elsewhere is this issue and in the contemporary party literature more generally. While, too, it has several advantages as a way of exerting influence on the shape of the emerging party systems, the application of a high threshold is a device that has the drawback of producing a large number of votes that are obviously wasted in terms of political representation. It also imposes a sharp all-or-nothing cut-off point in terms of access to the critical parliamentary arena. Relatively small parties that just clear the threshold can gain a disproportionately large number of seats, while parties that are only slightly less successful in attracting votes will remain wholly excluded from the parliamentary arena.

Another feature of the political systems in which parties develop in CEE, and one that is of some importance in the recently established democracies of post-communist Europe, is that of *presidentialism* and the influence of electoral contests for presidential office on the often weakly developed party systems of the region. The place of party has often vied with that of the presidency in the developing representative system, and the process of presidential competition has in some cases had a strong effect on the structure of party system. This could be true even when the constitutional role of the president was not particularly strong and the system was basically a parliamentary one – as was indeed the case in post-communist Poland, as Frances Millard demonstrates. The effect in Poland of the personal competition that dominates presidential elections has therefore been to amplify the weakness of the institutional development of the party system and overlay patterns of party competition with that between presidential candidates.

One of the key aspects of party organisation and activity (and not unrelated in terms of party system development to the effects of the electoral mechanism outlined above) is that of *state funding* and, more generally, the sources from which parties draw resources to support their operations. Ingrid van Biezen and Petr Kopecký thus examine the role of state money in financing party activity not just in CEE but also in the new democracies of southern Europe (Spain and Portugal). Their hypothesis that public funds will need to flow more strongly to support party activity in new democracies is largely confirmed, although there are some variations in how strongly this tendency emerges. It is less strong in the Czech Republic than in Hungary, for example, and longer-established parties like the Communist Party and Christian Democrats have been able to depend more on membership fees. A similar tendency could be seen in Portugal. Governing parties, too, have had some success in attracting funds from the business sector while a further significant factor is that of corruption and illicit funding. By their very nature the latter forms of funding are covert and largely hidden from public view. General perceptions suggest, however, that corrupt finance is less prevalent in established democracies and the democratic regimes of southern Europe and more prominent in the newer post-communist democracies of CEE (though less so in Hungary, as well as in Estonia and Slovenia).

Further distinctions were also drawn between new democracies and the established western regimes. Somewhat surprisingly, funds flowed more strongly to the parties' central office than to their parliamentary leadership while there was a tendency, particularly strong in central Europe, for resources to be directed more to electoral activities than regular organisational procedures. The latter effect may, indeed, be directly linked with the consequences of the electoral mechanism outlined above in the discussion of Birch's article, for high thresholds mean that a premium is placed on electoral success if parties are to gain access to state funds. But the picture here is not a uniform one, and it is not always the newer democracies of central Europe that exemplify this tendency, which is also pronounced in Spain. Nevertheless, there also seems to be a growing insistence in Czech governing parties on amending the institutional rules to protect their position and maximise income.

The theme of *state funding and cartelisation* is pursued and extended in the Polish context in Szczerbiak's article. He also hypothesises that state funding is likely to be a strong source of support in post-communist Poland and that, indeed, it could be a stronger basis for party activity than was the case at a comparable stage of west European democratic development. This view is broadly confirmed in the light of Polish experience, even though prior to 1997 the only form of direct state financial support for party activity was the system of reimbursement for electoral expenses introduced in 1993. It was hardly surprising, too, that all parties were enthusiastically in favour of the extension of state funding. This was as true of the successor Peasant Party as it was of the newer parties, even though its possession of a more extensive membership and organisational base might have been expected to give it a relative advantage over other parties in a situation where state funding was less extensive. Such views also correspond to the progressive cartelisation of party politics many observers see as a dominant trend in west European democracies. The evidence the Polish case offers in support of this hypothesis is, however, mixed. Entry to the political arena has by no means been blocked for new parties (shown not least by the parliamentary representation of four new parties or political organisations after the 2001 election to accompany just two established parties), and the new funding law of 1997 was actually rather favourable to non-parliamentary parties. The political system in Poland in this sense appeared to be considerably more open than that discerned in the Czech Republic.

The question of *party models* is more explicitly addressed in Hanley's article. He focuses less on the cartel model than on the idea of contemporary parties as electoral-professional organisations, and argues that the salience of the idea of the mass party as a broad characterisation of successor parties rooted in the old regime is overplayed. The articles both by van Biezen and Kopecký and by Szczerbiak also pay some attention to the particular position of the successor parties, although they do not suggest that their particular organisational characteristics have produced any distinctive features in the pattern of post-communist party politics. Hanley argues, on the basis of Czech experience, that parties in central Europe are most likely to follow a path-dependent line of development and to develop as hybrid organisations rather than as those embodying the characteristics of any particular west European model.

It is a view that relates not just to the ruling and satellite parties of the communist period but also to the organisational capital embodied in the short-lived mass movements of the transitional period and the resources passed to historic parties by emigrés and international actors. Yet here too there are reflections of some cartel tendencies, in that most dominant contemporary parties are understood to have developed from previously existing organisations that have monopolised organisational start-up capital and already choked off more authentically new parties. Nevertheless, he argues, there was a tendency by the mid- to late 1990s for Czech parties to converge on a broadly electoral-professional line of development.

The linkage between intra-party development and the institutional environment forms the topic of Boucek's chapter. Issues arising from the impact of electoral systems are again studied, this time in relation to the constraints and incentives they provide for intra-party behaviour and the development of factionalism. *Intra-party politics* in CEE - particularly in terms of conflicting pressures for unity or fragmentation, party factionalism or coherence - seem, on the basis of the relatively limited evidence so far available, to follow a pattern that suggests convergence with western Europe and thus affirm current theory derived from western experience. The major influence on the differing forms of intra-party behaviour derives, it is argued, from the nature of the electoral system. At one extreme is the single-member plurality system well entrenched in Britain (but hardly anywhere else). Despite signs of inner-party dissent in the 1980s and 90s the national parties in Britain remain concentrated and cohesive, although the implications of this for democratic representation and effective government remain less clear as third-party support has grown in the electorate. The hyper-representative systems seen in

Italy and Japan until the early 1990s produced strong factional tendencies. This created its form of immobilism as factions combined to block reform in the Italian Christian Democratic Party and sub-party preferences became similarly dominant in the Liberal Democratic Party of Japan. Aware of such problems, most new CEE democracies adopted mixed member electoral systems (as indeed did Italy and Japan following their experience of the more directly representative system). Evidence on the outcomes of the mixed systems is limited in view of the short period they have been in operation, although the judgement so far is that they have contributed to the rapid stabilisation of party systems and to forms of party behaviour not dissimilar to those seen in western Europe.

Sitter also directs attention to questions of *party system change* and the emerging relation between party strategy and system development in CEE. The question of whether western models can usefully be applied to the new CEE democracies is squarely addressed in a wide-ranging discussion of the well-known Lipset-Rokkan proposals concerning European cleavage structures and their relation to the freezing of party systems. The implication of the proposals for party system development has been the source of some debate in the west as, while some have understood this to embody a form of sociological determinism in reflecting and perpetuating cleavage structures, others have interpreted the 'freezing' hypothesis as one not akin to some process of nature but more the outcome of purposive political activity and the result of particular party strategies. Analysis of CEE developments confirms the second interpretation and directs attention to the active role of parties and their strategic choices in guiding the path of party system development. Party systems do not just 'emerge' but have proved rather to be the outcome of how individual parties choose to compete.

The configuration of different CEE parties is also a focus of attention for Taggart and Szczerbiak, who analyse the inter-relation of *party systems and the emergence of Euroscepticism* in the ten candidate states. In terms of party policy and voter preferences, patterns of Euroscepticism in CEE are similar to those in existing member states of the European Union. Some element of Euroscepticism is found in most countries (Bulgaria being the exception). Euroscepticism (particularly in its stronger variants) is a minority concern and policy line generally pursued by less mainstream parties, while soft

Euroscepticism is considerably more common than the harder kind. The nature of the party system and government tenure may also play a part in this pattern. As a tentative hypothesis it is argued, and at least partly confirmed, that Euroscepticism is greater in multi-polar systems, although it is bi-polar systems that are more likely to see (soft) Euroscepticism among governing parties.

While there are significant regional characteristics, then, it is at least reasonable to conclude that the path of party development in CEE, and indeed the operation of new European democracies more generally (or at least of the more developed central European systems of Hungary, Poland and the Czech Republic focussed on here), does not diverge greatly from the lines indicated by models derived from the experience of established western regimes. Contemporary democracies, whether new or old, provide broadly similar conditions for the development of political parties and offer similar kinds of incentives for their pattern of growth. The relatively high level of socio-economic development at which contemporary democracies operate - invariably now within some form of capitalist framework - affords a rapidly increasing range of technological facilities that permit rapid and extensive communication of political symbols and information (albeit at a fairly superficial level).[2] The need for a formally constituted mass membership and intensively structured party organisation is thus avoided, although the critical question of where the funds to support party activity and the increasingly expensive technological resources required to mount election campaigns come from remains pressing. The kind of party that emerges under these conditions may be variously defined - as modern cadre, catch-all, electoral-professional or even cartel (also some doubts will be expressed about the latter further on) - but all such models refer to broadly the same kind of party. The intensity of inter- and transnational communication and interaction, not least in the broad European arena, reinforces tendencies to uniformity.

There are undoubtedly costs involved in the dominance of such slimmed-down parties in terms of the roles they are able to perform and the nature of the contribution they are able to make to the operation of a modern democracy. They are less prominent as agencies of social integration, less capable of mobilising citizens for political participation, and less able to perform the pivotal roles of mediation that were prominent during the formative stages of modern mass democracy and which served to hold state and civil society in a relatively stable relationship in many countries. The parties such conditions have tended to produce throughout the democratic world seem nevertheless to be sufficient to sustain the operation of modern liberal democracies, albeit at a fairly basic level. But significant differences between established western democracies and the new post-communist systems are by no means absent, and they are variously identified in the different articles in this collection.

Parties in the new CEE democracies, as well as the institutional context within which they operate, have emerged and been consciously formed in the light of the ongoing experience of established as well as recently formed democracies. The electoral regimes applied in CEE are, in Birch's words, state-of-the-art and, it may be argued, both consciously adapted to the general conditions of the new post-communist democracies and also carefully amended by their designers to meet the interests of particular parties. The state, further, occupies a special position in CEE politics. State funding of parties is a process that has gained considerable prominence in west European party politics over recent decades but is a factor that has particular significance in CEE, as Szczerbiak points out, after the lengthy period of communist party-state domination (as well, indeed, as analogous configurations of state power in the pre-communist period). Corruption levels tend to be higher in at least some of the new CEE democracies, too, which may well be linked with the particular importance of state resources in post-communist politics. Some tendencies in organisational development seem to be rather different from the prevailing west European norm, with cash flows going more to the party central office than to its parliamentary leadership (van Biezen and Kopecký). There is also, as Hanley argues, a prevailing tendency towards the development of electoral-professional parties in CEE but one that is qualified by significant features of path-dependence and the persistence of certain hybrid organisational forms.

This mix of elements of similarity and difference points to the realistic, but somewhat messy and inelegant, conclusion that parties in the new CEE democracies are reasonably close to the relevant west European models - but nevertheless do not relate to them quite closely enough to eliminate continuing doubts about how well they encapsulate the major features of party development in the post-communist area. Certain regional factors may come into play here. The communist period is understood to have left a strong antipathy towards and mistrust of formally organised parties, and thus to contribute to an explanation for low membership levels and weakly structured parties. Recent scholarship nevertheless argues that membership levels have plummeted in the west and that the post-communist democracies are by no means alone in having low-population parties.[3] Corruption levels are generally seen to be higher in the east than in western Europe, although less so in Estonia, Slovenia and Hungary. This may be linked both with the deformation of the legal system under communism, but also with the relatively low level of socio-economic development in the east. National factors also hamper attempts to generalise across the post-communist region as a whole. Party politicians may well have tried to develop mass organisation during the early years of Czech democracy, as Hanley argues, but there is plenty of evidence to suggest that this objective was not generally shared by their Polish counterparts. Other discussions also suggest that the Czech pattern of party politics 'has always been distinctive and remains so today', and that there has been a striking concentration of power and collusion between major parties both during the pre-war and contemporary democratic periods.[4] Overall, then, regional factors point to some specific characteristics but do not seem to go very far in explaining the character of CEE parties in more general terms.

Is it possible to identify broader contextual or structural factors within CEE as a whole that shed light on national characteristics and help account for broader differences between parties in the new democracies and the established regimes of western Europe? As Szczerbiak points out at the beginning of his article, the leading models of party organisation currently in general use correspond to perceptions of an evolving relationship between parties and the state. Indeed, this view may be further broadened to include changing conceptions of state/civil society relations.[5] It promises to be a perspective worth examining further in the context of far-reaching post-communist change and its relation to party development. Mair, indeed, has suggested the social context of party development in post-communist CEE has been quite different from earlier cases of democratisation. The nature of the electorate and of pre-existing political organisations has been quite different, as has the context of party competition. Such characteristics were not thought to be conducive to effective party development.[6] Elsewhere I have pointed out in similar vein that, while the models currently discussed in the western party literature often seem to fit CEE developments quite well, the trajectory of party development has actually been quite different and it is the 'relative weakness of new parties against a background of a similarly impoverished civil society that is the most salient feature of party politics in the east'.[7] Independent social and political activity was highly circumscribed under the communist regime, and the process of marketisation and capitalist development that accompanied democratisation was destructive of established patterns of social interaction and existing networks that might have produced more strongly associative behaviour under the newly liberalised conditions of public life.

Neither should the other side of the equation be neglected, particularly in the post-communist CEE context. Discussion of party development in established democracies has generally tended to focus on the consequences of changes in civil society and the linkage problems experienced by parties in their survival and development in that respect, a perspective that is strongly reflected in the models currently discussed in the party literature. This helps explain the strong focus on the declining role of the mass-membership party, and the close attention paid to catch-all tendencies and electoral-professional variants. It is really only discussion of the cartel party that has directed attention to the state. This is surely one reason why that model - by no means otherwise obviously relevant to CEE conditions, as Szczerbiak has pointed out - has been such a prominent and popular topic of discussion where party developments in the region have been concerned. But the nature of the post-communist state is particularly problematic in a context where the relatively monolithic institutional complex of the former regime is subject to major processes of decomposition and change. It has happened in ways that are differentiated and still largely undefined as the institutions of a liberal democratic state are in the process of being designed. The empirical parameters of the state in CEE thus remain uncertain and are still being formed as concrete entities and defined in terms of conceptual analysis.

It is at least clear that the changing role and character of the post-communist state have been linked with the particular path taken by CEE party development. As well as helping to form the environment in which parties operate, in this indeterminate situation the nature of the state is also the object of party influence while parties have far greater access to the state and the resources it controls than did western parties at the equivalent stages of their development. The transformation of the intensively administered communist state has progressed in tandem with broader processes of political change. In terms of the prominence of party patronage, the relative timing of democratisation and state bureaucratisation has been critical in this respect: 'In general, when democratisation preceded bureaucratisation, parties were able to co-opt it as it grew for electoral advantage. When the opposite was true, the bureaucracy was able to protect itself and politicians were forced to adopt strategies of mass mobilisation'.[8] In the post-communist context, the particular role and importance of privatisation may also be usefully factored into the discussion of bureaucratisation.

It is certainly a perspective that has been developed in one case. Related views have become prominent in Poland in recent years, and attention has been directed to the nature of the 'soft state' that currently exists. It is a state in which leadership is weak and the effectiveness of rule and central government limited; in consequence the state is administered rather than effectively governed. It offers fertile ground for entrepreneurial party activity and provides the appropriate conditions for parties to colonise the state. Administrative structures and processes become politicised, and public interests tend to be supplanted by those of political parties.[9] The character of the post-communist state in this respect has particular importance for certain kinds of CEE parties like the main, though still relatively small, parties within the electoral coalition that assumed government after the 1997 Polish election. Within its broad form the main governing body, Solidarity Electoral Action (SEA), thus contained a number of parties with specific identities, a distinctive political history and their own objectives. They had generally been unable to win elections or gain major parliamentary representation on their own account, but the Solidarity coalition created a productive environment for them to pursue their specific objectives and particular interests.

The prominence of such an electoral coalition thus had particular implications for party development and the status of the small organisations operating within its broad framework. They highlight the general problems of organisational cohesion and institutional development in new democracies discussed by van Biezen and Kopecký in the context of Hungary and the Czech Republic. It was in such terms that they explained the otherwise surprising prominence of the party central office in some new democracies due to the pressing need for political cohesion at a critical stage of party development, a strategy not of course available for coalitions which have been unable to form organisationally unified parties. Yet the need for such groups to maintain unity and cohesion is both more difficult and more urgent than it is for the single party, especially if the coalition is actually in government. The assumption of a governing role, however, also presents the electoral coalition with unique opportunities in terms of access to state resources that can be distributed to buy the loyalty of individual party constituents to preserve and enhance the unity of the dominant political group as a whole.

The position of a number of such small parties within the Polish governing coalition installed in 1997 in particular thus became associated with preferential access to a range of state assets and diverse political resources. Accounts of party action in relation to such resources have included targets like the State Radiocommunication Agency (responsible for critical decisions about the allocation of broadcasting frequencies), the postal service and Communications Ministry as a whole (the latter finally disbanded before the 2001 election), State Railways, the central copper combine, and the privatisation of the health insurance agency. The process was one that concerned the growing practice of colonising public and private sector bodies - but especially those that span both sectors - by political 'families', which were to some extent but not exclusively party-based. If the organisational status of the governing coalition was problematic it could at least provide a home and useful base for a number of smaller groups which were indeed parties but had very limited resources, membership and structure in their own right. None of these small parties had any direct state funding, as that went to SEA as an electoral committee. Their accession to government office as constituent members of the coalition thus proved to be very advantageous in financial terms.

These developments raise important conceptual questions as, from another point of view, the process represents a distinctive variant of party cartelisation that casts further light on the critical area of party finance and material support. Polish developments in this respect reflect a specific form of the general cartelisation of party politics so frequently referred to in contemporary discussion of west European politics and often rather uncritically overlaid on CEE party developments. The difference here, though, is that growing Polish practice seemed to involve not a formal arrangement of established parties to consolidate their position on the basis of preferential access to state resources and an official budgetary basis, but more informal agreements within a broader coalition to monopolise and exploit state resources for a combination of party interest and private advantage. In the context of an electoral coalition like SEA, though, a permissive attitude to such activity provides a much-needed boost to the integration of a fractious and conflict-ridden party federation. It is a mechanism that may well be understood to act as a functional alternative to the prominence of the 'party in central office' identified elsewhere in CEE. The strategy of the parties and coalition involved were specific to Polish conditions but also directly related to the imperatives of institutionalisation facing competitive parties in new democracies as a whole, a combination that clearly signals caution to the comparativist concerned with fitting CEE developments to categories derived from west European experience of established democracies. The cartelisation of the governing coalition and exploitation of its politically privileged position could, of course, only work in this case so long as it held power - and control over media assets could have been expected to help it retain that power (an advantage that proved not to have the desired effect in the general election of 2001). Understandably enough in this context, too, the monopolisation of public assets is likely to turn from processes of party advantage to the satisfaction of personal interests and straightforward financial corruption, to the maximisation of particular interests in a relatively simple spoils system, a feature clearly identified by voters and thus an outright electoral disadvantage.

From a comparative perspective, then, it is likely to be in relations with the state that some of the more significant differences may be seen. But care should be taken not to draw premature conclusions about the intimacy of CEE parties with the state or, even less, to identify them in direct organisational terms. It is hardly the case, for example, that the parties are 'increasingly becoming similar to the state' or that 'parties may unambiguously become "state parties" in an extreme case'.[10] There are few signs that parties are failing to perform the core functions with which they are conventionally associated (although individual parties will, of course, be more or less successful in the democratic process as a whole), and party development in at least the central European area has been quite successful. Critical awareness needs to be maintained, too, not just of debates about the status of west European concepts of party development and the relation of established democratic parties to the state, but also of contrasting perceptions of the state itself and its performance in the west. Thus the original cartel party theory has been criticised for viewing developments too narrowly through the lens of an elite-centred political theory, and attention has been redirected to 'societal challenges and citizens' preferences as determinants of politicians' strategies'.[11] Clearly, neither state nor society can be neglected in discussion of party development and comparative analysis of the full range of party activity either in western or eastern Europe.

Consideration of CEE party development in the broader context of state and civil society relations thus points to similarities but also greater divergences from the general pattern of development in established democracies than initially might seem to be the case. The models derived from west European experience provide a reasonably good fit with CEE developments, and the institutional framework within which parties operate - like that provided by electoral systems - may work in ways not greatly different from those seen in established democracies. But the *path* by which the CEE parties have reached this position is quite different from that trod by west European democracies, and the *position* of parties in CEE with regard to state and civil society is also different in some significant respects. A broad focus on parties in relation to state and society thus promises to mark out fertile ground for further empirical analysis and detailed comparative study of CEE parties. It will be a challenging task as parties in established democracies also change their activities, structure and political role - often in ways that have provided the starting-point for the articles and analysis contained in this issue.

Notes

[1] H. Kitschelt, et al., *Post-Communist Party Systems: Competition, Representation, and Inter-Party Cooperation* (Cambridge: Cambridge University Press, 1999), pp. 401-3; P.G. Lewis, *Political Parties in Post-Communist Eastern Europe* (London: Routledge, 2000), p. 160.

[2] A. Ware, *Political Parties and Party Systems* (Oxford: Oxford University Press, 1996), p. 107.

[3] P. Mair and I. Van Biezen, 'Party Membership in Twenty European Democracies, 1980-2000', *Party Politics* 7(1) 2001, pp. 5-22.

[4] R.K. Evanson and T.M. Magstadt, 'The Czech Republic: Party Dominance in a Transitional System', in C.S. Thomas (ed.), *Political Parties and Interest Groups: Shaping Democratic Governance* (Boulder and London: Lynne Rienner, 2001), pp. 193-209, p. 193.

[5] Emphasised with particular strength by R.S. Katz and P. Mair, 'Changing Models of Party Organization and Party Democracy: The Emergence of the Cartel Party', *Party Politics* 1(1) 1995, pp. 5-28.

[6] P. Mair, 'What Is Different About Post-Communist Party Systems?', in *Party System Change: Approaches and Interpretations* (Oxford: Clarendon Press, 1997), pp. 175-98.

[7] Lewis, *Political Parties*, p. 162.

[8] D. Perkins, 'Structure and choice: the role of organizations, patronage and the media in party formation', *Party Politics* 2(3) 1996, pp. 361-2.

[9] P.G. Lewis, 'Organisational Change and Innovation in East-Central European Parties', paper delivered to a workshop on The Causes and Consequences of Organisational Innovation in European Political Parties at the Joint Sessions of the European Consortium for Political Research (Grenoble: 6-11 April 2001).

[10] T. Fricz, 'What Will Happen to the Parties? Crisis Phenomena of Parties and Their Possible Change of Function in the Twenty-First Century', *Central European Political Science Review* 1(2) 2000, pp. 108-9.

[11] H. Kitschelt, 'Citizens, Politicians, and Party Cartellization: Political Representation and State Failure in Post-Industrial Democracies', *European Journal of Political Research* 37(2) 2000, pp. 149-79, p. 175.

NOTES ON CONTRIBUTORS

Sarah Birch is a Lecturer in the Department of Government at the University of Essex. She has published on various aspects of the electoral process in Central and Eastern Europe, including a co-authored monograph entitled *Embodying Democracy: Electoral System Design in Post-Communist Europe* (Palgrave, 2002).

Francoise Boucek is a Researcher for the Public Policy Group at the London School of Economics and Political Science. Her doctoral thesis was a comparative study of the growth and management of factionalism in dominant political parties. Her other research interests include parties and party systems, electoral systems and electoral reform, and rational choice theory.

Frances Millard is Reader in the Department of Government of the University of Essex. Her books include *Polish Politics and Society* (Routledge, 1999) and *The Anatomy of the New Poland* (Elgar, 1994). She is co-author of *Embodying Democracy: Electoral System Design in Post-Communist Europe* (Palgrave, 2002) and the author of numerous articles on Polish politics and social policy.

Sean Hanley is Lecturer in Politics at Brunel University, West London. A specialist on Czech politics, his principal research interests include the problems of party formation and institutionalisation in post-communist East Central Europe, and the re-emergence of the centre-right in the region. He has published articles on these topics in various books and journals, including the *Journal of Political Ideologies*, and the *Journal of Communist Studies and Transition Politics*.

Petr Kopecký is Lecturer at the Department of Politics, University of Sheffield and a Research Fellow at the University of Leiden in the Netherlands, a position he also formerly held at the European University Institute in Florence. His main research interests include East European politics, political parties, civil society and democratization theory. He has published widely in journals and edited volumes on these subjects. His books include *Parliaments in the Czech and Slovak Republics: Party Competition and Parliamentary Institutionalization* (Ashgate, 2001) and (as co-editor) *Uncivil Society? Contentious Politics in Eastern Europe* (Routledge, 2003).

Paul G. Lewis is Reader in Central and East European Politics at the Open University. His publications range over diverse aspects of comparative and East European politics. His books include *Central Europe since 1945* (Longman, 1994), *Political Parties in Post-Communist Eastern Europe* (Taylor & Francis, 2000), and edited works on *Party Development and Democratic Change in Post-Communist Europe* (Frank Cass, 2001) and *Developments in Central and East European Politics 3* (Palgrave, 2003). His main research interests concern the continuing development of political parties in Central and Eastern Europe and the impact of EU enlargement on party systems.

Nick Sitter is Associate Professor of European Political Economy at the Norwegian School of Management, having worked previously at the Central European University, the American University in London, and as a political risk consultant. He took his doctorate at the London School of Economics and Political Science on party system development in East Central Europe, and has since published on West and East European party systems as well as on European Union public policy.

Aleks Sczczerbiak is Lecturer in Contemporary European Studies at the Sussex European Institute, University of Sussex. His current research interests include Central and East European party systems and electoral politics and the comparative party politics of Euroscepticism. He is author of *Poles Together? The Emergence and Development of Political Parties in Post-Communist Poland* (Central European University Press, 2001) and is Book Reviews Editor of *Party Politics*.

Paul Taggart is Senior Lecturer in Politics at the Sussex European Institute and co-editor of the journal *Politics*. Author of *The New Populism and the New Politics* (Macmillan, 1996) and *Populism* (Open University Press, 2000), he is co-convenor of the *Opposing Europe Research Network*, which is currently undertaking a comparative study of Euroscepticism in political parties.

Ingrid van Biezen is a lecturer in political science and international studies at the University of Birmingham, having previously taught and taken her PhD at the University of Leiden in The Netherlands. Her research interests lie in the fields of comparative politics, political parties, and democratic transitions and consolidation. She is currently involved in a cross-national research project on party organization and democracy in Eastern and Central Europe, having previously published on these themes in various books and journals, including *Party Politics* and *West European Politics*.

Paul Webb is Professor of Politics at the University of Sussex. His research interests focus on representative democracy, particularly party and electoral politics. The author or editor of several volumes, including *The Modern British Party System* (Sage Publications, 2000) and *Political Parties in Advanced Industrial Societies* (Oxford University Press, 2002), he is a co-editor of both *Party Politics* and *Representation*.